THE
BILL OF RIGHTS
PRIMER

THE
BILL OF RIGHTS
PRIMER

A CITIZEN'S GUIDEBOOK TO
THE AMERICAN BILL OF RIGHTS

AKHIL REED AMAR AND LES ADAMS

Skyhorse Publishing

Skyhorse Publishing books may be purchased in bulk
at special discounts for sales promotion, corporate gifts,
fund-raising, or educational purposes. Special editions can
also be created to specifications. For details, contact the
Special Sales Department, Skyhorse Publishing, 307 West
36th Street, 11th Floor, New York, NY 10018 or info@
skyhorsepublishing.com.

Skyhorse® and Skyhorse Publishing® are registered
trademarks of Skyhorse Publishing, Inc.®, a Delaware
corporation.

Visit our website at www.skyhorsepublishing.com.

10 9 8 7 6 5 4 3 2 1

Library of Congress Cataloging-in-Publication Data is
available on file.

ISBN: 978-1-62087-572-8

Printed in India

CONTENTS

ABOUT THIS BOOK

by Les Adams

In 1997, I wrote a little book entitled *The Second Amendment Primer*. It was more or less a labor of love, my hope being that perhaps a few thousand people or so would share my interest in an authoritative but easy-to-read book on the history and development of our right to keep and bear arms. Much to my surprise, the book became a bestseller. In just three years, sales have reached 500,000 copies, and the books continue to sell at a brisk pace.

Soon after my book on the Second Amendment was published, I began receiving letters from readers suggesting that I write a similar book on all the original amendments to the Constitution — the entire Bill of Rights. That seemed like a good idea to me, so I began my research and initial drafting of such a book in early 1998.

Readers suggested a primer on the Bill of Rights

Then several months later, Yale University Press published *The Bill of Rights: Creation and Reconstruction* by Akhil Reed Amar, professor of law at Yale Law School. Amar's book is a brilliant piece of work. It was selected to receive a Gavel Award Certificate of Merit in the Book Category in the 1999 Competition for the Media and the Arts, given by the American Bar Association. Here is a sampling of the reviews his book has been receiving in academic and legal circles:

One of the most important books about constitutional interpretation of its generation.

Jeffrey Rosen, *American Lawyer*

Commentary on Amar's book

Amar . . . takes us on a historical odyssey . . . . [He] offer[s] a striking and original analysis of the political values embodied in the amendments . . . . Amar's stimulating republican interpretation restores the states and the people to their rightful place in the constitutional story.

James Henretta,
New York Times Book Review

A methodological tour de force . . . . [O]ne of the most valuable works on constitutional scholarship written in the modern era.

Steven Calabresi, *co-founder of the Federalist Society*

Essential reading for anyone who claims to care about the history of liberty in America, from the ACLU to the NRA to the Federalist Society. Today's Bill of Rights, Amar shows, owes less to the Founding Fathers of the 1780s and more to the antislavery crusaders of the 1860s — women alongside men, blacks alongside whites — than many of us had realized.

Nadine Strossen, *professor, New York Law School, and national president, American Civil Liberties Union*

Akhil Amar is one of the most creative thinkers in the legal academy. Not surprisingly, he has produced the best book ever written about what we call the Bill of Rights.

Sanford Levinson, *professor,*
University of Texas Law School

Amar's argument is nothing short of brilliant: he recasts our understanding of the Bill of Rights in ways that have profound implications. No one presently writing is better able to combine legal and historical analysis.

Michael Les Benedict, *professor,*
Ohio State University

By viewing the Bill of Rights as a document with an evolving meaning shaped by history, and by stressing how the Civil War and Reconstruction transformed the Bill of Rights, Amar has made a major contribution to the history of American liberties.

Erie Foner, *professor,*
Columbia University

Authors agree to collaborate on a new book that will marry scholarly content with popular style

How could I possibly write anything that would achieve this level of acclaim? So, subscribing to the theory "if you can't beat 'em, join 'em," I contacted Amar and suggested that we collaborate on a new book combining the masterful scholarly content of his book with the demonstrably popular style and organization of mine. What if, I asked, we were to transform Amar's work (which, after all, is a scholarly treatise with a sophisticated organization, style, and vocabulary, aimed at a learned audience of judges, lawyers, and historians) into a more accessible and easily read book like *The Second Amendment Primer*? That is, what if we could create a book that would tell the great story of the Bill of Rights in a reader-friendly style without the loss of one whit of historical accuracy or legal erudition, but with an organization and vocabulary that most every-body would be comfortable with — a book that was easy to read and easy to refer to? Wouldn't that be something? We thought so, and hope you agree.

Easy to read. Easy to refer to.

The organization of *The Bill of Rights Primer* is similar to that of *The Second Amendment Primer*. The preface presents a short historical survey of the people, events, decrees, legislation, writings, and cultural milestones, in England and the American colonies, that influenced the Founding Fathers as they drafted the U.S. Constitution and the Bill of Rights. (Incidentally, this section is written solely by me, and the responsibility for any omissions, errors, or factual misinterpretations in the text is mine alone.) The remaining chapters, co-authored with Amar, are a condensation of his book.

New book includes features found to be popular in *The Second Amendment Primer*

The book also includes features that proved to be especially helpful to readers of *The Second Amendment Primer*:

- Important points are summarized in short notes at the side of the text.

- To present an uncluttered page that's easy to read, all reference and quotation sources are placed in a separate section of notes at the end of the book.

- Throughout the book, we have tried to provide synonyms for most of the fancy words that lawyers and scholars sometimes use and for obsolete words or words that no longer mean what their writers intended. However, since the Bill of Rights, is, after all, a legal and historical document, to discuss it adequately we simply cannot avoid the use of some legal or scholarly words and expressions for which there are no adequate synonyms. Therefore, we have provided a short glossary on page 389. (It might assist your comprehension if you briefly review this glossary before you begin reading the text.)

- Also at the back of the book are three reference sections: biographical profiles of all notable figures discussed or quoted in the text; endnotes; and an index.

- The work is designed in a pocket-size format for easy reference.

Akhil Amar and I hope you will find this small book handy and user-friendly . . . that you will come to regard it as an authoritative guidebook to your American freedoms.

A guidebook to your American freedoms

Thank you.

Les Adams

PREFACE

THE DEVELOPMENT OF THE CONCEPT OF POLITICAL FREEDOM IN ENGLAND AND THE AMERICAN COLONIES

I make no pretense that this chapter is a comprehensive history. My short review of the subject will necessarily be like a time machine, speeding through the course of English and American history, stopping only occasionally, and briefly at that, to examine a particularly significant development. Of the hundreds of writings, speeches, and legislative acts that contributed to the development of the concept of political freedom in England and America, I will be mentioning no more than a dozen or so.

A time machine speeding through history

So then, what is the freedom with which the Founding Fathers were concerned? When you think about it, there are many kinds of freedom — freedom from psychological or physical constraint, such as slavery or imprisonment, of course; but also freedom from want or fear; freedom to move; freedom to think; freedom to act; freedom to dream; and so on. But When Patrick Henry uttered his famous words during the Virginia debates, just what was the freedom for which he would give up his life? It was *political freedom*, the right of citizens to exercise free will in conformity with and under the protection of the rule of law.

The concept of our political freedom is the product of several thousand years of thought and development, from its birth in the civilizations of the ancient world up to the signing of the Magna Carta in the thirteenth century in England, followed by four centuries of relative inactivity, and then by an explosion of expression and action in England and the American colonies throughout the seventeenth and eighteenth centuries. Since that time, the concept of political freedom has matured into the foundation of governance for all the democratic societies of the western world.

Unfortunately, we don't have space in this little book to even catalog, much less discuss, all the people, wars, events, and cultural milestones that contributed to the development of the concept of political freedom during the thousands of years preceding the American Revolution. It's a massive body of knowledge whose mastery would have to include, at a bare minimum, the study of entire civilizations such as Sumeria, Babylonia, Israel, Egypt, Greece, Rome, and Byzantium; the analysis of significant cultural movements such as slavery, feudalism, the Renaissance, and the Reformation; the study and analysis of the thought of scores of great leaders and philosophers including Zoroaster, Homer, Herodotus, Solon, Socrates, Aristotle, Plato, Alexander the Great, Cicero, Caesar, Augustus, Livy, Tacitus, Jesus, Paul of Tarsus, Augustine, and St. Thomas Acquinas at the very least; and the reading of a number of great writings including the *Epic of Gilgamesh*, the *Code of Hammurabi*, the *Bible*, the *Funeral Oration of Pericles*, Justinian's *Institutes*, and so on.

Our focus, instead, will begin in England towards the close of the Middle Ages, when the heretofore largely theoretical concepts of political freedom began to be translated into practical, workmanlike documents and declarations of rights. **Our focus begins in England at the close of the Middle Ages**

ENGLAND'S PRINCIPAL DECLARATIONS AND WRITINGS

THREE GREAT DECLARATIONS OF LAW AND LIBERTY

Three documents, the Magna Carta of 1215, the 1628 Petition of Right, and the 1689 Declaration of Rights, are universally recognized as the cornerstones of political liberty in England. They're worth a closer examination.

Magna Carta

*Whenever mob or monarch lays
Too rude a hand on English ways,
A whisper wakes, the shadow plays
Across the reeds at Runnymede.*
Rudyard Kipling, 1891

In the 13th century, England was a feudal monarchy

In the thirteenth century, England was a feudal monarchy. The fortune, power, and influence of the king or queen derived principally from the Catholic Church and its top English representative, the Archbishop of Canterbury; and from a small group of barons and other noblemen who were the regional proponents of the king's or queen's will. These monarchs relied on a feudal structure in which their vassals, the barons, provided them with money for the royal treasury and armed soldiery for their military exploits.

King John's venality put the governing structure at risk

Whatever its shortcomings — and there were many as far as the common people were concerned — this governing feudal structure worked when England was ruled by relatively decent monarchs. But when an evil ruler such as King John assumed the throne, the monarch's venality and greed put the entire structure at risk.

In the gallery of heroes, statesmen, rogues, fools, idiots, and simpletons that make up the history of English royalty, John, the youngest son of Henry II and younger brother of Richard I ("the Lion-Hearted"), stands out as "a piece of work," as the popular expression goes.

In his landmark history of England published in 1778, David Hume wrote of John: "The character of this prince is nothing but a complication of vices, equally mean and odious; ruinous to himself, and destructive of his people. Cowardice, inactivity, folly, levity, licentiousness, ingratitude, treachery, tyranny, and cruelty, all of these qualities appear too evidently in the several incidents of his life."[1]

Incidents indeed there were. Early in his monarchy, in 1202, after being victorious in a rebellion waged against him in Normandy by his nephew, Arthur, the 16-year-old duke of Brittany, John imprisoned Arthur in the castle of Roüen. Then, according to most historians, he ordered Arthur's assassination. But failing to find a willing accomplice, John stabbed the young man to death with his own hands, fastened a stone about the dead body, and threw it into the Seine River. In later years, John ordered the death by starvation of the wife and son of William de Braose, the first English baron to take arms against him. He then kidnapped and held hostage twenty-eight young sons of Welsh barons, later hanging the boys when he became convinced of their fathers' treason. John's idea of a pleasant outing was to ride through the countryside, accompanied by his bodyguard of foreign mercenaries, raping and pillaging.

It was said of John that to know him well was to loathe him. When he died in 1216, it was accepted wisdom that it was the best service that he could do his kingdom.

It is one of the ironies of history that this thoroughly reprehensible monster played an instrumental role in the foundation of English constitutional government from which a number of the American concepts of freedom embodied in our Bill of Rights were to be drawn. You see, King John happened to be the most notable participant in an event that many historians regard as being one of the most important in the entire history of the western world.

The signing of Magna Carta

I refer, of course, to the signing of Magna Carta by King John and an assemblage of English barons on June 15, 1215, at Runnymede. Once called Running-Mead, this small creek runs through a meadow bearing the same name and flows into the river Thames between the towns of Windsor and Staines, southwest of London (not far from today's Heathrow Airport).

At this site, the principal barons of John's realm, armed and prepared to overthrow his monarchy if he did not accede to their demands, presented him with a document then popularly known as the Articles of the Barons, later entitled Magna Carta (or the Great Charter of King John).

Compared with John, the barons assembled at Runnymede might be regarded as quite decent fellows. But they were not choirboys. What they were seeking was not liberty for all, but relief from the oppressive financial demands (known as scutage) that John was making of them, as well as relief from a number of other feudal customs they found burdensome. The barons couched their demands in terms that might lead one to conclude that they were advocates of what we might today call democratic reform. But in fact, Magna Carta served to benefit primarily only the barons and their privileged friends.

At first glance, Magna Carta is indistinguishable from numerous other royal proclamations issued at the time. It consists of eighty-six lines in Latin, bears the Great Seal of King John, and is written on sheets of parchment measuring about fifteen by twenty inches. (There exist only four signed and sealed copies of this famous document: two are on display in London's British Museum; the other two are housed at the cathedrals of Lincoln and Salisbury.)

A quick glance at an English translation of Magna Carta can be misleading, particularly if one's eye is drawn to some of its chapters that today can only be regarded as quaint.

Take Chapter 23, for example:

> Neither a town nor any person shall be distrained to build bridges or embankments, excepting those which anciently, and of right, are bound to do it.

To provide a modern meaning: "The people shall not be compelled to make bridges unless

A document designed to benefit only the barons and their friends

they are bound to by ancient custom." Apparently, every time King John traveled on horseback outside London, in advance of his departure he forced the local folks to build bridges across the streams he intended to cross during his journey. The locals were much oppressed by this practice and found it an extreme hardship.

Despite the inclusion in Magna Carta of such relatively minor local grievances that would today be considered merely curious, it is nevertheless a profound, solemn document, reflecting the harsh realities of life in thirteenth-century England, and at the same time clearly anticipating republican reforms that would ultimately find expression almost five hundred years later in the English Declaration of Rights. Magna Carta has come to be recognized as the premier and fundamental document of English constitutional law.

Magna Carta announced the rule of law

For Americans, whose liberty depends upon the existence of laws limiting the authority and discretion of those in charge of the government, the importance of Magna Carta is that it announced *the rule of law*. This is evident in many of its chapters that established new rights for the barons and new standards for the conduct of the king. But in the development of both the English and American Bill of Rights, its most significant chapter is its famous Chapter 39:

No free man shall be taken or imprisoned or dispossessed, or outlawed, or banished, or in any way destroyed, nor will we go upon him, nor send upon him, except by the legal judgement of his peers or by the law of the land.

No clause of Magna Carta has been cited more often as a guarantee of personal liberties than this chapter. It was included in Magna Carta, many scholars believe, to codify a concept similar to the principle found in the Fifth and Fourteenth Amendments to the U.S. Constitution, that no person may be deprived of life, liberty, or property without due process of law.

Unquestionably Magna Carta played an essential part in the development of the U.S. Constitution and Bill of Rights. When the various American colonies took root in the seventeenth and eighteenth centuries, their governments embodied provisions of Magna Carta, particularly Chapter 39, into their legislation. And when in 1765 the British Parliament passed the Stamp Act (a notorious piece of punitive legislation that imposed various taxes upon the colonies to finance the maintenance of British troops in America), no less a figure than John Adams cited the provisions of Magna Carta in support of the principle "no taxation without representation."[2]

The Petition of Right

Several hundred years of English history were to pass after the signing of Magna Carta before England was presented with the next seminal document in its constitutional history, The Petition of Right, drafted by the English Parliament and presented to King Charles I in 1628. The petition reflected the gradual development of individual liberties that had been implied long before in the provisions of Magna Carta, and foretold the codification of those liberties, which would occur sixty-one years later with the passage of the English Bill of Rights.

A document declaring supremacy of law over the wishes of the king

The Petition of Right was a revolutionary document, declaring the supremacy of law over the personal wishes of the king and rejecting the doctrine known as the divine right of kings (the belief that monarchs obtain their ruling power directly from God, rather than from the consent of their subjects). Specifically, it demanded important restrictions upon monarchal power as it was being practiced by King Charles in violation of individual liberty. Among these were provisions that no longer could the king exact taxes without the consent of Parliament; that prisoners committed to jail at the king's command should be freed on bail before trial; that the quartering of troops in private homes was illegal; and that civilians could not be tried under martial law.

The Petition of Right thus contributed much to the establishment of some of the essential personal liberties of the English people. The eminent English historian William Holdsworth was later to characterize the petition as "the first of those great constitutional documents since Magna

Carta, which safeguard the liberties of the people by securing the supremacy of the law."[3]

Charles grudgingly accepted the Petition of Right, recognizing that he needed the cooperation of Parliament to raise money to fund his monarchy. But he had no intention of abiding by it. He dismissed Parliament the next year, not calling for its reconvention until 1640. During this time, a number of conflicts and the continuing struggle for power between Charles and Parliament led to the English Civil War in 1642 and Charles' conviction of treason and execution in 1649. *But King Charles had no intention of abiding by it*

Executive power in England then fell into the hands of Oliver Cromwell, who had commanded the forces of Parliament in the civil war. In 1653, Cromwell assumed the title of lord protector. Upon his death in 1658, his son Richard became lord protector, but Richard was an ineffective ruler and was forced into retirement in 1659. Parliament thereupon bestowed the monarchy upon Charles II, who ruled from 1660 until his death in 1685. James II then ascended to the throne, ruling from 1685 to 1688, when he was forced to flee to France after being ousted from power by armed forces under the command of Prince William of Orange.

Parliament then invited Prince William to become the new king of England, provided he and his wife, Mary, would accept the provisions of a new document Parliament had adopted on February 12, 1689, the English Declaration of

Rights. They did, and the declaration was signed the next day by the new king and queen.

The Declaration of Rights
(The English Bill of Rights)

The Declaration of Rights (which was later to be established in statutory form as the English Bill of Rights) reaffirmed the principles of the 1628 Petition of Right, denying the divine right of kings and setting forth thirteen basic rights that Parliament regarded as the "true, ancient, and indubitable rights and liberties of the people" of the English kingdom. In his classic *History of England*, Lord Macaulay summed up the significance of the Declaration of Rights as follows:

The Declaration of Rights contained the seeds of every good law needed to promote the public welfare

The Declaration of Right[s], though it made nothing law which had not been law before, contained the germ of the law which gave religious freedom to the Dissenter, of the law which secured the independence of the Judges, of the law which limited the duration of Parliaments, of the law which placed the liberty of the press under the protection of juries, of the law which prohibited the slave trade, of the law which abolished the sacramental test, of the law which relieved Roman Catholics from civil liabilities, of the law which reformed the representative system, of every good law which has been passed during more than a century and a half, of every good law which may hereafter, in the course of ages, be found necessary to promote the public weal, and to satisfy the demands of public opinion.[4]

THREE INFLUENTIAL
PRIVATE WRITINGS

During the seventeenth and eighteenth centuries, the private writings of a number of jurists and political philosophers were to advocate republican ideals and further the growth of political freedom in England. My discussion will be confined to the most influential of the time: the writings of members of the Whig Party, as well as those of John Locke and William Blackstone.

The Whig Writers

The Whig writers — relatively unknown by the general public today — included such non-household names as Charles Lawson, Algernon Sidney, James Burgh, John Trenchard, Andrew Fletcher, Robert Molesworth, Thomas Gordon, Joseph Addison, James Harrington, Henry Neville, and too many more to name. They were members of a political party commonly referred to as "Whigs," or "Commonwealthmen," or "classical republicans" which from the late seventeenth century until 1760 exercised considerable political power in England. (*Whig* is the short form of the word *whiggamore*, a name applied to a Scotch word once used to describe the people from west Scotland who opposed King Charles I of England in 1648.) The political philosophy of the Whigs had been strongly influenced by the writings of a number of philosophers from ancient times,

The Whigs advocated more political power for the House of Commons

including Aristotle, Cicero, Livy, and Tacitus, as well as those of the Italian Renaissance writer Machiavelli. The Whigs advocated granting more political power to the House of Commons. They had been largely responsible for the Glorious Revolution of 1688 that established the supremacy of Parliament over the king. They were also instrumental in the drafting and enactment of the English Bill of Rights.

John Locke

John Locke was the author of *Two Treatises on Government*, one of the great books in the history of the world. The second treatise in the book, entitled "An Essay Concerning the True Original, Extent and End of Civil Government," is Locke's landmark contribution to constitutional law, political theory, and the establishment of democratic government and political freedom in England. Although published towards the close of the seventeenth century in 1689, it was to exert a powerful influence upon the momentous events that were to take place in England (as well as in the American colonies) during the next century.

In Locke's view, the people, not the king, were sovereign

Locke believed that by nature people had certain rights and duties. These rights included life, liberty, and ownership of property. In exercising these rights, the people had the right to govern themselves in the way they judged to be for the common good. In other words, the people, not the king, were sovereign, a sovereignty based upon a virtual mutual contract on the part of the people to govern themselves. If the terms of the contract needed to be changed to accommodate changing circumstances, only the people, not the government, could make such changes.

In Locke's view, civil rulers hold their power not absolutely but conditionally, government being essentially a moral trust. And if in the exercise of its power as trustee the government fails to live up to this trust, that is, to protect the life, liberty and property of the people, the people and only the people had the right and power to dissolve the government and select a new one.

Also, a principal point in Locke's system is that the government may be dissolved while society remains intact. In other words, the people constitute in themselves a power superior to that of the government.

William Blackstone

William Blackstone was an English judge, professor, and author of the monumental *Commentaries of the Laws of England*, published in 1765–1769. This four-volume work presented a comprehensive picture of the English law of his time, and became the most influential work in the history of English law. Blackstone was a member of the political opposition to the Whigs, the Tory Party, yet he agreed with many of the Whig republican philosophies. Blackstone's masterly exposition of the English common law joined with

The great exposition of the English common law

England's majestic history of constitutional law to create a strong foundation upon which the Founding Fathers were soon to erect the framework of political freedom in America.

AMERICA'S PRINCIPAL DECLARATIONS AND WRITINGS

INTRODUCTION

As heirs to English common law and its constitutional history, the early American colonists who drafted colonial charters and laws throughout the seventeenth century and their descendants — the Founding Fathers of the eighteenth century — intended nothing less than to incorporate into their new governments the laws and liberties of Englishmen.

It is well to remember that the early colonists of the seventeenth century were born in England, and would have been exposed to family dialogues steeped in English thought, custom, and values. In turn, after traveling to America they would have passed English traditions along to their soon-to-be-famous sons and grandsons. Of these forebears of the Founding Fathers, the French observer Alexis de Tocqueville commented:

> Born in a country [England] which had been agitated for centuries by the struggles of faction, and in which parties had been obliged in their

turn to place themselves under the protection of the laws, their political education had been perfected in this rude school, and they were more conversant with the notions of right, and the principles of true freedom, than the greater part of their European contemporaries.[5]

The early American colonists, as well as their sons and grandsons, were educated in the classical European tradition. Their curriculum emphasized a thorough schooling in world history, including study of the birth of the concept of political freedom in the ancient civilizations of the Middle East and in the classical civilizations of Greece and Rome. They studied the growth of the concept of political freedom throughout Europe in the historical eras to follow: successively the Middle Ages and the rise of feudalism, the Renaissance, the Reformation, and the Age of Enlightenment.

Colonists were educated in the classical European tradition

In particular, they were thoroughly schooled in English history, and knew the Whig writers. As historian David Hardy observes:

They were thoroughly schooled in English history

The Whig writers have more than purely historical interest. John Adams estimated that ninety percent of Americans were Whig sympathizers at the time of the American Revolution, and many of these Americans were deeply familiar with the writings of their English predecessors. John Adams held special regard for Harrington, although he probably did not endorse the 1779 proposal to change Massachusetts' name to *Oceana* (from the title of Harrington's most celebrated work). Adams and Madison both studied Molesworth in detail. Jefferson's library boasted copies of Sidney, Molesworth and Harrington. These works, and those of Fletcher, were also owned by the likes of Benjamin Franklin, John Hancock, and George Mason. When Burgh's *Political Disquisitions* was printed in the [c]olonies, Benjamin Franklin served as editor, and the subscription list for the first edition included George Washington, John Adams, John Hancock, and John Dickinson.[6]

They were conversant with the works of John Locke. His words resonate throughout all the political debates and documents of the American Revolution.

They knew Blackstone and the common law

Also, since most of the colonial political leaders were lawyers, they knew their Blackstone. As Professor Joyce Malcolm points out:

> The influence of the radical Whigs on Americans of the founding era is generally acknowledged, but the profound impact of a more moderate English author [Blackstone] has usually been underestimated. The first volume of William Blackstone's *Commentaries on the Laws of England* did not appear in Britain until 1765, and the fourth and last volume did not appear until 1769, yet nearly 2500 copies had been sold in America by the start of the American Revolution in 1775.[7]

And, of course, they knew their common law. Chief Justice Howard Taft observed that

[t]he Framers of our Constitution were born and brought up in the atmosphere of the common law, and thought and spoke its vocabulary. They were familiar with the other forms of government, recent and ancient, and indicated in their discussions earnest study and consideration of many of them; but, when they came to put their conclusions into the form of fundamental law in a compact draft, they expressed themselves in terms of the common law, confident that they could be shortly and easily understood.[8]

COLONIAL OR STATE-SPONSORED WRITINGS PRIOR TO THE CONSTITUTIONAL PERIOD

The Colonial Charters

The first manifestations of English influence upon the development of political freedom in the American colonies were evidenced in the colonial charters granted to individual colonies by the British Crown (the first to Virginia in 1606, the last to Georgia in 1732). A notable example is Pennsylvania's Charter of Privileges of 1701, regarded by many historians as the most famous of all colonial constitutions because of the influence exerted upon its drafting by Quaker William Penn.[9] The Pennsylvania Charter placed emphasis upon safeguarding individual rights. Its influence was widespread, and its guarantees of individual rights were to influence the drafting of constitutions in other colonies (soon to be called states).

Colonial charters declared that the rights of Englishmen applied to the American colonists

The relevance of these charters to the American Bill of Rights is that each declared that American colonists should enjoy the rights of Englishmen (other countries viewed the inhabitants of their colonies as persons outside the constitutional and legal system of the home country). As the noted legal historian, Bernard Schwartz observes:

> The Virginia Charter [and others soon to follow] thus established the vital precedent that the colonists were entitled to all the "rights of Englishmen." Had that principle not been established, it may be doubted that the history of the American [c]olonies would have developed as it did.[10]

This guarantee was frequently cited by the American revolutionists in opposing English colonial policy. Even a century and a half after its publication, the First Charter of Virginia was quoted by Patrick Henry in a speech before the Virginia House of Burgesses in 1765 as an argument against the imposition of the Stamp Act.[11]

Thomas Paine's Common Sense

Before examining the most significant public documents and declarations that were to be published during the pre-revolutionary and constitutional periods, I'd like to reacquaint you with a very important private writing that had substantial influence upon the legislative debates taking place throughout all the colonies, Thomas Paine's *Common Sense.*[12]

An important and influential private writing

Most Americans probably recall only one quotation of Thomas Paine's: "These are the times that try men's souls." These words were first set forth as the lead sentence of Paine's pamphlet *The American Crisis,* that Paine published on December 23, 1776 while he was serving in General George Washington's Continental Army at its winter headquarters in Morristown, New Jersey. Not only the celebrated first sentence but the entire pamphlet remains worthy of our attention today. Here is its stirring first paragraph:

> These are the times that try men's souls. The summer soldier and the sunshine patriot will, in this crisis, shrink from the service of their country; but he that stands it *now* deserves the love and thanks of man and woman. Tyranny, like hell, is not easily conquered; yet we have this consolation with us, that the harder the conflict, the more glorious the triumph. What we obtain too cheap, we esteem too lightly; it is dearness only that gives everything its value. Heaven knows how to put a proper price upon its goods; and it would be strange indeed if so celestial an article as *Freedom* should not be highly rated. (Italics in original)[13]

As felicitous a statement on the value of patriotism as this is, the impact of *The American Crisis* is overshadowed by another of Paine's writings, *Common Sense,* which was written just as hostilities were beginning in the American Revolution. *Common Sense* first appeared in print in January, 1776. It quickly became one of the most successful and influential pamphlets in the history of political writing, selling, by Paine's estimate, some 150,000 copies. (Paine directed that his share of the profits be used to buy supplies for the Continental Army.)

Common Sense presents a powerful argument for American independence. It is also a vigorous attack on the British Constitution and the principle of hereditary rule. Paine later wrote that the aim of his work was "to bring forward and establish the representative system of government."

A vigorous attack on Britain and the principle of heredity rule

The language of *Common Sense* is powerful stuff. "Of more worth is one honest man to society, and in the sight of God," Paine wrote, "than all the crowned ruffians that ever lived." George III is "the royal brute of England." On the issue of independence, he wrote, "There is something absurd in supposing a continent to be perpetually governed by an island." Towards the end of the pamphlet, he offered an awesome view of the significance of the American Revolution. "We have it in our power to begin the world over again." In a world "overrun with oppression," America alone would be the home of freedom, "an asylum for mankind."

However, *Common Sense* was important to its readers in the colonies (and survived as one of the most important documents in American history) not because of the ideas that Paine advocated — they were the common currency among a number of American patriots — but the way in which he presented them. Here was a new style of political writing directed not merely to the educated elite. Paine assumed knowledge of no authority but the Bible, with which all citizens were familiar, and avoided the florid language common to political pamphlets of the era. His style was the equal of his argument: anyone could grasp the nature of politics and government; all that is required is common sense.

One of the most important documents in American history

No less a personage than John Adams observed in 1806: "I know not whether any man in the world has had more influence on its inhabitants or affairs in the last thirty years than Thomas Paine."[14]

State Constitutions and Bills of Rights

Next in our chronology of documents that served as foundations of the American Bill of Rights were the state declarations of rights and constitutions that proclaimed the rights and privileges of citizens, as well as the laws under which they chose to govern themselves. Of these, by far the most noteworthy was Virginia's Declaration of Rights of 1776. Drafted by a committee that included such prestigious figures as Edmund

State declarations of rights and constitutions were the principal models for our Bill of Rights

Randolph, Patrick Henry, George Mason, and James Madison, the Virginia declaration directly influenced the drafting and adoption of bills of rights in many of the other states. According to Bernard Schwartz:

> The Virginia Declaration of Rights of 1776 is the first true Bill of Rights in the modern American sense, since it is the first protection of the rights of the individual to be contained in a Constitution adopted by the people acting through an elected convention.[15]

FEDERAL DOCUMENTS PUBLISHED PRIOR TO ADOPTION OF THE U.S. CONSTITUTION

Acting in concert, during this period the states also drafted and adopted five landmark federal documents: the Declaration of Rights and Grievances of the Stamp Act Congress (1765), the Declarations and Resolves of the First Continental Congress (1774), the Declaration of Independence (1776), the Articles of Confederation (1777), and the Northwest Ordinance (1787).

The Declaration of Rights and Grievances of the Stamp Act Congress

The Stamp Act Congress was convened in New York in October, 1765. The Congress was organized by the state of Massachusetts, and was attended by nine of the thirteen states. The purpose of the meeting was to draft a protest to the British king and Parliament against enforcement of the British Stamp Act, which had been passed by Parliament on March 22, 1765, and which was to go into effect in November of that year. The British Stamp Act placed stamp duties (or taxes) on various items of commerce in the colonies such as legal documents, newspapers, almanacs, and licenses. The legal question the delegates debated was whether Englishmen in the colonies could be taxed by Parliament, a body in which they were not represented, in view of the fact that the right of the people to participate in the levying of taxes had long been established as a fundamental part of the English Constitution.

A protest against the British Stamp Act

The protest drafted by the Stamp Act Congress, the Declaration of Rights and Grievances, was successful. The Stamp Act was repealed by Parliament on March 18, 1766. And while the colonists were undoubtedly pleased to have won this victory, it also portended events that were to come, as predicted by a British observer, James Scott:

The Americans imbibe notions of independence and liberty with their very milk, and will some time or other shake off all subjection. If we yield to them in this particular, by repealing the Stamp-Act, it is all over; they will from that moment assert their freedom.[16]

"Americans imbibe notions of liberty along with their milk"

Declarations and Resolves of the
First Continental Congress

Nine years later, in September 1774, in response to growing British oppression throughout the colonies (most recently demonstrated by the British Parliament's passage earlier that year of the Intolerable Acts[17]), delegates from all the states gathered in Philadelphia and convened the First Continental Congress. On October 14, they approved and adopted the Declarations and Resolves of the First Continental Congress. This document based the rights of the colonists not only upon the principles of the English Constitution and the colonial charters, but also upon the law of nature. It cited a number of acts instituted by the British Parliament over the previous ten years that had violated these principles. It condemned standing armies. It reiterated the principles that Americans were entitled to all English liberties, including no taxation without representation, the right of trial by jury, and freedom to petition the king and Parliament for the redress of grievances. The Declarations and Resolves of the First Continental Congress was one of the most important forerunners of the Declaration of Independence and the revolutionary declarations (or bills of rights) and constitutions that the states adopted in the period 1776 to 1787, as we have discussed above.

An important forerunner to the Declaration of Independence

On May 10, 1775, the delegates met again as the Second Continental Congress. They adopted two landmark documents: the Declaration of Independence and the Articles of Confederation.

The Declaration of Independence

The principal purpose of the Declaration of Independence was to declare the freedom of the American colonies from Britain. But as envisioned by its author, Thomas Jefferson, the scope of the Declaration was far greater. Combining his own rhetoric with language he cribbed from several earlier sources,[18] Jefferson created the most memorable document in our American heritage, one that expresses two universal principles that have been important to developing democracies throughout the world ever since. The first principle is that government exists for the benefit of the people and not their rulers and that when a government turns to tyranny, the people of the country have a right to resist and overturn the government. The second principle, that "all men are created equal," has come to be read as a powerful reminder that all members of a society are entitled to full protection of the law and to the right to participate in public affairs. The Congress adopted the Declaration on July 4, 1776, a date that has been celebrated ever since as the birthday of the United States.

The most memorable document in our heritage

The Articles of Confederation

The Articles of Confederation was an agreement whereby the thirteen original states established a confederation called the United States of America, and established a Congress of the Confederation to operate the government. After more than a year of debate and almost five years beyond that (the time needed for ratification by all thirteen states), the Articles of Confederation was adopted on March 1, 1781. It served as America's basic charter until the Constitution of the United States was ratified in 1788.

A flawed piece of legislation

The Articles of Confederation turned out to be a severely flawed piece of legislation. It contemplated that the states should assume the primary responsibility for the protection of their citizens, and only a few powers were given to the central government. Among its many deficiencies, the Articles did not grant the government the power to tax, to raise troops, to regulate commerce, or to enforce its own laws or treaties. It set up a cumbersome and practically unworkable amendment process: for any suggested change to be made, all thirteen states had to give unanimous approval. Even at the time it went into effect, many political analysts argued that it did not give Congress sufficient power to operate effectively. George Washington observed that "the confederation appears to be little more than a shadow without the substance; and congress a nugatory body, their ordinances being little attended to."[19]

The Northwest Ordinance

Although not as well known as America's other seminal declarations of freedom, the Northwest Ordinance deserves our attention. It contains the first bill of rights enacted by the federal government of the United States. More important, it established as part of the colonial policy of the United States the principle that the settlers of uninhabited territories should enjoy the same personal liberties as the citizens of the parent country. Operating under the authority of the Articles of Confederation, Congress passed the ordinance in July 1787, just two months before the U.S. Constitution was adopted. Its provisions provided for the future of the great territory west of the Appalachian Mountains, including, importantly, a provision that settlers of the uninhabited territories should enjoy the same personal liberties as citizens of the parent country. Probably the most famous clause in the Northwest Ordinance is Article VI, which prohibited slavery in the territory. Of course, as we know, no comparable provision appears in either the U.S. Constitution or the Bill of Rights. And, as you will be reading later in the book, when slavery was abolished throughout the United States by means of

First abolition of slavery

the Thirteenth Amendment, the language of that amendment is similar to that found in Article VI of the Northwest Ordinance.

DRAFTING, ADOPTION, AND RATIFICATION OF THE U.S. CONSTITUTION

Congress called for the states to meet in Philadelphia in May, 1787, for the purpose of convening a Constitutional Convention. Congress directed that this convention was to meet "for the sole and express purpose of revising the Articles of Confederation and reporting to Congress and the several [state] legislatures such alterations and provisions therein as shall when agreed to in Congress and confirmed by the states render the federal constitution adequate to the exigencies of Government & the preservation of the Union."[20]

The eventful summer of 1787

Fifty-five state delegates gathered in Philadelphia that eventful summer. Although John Adams and Thomas Jefferson — two of the most eminent Americans on the political scene that year — were abroad at the time of the Constitutional Convention, "nevertheless there gathered at Philadelphia in 1787 such men of mark as could not well be assembled in any convention near the end of the twentieth century."[21] Included were such well-known figures as George Washington, James Madison, Benjamin Frank-

lin, and Alexander Hamilton. The delegates —
now the Founding Fathers — met to examine the
defects of the Articles of Confederation and to
develop a plan to remedy those defects. Under
the stewardship of James Madison, the Convention accepted for deliberation a series of fifteen
resolutions, known as the Virginia Plan, most of
which ultimately came to comprise the structural
framework of the new federal constitution. After
considerable debate and compromise, the delegates agreed to adopt the Constitution of the
United States and it was signed on September
17, 1787. Ratification by at least nine states was
then required. After nine months of debate in the
state legislatures and editorial commentary in the
press (the most influential of which, *The Federalist,* is discussed below), ratification was accomplished on June 21, 1788 with the affirmative
vote of New Hampshire.

**The Vir-
ginia Plan
provided
the
structure
for our new
Constitu-
tion**

An Influential Writing of the Time,
The Federalist

The ratification period was witness to a huge out-
pouring of commentary and debate, not only in
state legislatures and conventions, but also in the
private correspondence of influential politicians
and public commentary in the press. The most
influential publication was by far *The Federalist*.
According to noted constitutional scholar Edward
Earle Mead:

There are, indeed, few documents of American history which offer so rich a reward to the citizen who reads [*The Federalist*] with care and thoughtfulness. The spirit of the Federal Constitutional Convention — to establish a government sufficiently vigorous to assure political union and economic prosperity without infringing too far on the rights of the States and of individuals — is here revealed in striking fashion. And this is of no mere academic interest; it is the immediate concern of every intelligent American."[22]

The Federalist stands as the first authoritative interpretation of the Constitution and the first step in the long process of development that has given the Constitution its life, meaning, and importance. It has acquired all the weight and authority of a judicial decision and has been frequently cited in settling constitutional questions. Thomas Jefferson described *The Federalist* in 1825 as "an authority to which appeal is habitually made by all, and rarely declined or denied by any as evidence of the general opinion of those who framed and of those who accepted the Constitution of the United States on questions as to its genuine meaning."[23] Chief Justice John Marshall wrote, "Its intrinsic merit entitles it to this high rank [as a complete commentary on the Constitution], and the part two of its authors performed in framing the Constitution, put it very much in their power to explain the views with which it was framed."[24]

A complete commentary on the Constitution

The Federalist consists of eighty-five essays that originally appeared in several New York newspapers between the autumn of 1787 and the spring of 1788. The essays were political campaign documents designed to persuade the people of the state of New York to ratify the Constitution, which had just been drawn up in Philadelphia. Although the essays were written hurriedly for newspaper publication, they were the products of prolonged study, much thought, and extensive experience. Its three authors were quite young — Alexander Hamilton was 30, James Madison, 36, and John Jay, 42 — but whether viewed as statesmen, political thinkers, or practical politicians, they were among the most esteemed men of their age.

Chief credit for the work goes to Alexander Hamilton, who originated the idea and enlisted the help of James Madison and John Jay for its execution. Hamilton had distinguished himself as a regimental commander at Yorktown, as military secretary to General George Washington, and as a successful New York lawyer. His prominence was increased by his marriage into one of the richest and most powerful families in New York, that of General Philip Schuyler.

Alexander Hamilton originated the idea

The importance of Madison's contribution, considerable from any viewpoint, was enhanced by the commanding role he had played in the work of the Constitutional Convention. In that assemblage, Madison took the floor to debate on

virtually every important issue and gained a fab-
ulous reputation for scholarship. His political
astuteness was evident not only on the floor of the
convention, but even more so in his tireless and
adroit work in committees. He displayed a range
of statecraft and theoretical insight that not even
his closest friends could have foretold, and
for which historians have almost unanimously
dubbed him "the father of the Constitution."

Jay's contribution, while minor in comparison
to that of Hamilton or Madison, was nevertheless
significant. Older than either of his co-authors, his
prestige at the time was far greater than either
Hamilton's or Madison's. A prosperous New
York lawyer, Jay had been secretary of foreign
affairs for the United States under the Confederation. His diplomatic experience especially qualified him to discuss the advantages that the new
Constitution would provide the nation in the conduct of foreign affairs

**Madison
and
Hamilton
did not
person-
ally agree
with
every-
thing in
the new
Constitu-
tion**

Neither Madison nor Hamilton altogether approved of the shape the new Constitution had
taken. Madison was disappointed that some of
the provisions of his Virginia plan — for example,
the concept of proportional representation of the
several states in the Senate, and the federal legislature's power to negate state laws — had failed
to be included. Hamilton went even further. He
believed, for example, that the Constitution
should have included provisions that federal
authority should be strengthened at the expense

of the states, that members of the Senate and the
president should hold office for life, and that the
U.S. Constitution should more closely resemble
the English model.

Nonetheless, in *The Federalist* Madison and
Hamilton defended the whole of the Constitution
arrived at by the delegates in Philadelphia, giving
no hint of dissatisfaction. It was presumably their
view that while the new Constitution was flawed,
it was infinitely superior to the widely discredited
Articles of Confederation of 1781; and in the
political climate of the times there seemed little
chance of getting anything better.

Hamilton commented:

> I never expect to see a perfect work from imper-
> fect man. The result of the deliberations of all
> collective bodies must necessarily be a com-
> pound, as well of the errors and prejudices as of
> the good sense and wisdom of the individuals of
> whom they are composed. The compact which
> are to embrace the thirteen distinct States in a
> common bond of amity and union, must neces-
> sarily be a compromise of as many dissimilar
> interests and inclinations. How can perfection
> spring from such materials?[25]

**But an
imperfect
compro-
mise
was better
than
nothing**

Although the essays in *The Federalist* were
written long ago to address an immediate issue,
they have proved to be a permanent reservoir of
political wisdom, to be drawn on as new problems
arise. *The Federalist* reminds us that in a government by the people, everything must yield

sooner or later to the will of the people. The battle for the preservation of our political institutions
and our individual rights must be fought out not
in the courts but in the forum of public opinion. Even though *The Federalist* was originally
directed "To the People of New York," its chief
function is the same today as it has been for more
A guide than 200 years — not the guidance of the courts
for over
200 years but the shaping of public sentiment.

The Federalist has come to rank alongside
three public documents (the Declaration of Independence, the Constitution of the United States,
and its accompanying Bill of Rights) as one of the
most important writings in the history of the
American republic.

The Federalist and
Antifederalist Positions

Central to an understanding of the Constitution's
ratification process (and the later debate, adoption, and ratification of the Bill of Rights) is famil-
iarity with the alignment of the convention delegates into two opposing blocs: the Federalists, as
the pro-Constitution delegates called themselves,
and the Antifederalists, who opposed the ratification of a constitution which failed to include a
declaration of rights.

The Federalists, whose early leaders included
Alexander Hamilton, John Jay, James Madison,
and George Washington, believed that the strong

national government the Constitution provided should be ratified without change. In fact, some Federalists even believed the Constitution to be a perfect instrument, divinely inspired. The Federalists' opposition to the inclusion of a bill of rights in the Constitution was based upon the argument that a bill of rights was unnecessary and dangerous. This argument was put forward by Alexander Hamilton. As to a bill of rights being unnecessary, Hamilton argued:

Hamilton and the Federalists believed a bill of rights was unnecessary and dangerous

> It has been several times truly remarked that bills of rights are in their origin, stipulations between kings and their subjects . . . Such was Magna Carta . . . Such was the petition of right . . . Such also was the [English] bill of rights. It is evident, therefore, that according to their primitive signification, they have no application to constitutions professedly founded upon the power of the people, and executed by their immediate representatives and servants. *Here, in strictness, the people surrender nothing, and as they retain every thing, they have no need for particular reservations.* 'We the people of the United States, to secure the blessings of liberty to ourselves and our posterity, do ordain and establish the constitution of the United States of America.' Here is better recognition of popular rights than volumes of those aphorisms which make the principal figure in several of our state bills of rights. (Italics supplied)[26]

As to a bill of rights being dangerous, Hamilton argued:

> Bills of rights, in the sense and in the extent in which they are contended for . . . in the proposed constitution . . . would even be dangerous. They would contain various exceptions to powers which are not granted; and on this very account, would afford a colourable pretext to claim more than were granted. For why declare that things shall not be done which there is no power to do?[27]

There were some Federalists, of course, who did support adding a bill of rights, but the rules under which the proposed constitution had been signed prohibited any amendment to the document before ratification.

Antifederalists were highly suspicious of the power being granted to the federal government

The Antifederalists — among them Richard Henry Lee, Elbridge Gerry, George Mason, and Patrick Henry — were militant advocates for the inclusion of a bill of rights in the new Constitution. They were suspicious of the extraordinary powers that were to be granted to the federal government by a constitution lacking a bill of rights that would clearly and unequivocally protect certain rights and freedoms. Moreover, as Bernard Schwartz observes,

> The Federalist answer [to the objections of the Antifederalists] became increasingly less persuasive. Even if, in technical law, the Federalists were correct, it did not quiet the popular apprehension. Even if a Bill of Rights was not necessary, legally speaking, it could certainly do no harm. At the least, it would provide additional assurance that the new government would not

swallow up the liberties of the people. Thus the debate on the Constitution led to increasing popular pressure for a Bill of Rights to be added to the instrument. Even the Federalists were to yield to the pressure and admit the need for some amendments to protect fundamental rights.[28]

DRAFTING, ADOPTION, AND RATIFICATION OF THE BILL OF RIGHTS

When the first Congress assembled under auspices of the new Constitution, one of its early items of business was consideration of a federal bill of rights. Formulation of an initial draft of a bill of rights was under the leadership of James Madison, who had initially been lukewarm to the idea of adding a declaration of rights to the Constitution (a position he later modified under the political pressures of his closely contested campaign against the Antifederalist James Monroe for election to Congress). On June 8, 1789, Madison initiated the debate with his famous speech explaining the proposed amendments and why they were necessary. He pointed out that

Madison initially opposed a bill of rights but later changed his position

the great mass of the people who opposed [the Constitution], disliked it because it did not contain effectual provisions against encroachments on particular rights, and those safeguards which they have long been accustomed to have interposed themselves between them and the magistrate who exercises the sovereign power.[29]

Madison had begun work with a file of nearly one hundred suggested amendments (not counting duplications) proposed by eight states to be considered for inclusion in a bill of rights. As Bernard Schwartz reports:

> All eight of the states which proposed amendments (either officially or otherwise) recommended a provision like that ultimately contained the Tenth Amendment, reserving to the states powers not delegated to the Federal Government. Seven states recommended a right of jury trial in civil cases. Six urged protection for religious freedom. Five sought guarantees of freedom of the press (with three adding freedom of speech as well), the right to bear arms, trial by jury of the vicinage, prohibitions against quartering of troops, and unreasonable searches and seizures. Four states asked for protection of the right to "the law of the land" or due process, speedy public trial, assembly and petition, and against excessive bail and fines and cruel and unusual punishments. . . . Of twenty-two amendments which were supported by four or more states, fourteen were incorporated by Madison in his [final] recommendations to Congress.[30]

Twelve amendments were first proposed

Debate and redrafting began on June 8, 1789. Congress reduced that number to twelve and adopted the slate of amendments on September 25, 1789. Two amendments failed to be ratified, and the remaining ten, now called the Bill of

Rights, were ratified and placed into law on December 15, 1791.

A Modern Analysis of the Origins of the Rights Contained in the U.S. Bill of Rights

In the preceding pages, I have endeavored to give you an abbreviated history of the growth and development of the concepts of political freedom that influenced the drafting of our Bill of Rights. Our review included three English documents (Magna Carta, the Petition of Right, and the Bill of Rights), a number of American documents (the colonial charters, the state constitutions and declarations of rights, the Declaration of Rights and Grievances of the Stamp Act Congress, the Declarations and Resolves of the First Continental Congress, the Declaration of Independence, the Articles of Confederation, the Northwest Ordinance, and the U.S. Constitution), various private writings from England (those of the Whig writers as well as John Locke and William Blackstone), and two American writings (Thomas Paine's *Common Sense* and *The Federalist* of Hamilton, Madison and Jay).

Of course, James Madison and his fellow members of Congress were well acquainted with all of these documents. The question then arises: which were the primary sources from which Madison and his colleagues drew their inspira-

A
thought-
ful
study on
the
origins
of the Bill
of Rights

tion? One of our leading constitutional scholars, Donald S. Lutz,[31] has provided us with a thoughtful, innovative study[32] of the origin of the Bill of Rights. I'd like to share his thoughts with you.

"When Americans think and write about the U.S. Bill of Rights today," writes Professor Lutz, "one of three assumptions is usually made about its origin: 1) the Bill of Rights was the original, spontaneous product of a few minds in 1789; 2) the Bill of Rights was an updated American version of Magna Carta; or 3) James Madison simply compiled the Bill of Rights from the suggestions for amendments made by the state conventions that constitutionally ratified the U.S. Constitution. As it turns out, none of these working hypotheses is correct. Instead the Bill of Rights resulted more from a long political process on American shores, a process in which the states, and their respective colonial predecessors, played a key role.

States
played a
critical
role

"To deal with the second hypothesis first, it is possible to demonstrate the relatively minor influence of Magna Carta through a simple count of overlapping provisions. The Bill of Rights has twenty-six separate rights listed in its ten amendments:

> Establishment of Religion
> Free Speech
> Assembly
> Right to Bear Arms
> Searches

Grand Jury
Self-Incrimination
Just Compensation
Free Exercise of Religion
Free Press
Petition
Quartering Soldiers
Seizures
Double Jeopardy
Due Process
Speedy Trial
Jury Trial
Witnesses
Jury Trial (Civil)
Fines
Rights Retained by the People
Cause & Nature of Accusation
Counsel
Bail
Punishment
Reserved Powers

"Of these twenty-six rights, only four can be traced to Magna Carta using the most generous interpretation of that famous document. Looking at it from the other direction, only four of the sixty-three provisions of Magna Carta ended up in the U.S. Bill of Rights. This lack of overlap is not surprising since Magna Carta and the U.S. Bill of Rights have enormously different functions. The former defined the relationship between a king and his barons, whereas the latter placed limits on all branches of government vis-à-vis the entire citizenry.

"Despite the enormous historical importance of Magna Carta in content, form, and intent, it is only a distant forerunner of the U.S. Bill of Rights. Nor is the overlap with the rest of English common law, although important, that extensive. In addition to the four rights that can be traced to Magna Carta, another right in the U.S. Bill of Rights can be traced to the 1628 English Petition of Right, and two to the 1689 English Bill of Rights.[33] This brings to seven the number of rights among the twenty-six in the U.S. Bill of Rights that can be traced to a major English common law document, although the respected scholar Bernard Schwartz is only willing to make such a linkage for five of these seven rights.

Only seven rights can be traced to English common law documents

"Furthermore, as writers on the English common law always point out, Magna Carta had to be continually reconfirmed, at least forty-seven times by one count, because the document was ignored for long periods of time, and its contents were at best honored in the breach.[34] Indeed, despite the written guarantees for certain rights contained in major documents of English common law, at the time of the American revolution these rights were either not protected at all, or were not protected to the level that had become the case in America.[35]

"Even in those instances where protection of a right in England approached that in America, there was a fundamental difference in whose actions were limited. Partly for this reason,

James Madison said that there were too many differences between common law and the U.S. Bill of Rights to warrant comparison.

[The] truth is, they [the British] have gone no farther than to raise a barrier against the Crown; the power of the Legislature is left altogether too indefinite. Although I know whenever the great rights, the trial by jury, freedom of the press, or liberty of conscience, come in question [in Parliament] the invasion of them is resisted by able advocates, yet their Magna Carta does not contain any one provision for the security of those rights, respecting which the people of America are most alarmed . . . those choicest privileges of the people are unguarded in the British Constitution. But although . . . it may not be thought necessary to provide limits for the legislative power in that country, yet a different opinion prevails in the United States.[36]

Major differences between the English common law and our Bill of Rights

"At the very least, then, the attribution of the American Bill of Rights to English common law and its major documents such as Magna Carta must be supplemented with documents written on American shores, specifically, to state and colony documents."

Lutz also relies on this analysis to refute his first working hypothesis, that the Bill of Rights was the original, spontaneous product of a few minds in 1789. As he explains, "[Earlier state constitutions contained all but] the last two rights in the U.S. Bill of Rights [rights retained by the people and reserved powers] and sixteen of the twenty-six rights were *first* codified and protected in a document written by a colony's government (four more were first codified and protected in documents written by the [First] Continental Congress). . . . If the Bill of Rights was made up from nothing in 1789, then how do we explain the presence of these rights in the already existing state and colonial documents?"

Turning to his third working hypothesis, that James Madison simply used the one hundred amendments that had been proposed by the state ratifying conventions as the basis of his draft of the Bill of Rights, Lutz concludes otherwise. He reasons that ". . . while there is a modest relationship between what Madison put in his list and what the states proposed, Madison avoided almost all of the proposed amendments that the state ratifying conventions wanted most."

Madison avoided most of the amendments proposed by the states

"Madison needed to make some connection with state interests to mollify the Antifederalists, but he did not like most of [the amendments] the states proposed. The tactic he fastened upon was to exploit seams in the Antifederalist position on what amendments to make.

"[The Antifederalists] who argued most vigorously against the proposed Constitution offered three different kinds of amendments that were often intertwined and confused. One type of amendment was aimed at limiting the national government by withholding a specific power.

Examples included prohibitions on direct taxes, monopolies, and borrowing money on credit.

"A second type of amendment altered an institution in such a way as to pull its teeth. Examples included making senators ineligible for concurrent terms, giving state and national courts concurrent jurisdiction, and requiring a two-thirds vote in both houses for any bill dealing with navigation or commerce.

"A third type of amendment was one suitable for a bill of rights as we now understand it. Examples included protection of the rights to speak, write, publish, assemble, and petition (rights that safe-guarded the ability of the people to organize politically); as well as prohibitions on self-incrimination, double punishment, excessive bail, and [unreasonable searches] (rights that defined an impartial legal system). One can see in Madison's process a clear inclination toward the third over the first two kinds of amendment.

"[In effect, Madison finessed the Antifederalists, upsetting] some Antifederalists who argued that he had 'thrown a tub to the whale' (that is, had created a distraction to deflect public attention from the real issue), but it worked very well for one critical reason — Madison used the bills of rights attached to the state constitutions as his model." **Madison finessed the Antifederalists**

You will recall that earlier we had pointed out that Madison and Hamilton considered the declarations of rights contained in state constitutions to be ineffective in protecting rights, because state bills of rights did not prevent majorities from doing whatever they wished. So, in effect, they said to the Antifederalists, "This is a useless idea but if you want one, here it is, just like the nice ones you have in your state constitutions that won't work." The Antifederalists thus had difficulty opposing Madison's use of this model, since it was a model of their own making and was part of what they were demanding.

The Antifederalists were unable to oppose Madison's model

What happened then is this, according to Professor Lutz's analysis: "An examination of the state bills of rights written between 1776 and 1787 shows that Madison effectively extracted the least common denominator from them as the basis for his proposed list of amendments, excepting those rights which might reduce the power of the national government. *Almost every one of the twenty-six rights in the U.S. Bill of Rights could be found in two or three state documents, and most of them in five or more.*"[37] (Italics supplied)

He then concludes: ". . . The state constitutions and their respective bills of rights, not the amendments proposed by state ratifying conventions, are the immediate source from which the U.S. Bill of Rights was derived.

The idea of a written bill of rights came from the states

"Students of American politics sometimes speak of the states as laboratories for innovative policies that, after an initial trial at the state level, eventually form the basis for much legislation at the national level. On the other hand, innovation in American rights is usually portrayed as beginning with the United States Supreme Court and being imposed on the states. It is worth remembering that the very idea of a written bill of rights attached to a constitution, as well as the content of the U.S. Bill of Rights, developed first at the state level."

CREATION AND RECONSTRUCTION: AN OVERVIEW

How the Bill of Rights should be understood to contain eleven amendments: the ten ratified in 1791, plus an eleventh, the Fourteenth Amendment adopted in 1868 . . . The relationship between the Constitution and the Bill of Rights . . . The development of the doctrine of "incorporation," and how it has radically altered the meaning of the original Bill of Rights.

The Bill of Rights is traditionally identified as the first ten amendments to the U.S. Constitution. But to understand its meaning today, we should see the Bill of Rights as including *eleven* amendments: the first ten ratified in 1791, plus the Fourteenth Amendment — the "Reconstruction Amendment" — adopted in 1868 during the Reconstruction era following the Civil War. In effect, although they are not always aware of it, modern Americans read the

Founders' Bill of Rights through the lens of the later Reconstruction Amendment.

Let's first discuss the relationship between the original Constitution and the Bill of Rights. The Bill of Rights stands as the high temple of our constitutional order, yet we lack a clear view of it. The conventional view, endorsed over the years by a substantial segment of our legal community, is that the original Constitution proposed by the Philadelphia convention focused primarily on the *structure* of government — the relationship between the federal and state governments (federalism); the organization of the federal legislature into two houses (bicameralism); the separation of powers among the three branches of government; the amendment process and so on. By contrast, the Bill of Rights proposed by the first Congress is conventionally thought to have had little to say about such *structural* issues and to have focused instead on *rights* — vesting individuals and minority groups with substantive rights against popular majorities.[1]

This book offers a different perspective. Individual and minority rights were indeed a distinctive feature of the Bill of Rights, but not the sole, or even the dominant, feature. A close look at the Bill reveals structural ideas tightly interconnected with the language of rights — states' rights and majority rights alongside individual and minority rights — and also protection of various important organizations and institutions: church,

The relationship between the original Constitution and the Bill of Rights

This book offers a different perspective

militia, and jury. The genius of the original Bill of Rights was not to downplay organizational structure but to deploy it, not to impede popular majorities but to empower them.

Consider, in this regard, James Madison's famous assertion in *The Federalist* No. 51 that "[i]t is of great importance in a republic not only to guard the society against the oppression of its rulers, but to guard one part of the society against the injustice of the other part."[2] The conventional understanding of the Bill seems to focus almost exclusively on the second issue presented by Madison (protection of minority against majority) while ignoring the first (protection of the people against self-interested government). Yet as we shall show, the first issue was indeed first in the mind of those who framed the Bill. In their view, the Bill of Rights' central purpose was to assure that *the people maintained control over government.* They recognized that after the people have delegated power to a small set of specialized officials to run the government's day-to-day affairs, the danger exists that those officials might try to rule in their own self-interest, contrary to the interests and expressed wishes of the people. To minimize such self-dealing on the part of government officials, the Bill of Rights protected the ability of local governments to monitor and deter such federal abuse; it ensured that ordinary citizens would participate in the federal administration of justice through various jury provisions;

Madison's famous *The Federalist* No. 51

and it preserved the sovereign right of a majority of the people themselves to alter or abolish government and thereby pronounce the last word on constitutional questions. The essence of the Bill of Rights was more structural than not, and more supportive of majority rights than not.

The essence of the Bill of Rights

If this is so, how can we account for the conventional wisdom that the Bill of Rights is overwhelmingly about individual rights rather than structure?

This confusion has been perpetuated in our law schools, where instead of studying the Bill of Rights as a complete document, many law professors and legal scholars break up the Bill into separate blocks of text and examine each segment in isolation. Some amendments — the Second and Third — are even ignored.[3] Law professors often neglect to inquire into the rich interplay between the Constitution and the original Bill of Rights. When they write textbooks on constitutional law, they typically treat "the structure of government" by examining the Constitution and then treat "individual rights" by examining the Bill of Rights. If legal scholars and their disciples (law students and lawyers) have such a distorted vision of the Bill of Rights, is it any wonder the general public is confused?

Law professors perpetuate the confusion

In Part I of this book — "Creation" — we will challenge prevailing practice by offering an integrated survey of the Bill of Rights as it was originally conceived by the Founders, a survey that will illustrate how its provisions related to each other and to those of the original Constitution. In the process we hope to refute the prevailing notion that the original Bill of Rights and the Constitution represented two very different schemes for regulating government.

Our survey will also serve to clear up the misconception held by many Americans that the Constitution and Bill of Rights have always protected our most basic liberties against states. Rather, the original Bill of Rights restrained only the conduct of the federal government, not state governments. Consider for example the administration of criminal justice in state courts. While today we take for granted a number of freedoms associated with the criminal trial in state court — "right to a jury trial," "right to legal counsel," "right against self-incrimination," etc. — such rights were not protected by the federal government until the ratification of the Fourteenth Amendment in 1868, and the subsequent birth and development of the judicial doctrine of "incorporation." **The original Bill of Rights restrained only the conduct of the federal government**

Incorporation is a doctrine, as well as a process, by which the federal courts apply the provisions of the Bill of Rights to the states by interpreting the Fourteenth Amendment as encompassing — "incorporating" — those provisions. Stated another way, incorporation uses the words of the Fourteenth Amendment to make applicable against the states many of the provisions contained in the Bill of Rights. The process **Incorpor-** of incorporation began in 1897, gained momen- **ation** tum between the world wars, and climaxed dur- **began in** ing the Warren Court era in the 1960s. When the **1897** dust settled, the Court had read the Fourteenth Amendment to require that states, as well as the federal government, must observe most of the specific rights in the Bill of Rights.

In Part II — "Reconstruction" — we will try to show how, through the process of incorporation, the gravitational pull of the Fourteenth Amendment has altered the trajectory of the original Bill of Rights in area after area: freedom of speech and of the press, the right to keep and bear arms, the right of jury trial, the unenumerated rights retained by the people, and so on. In other words, we will show how the general concept of a "Bill of Rights" — indeed, the very phrase itself — has been reshaped (reconstructed, if you will) by the Fourteenth Amendment.

In short, in Part I we will *contest conventional wisdom* about the meaning of the original Bill of Rights by exploring its "Creation" (how it was originally conceived in tandem with the U. S. Constitution). Then in Part II we will *confirm conventional wisdom* about the Bill of Rights as it exists today by exploring its "Reconstruction" (how its meaning changed after going through the process of incorporation into the Fourteenth Amendment).[4]

I

Creation

I

FIRST THINGS FIRST

How our nationalist and states'-rights traditions, and the precise way judges have "incorporated" the Bill of Rights into the Fourteenth Amendment, have slanted our view of the original Bill of Rights . . . How the first two amendments proposed by the First Congress failed to achieve ratification . . . How debate over their provisions revealed the philosophical differences between Federalist and Antifederalist forces that were to influence the content of the other amendments.

The Founders' Bill of Rights was, unsurprisingly, a creature of its time. Yet because its eighteenth-century words play such an active role in twenty-first-century legal discourse, we may at

More than two centuries separate us from the world that birthed the Bill

times forget that more than two centuries separate us from the world that birthed the Bill. Before we fix our gaze on this eighteenth-century document, let us briefly consider how nineteenth- and twentieth-century events and ideas have organized our legal thinking, predisposing us to see certain features of the original Bill of Rights and to overlook others. And before we rush to examine the words that are first in our modern Bill of Rights, let us briefly consider the words that were first in the original Bill of Rights.

MODERN BLINDERS CONSTRICTING OUR VIEW OF THE ORIGINAL BILL OF RIGHTS

OUR NATIONALIST AND STATES'-RIGHTS TRADITIONS

Modern Americans inhabit a world whose constitutional terrain is dominated by a series of landmark Supreme Court cases that invalidated state laws and administrative practices in the name of individual constitutional rights. Many Americans now embrace a tradition that views state governments as a major threat to individual and minority rights, and federal officials — especially federal courts — as the special guardians of those rights.[1]

This nationalist tradition has deep roots. Over

the course of two centuries, the Supreme Court has struck down state and local action with far more regularity than it has invalidated acts of our federal government.[2] Early in the twentieth century, Justice Oliver Wendell Holmes declared, "I do not think the United States would come to an end if we lost our power to declare an Act of Congress void. I do think the Union would be imperiled if we could not make that declaration as to the laws of the several States."[3] Justice Holmes had reached maturity during the Civil War era, and he understood from firsthand experience that the constitutional amendments adopted following the war — particularly the Fourteenth Amendment — reflected a similar suspicion of state governments.

The nationalist tradition, however, is far older than Reconstruction; its deepest roots lie in Philadelphia, not Appomattox. An important goal of the Federalist framers in the Philadelphia convention was to forge a strong set of federally enforceable rights against abusive state governments. Several of these limits on states appear in Article I, section 10 of the original Constitution. Indeed, the Federalists' effort to create a strong central government drew much of its life from their dissatisfaction with small-scale politics and their belief, as exemplified in James Madison's *Federalist* No.10, that an "enlargement" of the government's geographic "sphere" would improve the caliber of public decision making.[4]

Alongside this nationalist tradition, however, lay a states'-rights tradition — also championed by Madison — that extolled the ability of local governments to protect citizens against abuses by central authorities. The foundations of this states'-rights tradition are even older than those of the nationalist tradition — indeed, older than the Union itself. In the seventeenth century, British North America began not as a single continent-wide entity but as a series of different and distinct colonies, each founded at a different moment with a distinct charter, a distinct history, a distinct immigration pattern, a distinct set of laws and legal institutions. For example, in 1760 "Virginia" was, legally speaking, an accomplished fact — its House of Burgesses had been meeting since the 1620s — but "America," as a legal entity, was still waiting to be born. Also, during the fateful years between the end of the French and Indian War and the beginning of the Revolutionary one, colonial governments took the lead in protecting their citizens from perceived abuses of the English Parliament. Colonial legislatures kept a close eye on the central government; sounded public alarms whenever they saw oppression in the works; and organized political, economic, and (ultimately) military opposition to perceived British evils.[5]

In helping to draft the Constitution and Bill of Rights, Madison was quite careful to identify the limits, as well as the affirmative scope, of

(margin note) Our states'-rights traditions are older than the Union itself

states' rights. State governments could monitor the federal one and mobilize political opposition to federal laws seen as oppressive, but no state entity could unilaterally nullify those laws or secede from the Union.[6] Moreover, Madison's scheme gave the federal government a crucial role in protecting citizens from abusive state governments. Later spokesmen for the states'-rights position, like John C. Calhoun and Jefferson Davis, disregarded these vital limits. Not only did their arguments on behalf of nullification and secession misread the Constitution's federal structure,[7] but these arguments were deployed on behalf of slavery, the ultimate violation of human dignity. The Civil War was the second war fought on American soil over the intertwined issues of states' rights and human rights, but this time the relation between the two sets of rights was different. In sharp contrast to the Revolutionaries' rhetoric of the 1770s, the Rebels' rhetoric of federalism in the 1860s came to be seen as conflicting with, rather than supportive of, true freedom.

Modern Americans are still living with the legacy of the Civil War, with modern rhetorical battle lines tracking those laid down more than a century ago. Nationalists recognize the need for a strong national government to protect individuals against abusive state governments, but often ignore the threat posed by a monstrous central regime unchecked by competing power centers.

Modern Americans are still living with the legacy of the Civil War

Conversely, states' rightists wax eloquent about the dangers of a national government run rampant, but regularly deploy the rhetoric of states' rights to defend states' wrongs. What has been lost in this modern debate is the crucial Madisonian insight that localism and liberty can sometimes work together rather than at cross-purposes. This is one of the themes that we hope will emerge from our fresh look at Madison's Bill of Rights.

Localism and liberty can sometimes work together

THE INCORPORATION PROCESS

As noted earlier, through the Fourteenth Amendment almost all the provisions of the Bill of Rights have come to be incorporated against the states, effectively changing its meaning. Whereas the Bill of Rights was originally a set of largely structural guarantees applying only against the federal government, it has now become a bulwark of rights against all government conduct, both federal and state. Whereas the Bill of Rights was originally drafted to protect the general citizenry from a possibly unrepresentative government, it has now has been pressed into the service of protecting vulnerable minorities from dominant social majorities. In addition, the precise way in which judges have "incorporated" the Bill of Rights into the Fourteenth Amendment has had the unfortunate effect of blinding us to the ways in which the Bill has been transformed. Courts and legal scholars now appear to be applying the Bill of Rights directly against states. The Fourteenth Amendment is mentioned only in passing if at all.[8] Like people with glasses who often forget that they are wearing them, most people read the Bill of Rights through the lens of the Fourteenth without realizing how powerfully that lens has refracted what they see.

It is time, then, to take off these glasses and see how the Bill of Rights looked before Reconstruction. Only then can we fully appreciate some of its most important features as originally conceived. When we remove our modern blinders, a rather different Bill of Rights comes into view. What follows in the upcoming chapters may sometimes startle modern readers. But upon reflection, we should not be surprised to learn that those present at the Creation inhabited a world very different from our own. And only after we understand their world and their original vision can we begin to assess, in a self-conscious and systematic way, how much of this vision, if any, has survived — or should survive — subsequent constitutional developments.

The Founders inhabited a world very different than our own

THE FIRST TWO FAILED AMENDMENTS

The Bill of Rights proposed by the First Congress consisted of twelve amendments. Yet only the last ten were ratified by the requisite three-fourths of state legislatures in 1791, thereby becoming "valid to all Intents and Purposes, as Part of [the] Constitution."[9] The first two failed amendments are nevertheless worthy of brief examination for the insights they provide into the thinking of the Federalists and Antifederalists in the First Congress.

An examination of the first two failed amendments

THE ORIGINAL FIRST AMENDMENT: SIZE AND REPRESENTATIVE CHARACTER OF THE HOUSE OF REPRESENTATIVES

The words that modern Americans refer to as the "First Amendment" really weren't "first" in the minds of the First Congress. Read the words that began their Bill of Rights:

> Article the first. . . . After the first enumeration required by the first Article of the Constitution, there shall be one Representative for every thirty thousand, until the number shall amount to one hundred, after which, the proportion shall be so regulated by Congress, that there shall be not less than one hundred Representatives, nor less than one Representative for every forty thousand persons, until the number of Representatives shall amount to two hundred, after which the proportion shall be so regulated by Congress, that there shall not be less than two hundred Representatives, nor more than one Representative for every fifty thousand persons.[10]

This would-be First Amendment obviously deals with the structure and organization of government, not individual rights. It is an explicit modification of the structural rule set out in Article I, section 2 of the Constitution, which mandates that the "Number of Representatives shall not exceed one for every thirty Thousand" constituents.[11]

Antifederalist Objections, Federalist Responses

This amendment responded to one of the Antifederalists' most important cluster of concerns: demography and geography — the numerical size of the citizenry and the spatial sweep of the nation. The Antifederalists adhered to classical political theory that suggested that republics could thrive only in geographically and demographically small societies, where citizens would be shaped by a common climate and culture, would hold homogeneous world views, would know each other, and could meet face-to-face to deliberate on public issues. Models of such republics included the Greek city-states and pre-Imperial Rome.[12]

James Madison and the Federalists stood this classical view on its head by claiming that a large and modestly diverse society could actually produce a more stable republic than could a small and homogeneous city or state. Madison's *Feder-*

One of the Antifederalists' most important concerns

alist No.10 is today recognized as the most elegant and incisive presentation of this revolutionary idea, but in fact the entire introductory section of *The Federalist* sought to confront squarely the Antifederalist concern about size. In *The Federalist* No. 2, for example, John Jay noted the many ways in which (white) Americans shared a basic uniformity that constituted them as one people, ethnically, culturally, linguistically, historically, commercially, and geographically.[13]

A related Antifederalist objection to the Constitution was that Congress too small, too rich, too "refined." The Antifederalists feared that because the legislature was so small, only great men with reputations spanning wide geographic areas could secure election.[14] Thus for Antifederalists the Constitution was at heart an aristocratic document, notwithstanding its ringing populist proclamations ("We the People . . . ") and dramatic ratification by specially elected popular conventions. Antifederalists feared that the aristocrats who would control Congress would have an insufficient sense of sympathy with, and connectedness to, ordinary people. Unlike state legislators, these lordly men in Congress would disdain their lowly constituents, who would in turn lose faith in the national government. In the end, the new government would be obliged to rule through corruption, force, and fear — with monopolies and standing armies — rather than through mutual confidence.[15]

For Antifederalists, the Constitution was at heart an aristocratic document

The Antifederalists were not simply concerned that Congress was too small relatively — too small to be truly representative of the great diversity of the nation. Congress was also too small absolutely — too small to be immune from secret plots and intrigue.

The Federalists were not oblivious to these concerns, as Madison's own language in *The Federalist* shows.[16] In fact, at the Philadelphia convention Madison had championed a motion to double the initial size of the House of Representatives from 65 to 130 members: "A *majority* of a *Quorum* of 65 members, was too small a number to represent the whole inhabitants of the U. States; They would not possess enough of the confidence of the people, and w[oul]d be too sparsely taken from the people, to bring with them all the local information which would be frequently wanted."[17] However, this motion went down to defeat in July.

But after the Constitution was ratified, Madison returned to the issue of congressional size, with a proposed first amendment that (at least in the short run) promised a larger — more representative, less aristocratic — Congress. Despite the Federalists' attempt to reach a compromise with the Antifederalists on these size-related issues, the amendment fell one state short of ratification. The key state appears to be Delaware, the only state that ratified the last ten amendments while rejecting the first.[18] Whatever its

The original First Amendment fell one state short of ratification

reasons for spurning the First Congress's First Amendment (the legislative history is sparse, but because of its tiny population and limited room for growth, Delaware had selfish reasons to favor as small a House of Representatives as possible), we do well to remember that only a single state — and a tiny one at that — stood between the ten success stories of Amendments III-XII and the failure of the original Amendment I.

THE ORIGINAL SECOND AMENDMENT: RESTRICTING ECONOMIC SELF DEALING

One of the principal objectives of the Bill of Rights' framers was to insure that the officials to whom the people have delegated power to run the government's day-to-day affairs would be restrained from self-dealing contrary to the interests and expressed wishes of the people. The original Second Amendment was obviously directed to minimize such activity: "Article the second. . . . No law, varying the compensation for the services of the Senators and Representatives, shall take effect, until after an election of Representatives shall have intervened."[19]

The original Second Amendment also went down to defeat

This amendment went down to defeat in the 1790s. Only six state legislatures ratified its words. The likely reason for its failure to achieve ratification is that whereas the original First

Amendment had focused on a key difference between an "aristocratic" Congress and more "democratic" state legislatures (so that the state legislators could cheerfully support the First Amendment without calling into question their own legitimacy), the original Second Amendment's issue of legislative salaries hit closer to home — close to their own pocketbooks. How could state legislators vote for this amendment without also triggering public demand for similar amendments to their respective state constitutions regulating their own salaries?[20]

However, the original Second Amendment apparently lived to fight another day. After lying dormant — and presumed dead — for nearly two centuries this Rip Van Winkle Amendment reawoke to a burst of attention and a flurry of ratifications in the 1980s and 1990s. In 1992, more than two hundred years after being proposed, the amendment was officially proclaimed valid — as the Twenty-seventh rather than the Second Amendment to the United States Constitution.

But the original Second Amendment lived to fight another day

II

OUR FIRST AMENDMENT

An examination of the original Third (our First) Amendment protecting religion and expression (speech, press, assembly and petition).

"Congress shall make no law respecting an establishment of religion, or prohibiting the free exercise thereof; or abridging the freedom of speech, or of the press; or the right of the people peaceably to assemble, and to petition the government for a redress of grievances."

The framers' Third — our First — Amendment affirmed vital rights of religion and expression; but it did so with a distinct tilt towards the rights of the majority and the protection of local interests.

Let's begin by considering the second half of the amendment: "Congress shall make no law . . . abridging the freedom of speech, or of the press; or the right of the people peaceably to assemble, and to petition the Government for a redress of grievances."

SPEECH AND PRESS

Our First Amendment provides for the freedom of speech and press in a working democracy.[1] However, the amendment's precise definition of those freedoms has undergone significant change over time. Like the two preceding failed amendments, the speech and press amendment in 1791 focused (at least in part) on the structure of the federal government and the linkage between the representatives in Congress and their constituents. Today, many scholars tend to view First Amendment rights as fundamentally *minority* rights — the rights of unpopular individuals or groups to speak out against a hostile and repressive majority.[2] But bear in mind that the body **The body that is restrained by this amendment is Congress** that is restrained by this amendment is not a hostile and repressive *majority of the people*, but rather *Congress*. Indeed, the earlier two failed amendments reflected the concern that congressional majorities may in fact have "aristocratical" and self-interested views in opposition to views held by a majority of the people. While it's true that the text of the First Amendment is surely broad enough to protect the rights of unpopular minorities (like Jehovah's Witnesses and Communists),[3] originally the amendment's historical and structural core was to safeguard the rights of popular *majorities* against a possibly unrepresentative and self-interested Congress.

Recall Madison's distinction in *The Federalist* No. 51 between the two main problems of republican government — first, protecting citizens generally from government officials pursuing their own self-interested agendas at the expense of their constituents; and second, protecting individuals and minorities from tyrannical majority factions of fellow citizens.[4] As did the First Congress's first two failed amendments, their next amendment evidenced more concern about a self-serving Congress than a tyrannical majority of citizens.

The two main problems of republican government

For as Madison was well aware, and as he reminds us in *Federalist* No. 10, the second issue, the danger of majority oppression of minorities, was far greater at the state than at the national level. In part, this was because congressional majorities operated at long distance — both geographically and emotionally — from their constituents, whereas state legislators were much closer to and more involved with their constituents' immediate concerns, making it far more likely that state legislative majorities would simply reflect the unrefined sentiments of popular majorities. Congress was singled out to be restrained by the First Amendment precisely because it was *less* likely to reflect majority will.

It becomes even more clear that the protection of popular majority speech was a central purpose of the original First Amendment when we recall its historic connection to jury trial: popular bodies outside regular government would protect popular speech criticizing government. Madison and his fellow drafters of the amendment were well aware of the historic common-law rule against "prior restraint"[5] — courts could not enjoin a publisher from printing offensive material but could entertain civil and criminal prosecutions for libel and sedition after publication. This rule worked to enhance the role of the jury: unlike prior restraints issued by judges — permanent government officials on the government payroll — libel and other post-publication prosecutions required jury trials in which ordinary citizens would be free to vote for publishers without fear of reprisal from the government.

The First Amendment's historic connection to jury trial

In the colonies, the celebrated 1730s trial of the New York publisher John Peter Zenger had placed the jury at center stage in libel cases, and it remained there even after the Revolution and Constitution.[6] As we shall see in more detail in Chapter 5, publishers prosecuted under the Alien and Sedition Acts in the late 1790s tried to plead their First Amendment defense directly to jurors. The judges, after all, had been appointed by the very same (increasingly unpopular) Federalist administration that the defendants had attacked in the press.

The Zenger libel trial contrasts sharply with modern First Amendment discourse, in which lawyers often seek to limit the power of juries on speech questions by appealing to federal judges. As the First Amendment's center of gravity has shifted to protection of unpopular, minority speech in the modern era (appropriately, in light of the Fourteenth Amendment), its natural institutional guardian has become an insulated judiciary rather than the popular jury.[7]

ASSEMBLY AND PETITION

When we turn our attention to the assembly and petition clauses of the First Amendment (". . . the right of the people peaceably to assemble, and to petition the government for a redress of grievances."), a similar pattern emerges. Both of these clauses plainly protect individuals and minority groups, but the clauses contain a *majority* protection that many modern scholars have overlooked. The right of the people to assemble does not simply protect the ability of self-selected clusters of individuals to meet together; it is also an express reservation of the collective right of We the People to assemble in a future convention and exercise our sovereign right to alter or abolish our government. In the words of Rousseau's 1762 treatise on the social contract, "the sovereign can act only when the people are assembled."[8]

Read carefully these remarks of presiding offi-

These clauses contain a protection of the majority that is often overlooked

cer Edmund Pendleton at the Virginia ratifying convention of 1788:

> We, the people, possessing all power, form a government, such as we think will secure happiness: and suppose, in adopting this plan, we should be mistaken in the end; where is the cause of alarm on that quarter? In the same plan we point out an easy and quiet method of reforming what may be found amiss. No, but, say gentlemen, we have put the introduction of that method in the hands of our servants, who will interrupt it from motives of self-interest. What then? . . . Who shall dare to resist the people? No, we will assemble in Convention; wholly recall our delegated powers, or reform them so as to prevent such abuse. . . . [9]

This rich paragraph has it all: primary attention to the problem of the self-dealing of government officials, dogged unwillingness to equate Congress with a majority of the people, and keen appreciation of the collective right of the people to bring wayward government to heel by assembling in convention.

Constitutional conventions were typical models for the exercise of the right of assembly

Members of the First Congress shared Pendleton's understanding that constitutional conventions were typical models for the exercise of the right of assembly.[10] As Gordon Wood has observed, "conventions . . . of the people . . . were closely allied in English thought with the people's right to assemble."[11] For example, we find Blackstone describing how, in 1688, the British people, through Parliament, "assemble[d]" in "convention."[12] And in Revolutionary America, we almost invariably find the words *people*, *assemble*, and *convention* tightly clustered in discussions of popular sovereignty and the right to alter or abolish government — in state constitutions and bills of rights,[13] in early state and federal case law,[14] in the wording of the Philadelphia convention's initial version of Article VII of the Constitution,[15] and throughout the ratification debates.[16]

Regarding petition, the amendment explicitly guarantees "the right of the people" to petition — phraseology that also connects the right of petition with the idea of popular sovereignty. Indeed, the ideas of petition, assembly, and convention were tightly intertwined in eighteenth-century America.[17] In the Continental Congress's 1774 Declaration of Rights, and in all six of the Revolutionary-era state constitutions affirming a right of the people to assemble, the right was explicitly yoked to the right of petition.[18]

To be sure, like its companion assembly clause, the petition clause also protects individuals and minority groups. But to focus only on minority invocations of the right to petition is to miss at least half of the clause's meaning. Like the other provisions of the First Amendment, the right of petition addresses the special concern that, given Congress's small size and elite status, representatives would not have adequate knowledge of local conditions, popular sentiments and

The petition clause also protects individuals and minority groups

their constituents' — the majority's — wants and needs.[19]

RELIGION

The establishment clause of the First Amendment ("Congress shall make no law respecting an establishment of religion, or prohibiting the free exercise thereof . . .") did more than prohibit Congress from establishing a national church. Its mandate that Congress shall make no law "*respecting* an establishment of religion" also prohibited the national legislature from interfering with, or trying to *dis*-establish, churches established by state and local governments.[20] In 1789, at least six states had government-supported churches — Congregationalism held sway in New Hampshire, Massachusetts, and Connecticut under local-rule establishment schemes, while Maryland, South Carolina, and Georgia each featured a more general form of establishment in its state constitution.[21] Even in the remaining states, church and state were hardly separate; at least four of these states, for example, barred non-Christians or non-Protestants from holding government office.[22] According to one tally, eleven of the thirteen states had religious qualifications for officeholding.[23] In fact, commenting on the First Amendment in his celebrated *Commentaries on the Constitution*, Joseph Story observed that "the whole power

The establishment clause also prohibited Congress from *dis*-establishing churches established by state and local governments

over the subject of religion is left exclusively to the state governments."[24]

Thomas Jefferson, often invoked today as a strong opponent of religious establishment, appears to have understood the states'-rights aspects of the original establishment clause. Although he argued for an absolutist interpretation of the First Amendment — that the federal government should have nothing whatsoever to do with religion in the states — he was more willing to flirt with governmental endorsements of religion at the state level, especially where no state coercion would impinge on dissenters' freedom of conscience.

Thus, *President* Jefferson in 1802 refused to proclaim a day of religious Thanksgiving, but *Governor* Jefferson had agreed to do so some twenty years before.[25] In defending his practice to the Reverend Samuel Miller in 1808, Jefferson quoted both the First and Tenth Amendments and explained: "I am aware that the practice of my [presidential] predecessors may be quoted. But I have ever believed that the example of state executives led to the assumption of that authority by the general government, without due examination, which would have discovered that what might be a right in a state government, was a violation of that right when assumed by another."[26]

Interestingly, a virtually identical view was voiced in the First Congress on September 25,

Jefferson understood the states'-rights aspects of the original establishment clause

1789 — the very day the Bill of Rights cleared both houses. When New Jersey Representative Elias Boudinot introduced a bill recommending "a day of public thanksgiving and prayer," South Carolina's Thomas Tucker rose up in opposition: "[I]t is a religious matter, and as such, is proscribed to us. If a day of thanksgiving must take place, let it be done by the authority of the several States. . . ."[27]

Like the general topic of state religious policy, restrictions on speech and press were also seen by many friends of the Constitution as falling beyond Congress's Article I enumerated powers. Thus, our First Amendment opened with words suggesting an utter lack of enumerated congressional power to regulate religion in the states or restrict speech: "*Congress shall make no law*" — a phrase that precisely tracked and inverted the exact wording of the Article I clause declaring that "*Congress shall* have power . . . to *make all laws* which shall be necessary and proper" to meet legitimate federal goals. No other Amendment in the Bill of Rights used this "Congress shall make no law" phrase, and no state constitution in 1789 linked religion with expression. Both of these telling facts suggest that the framers' Third (our First) Amendment was in part a federalism provision designed to reinforce the idea that Congress enjoyed only limited enumerated power, and that such power simply did

The framers' Third (our First) Amendment was in part a federalism provision

not extend to religious regulations or censorship in the several states.

This states'-rights understanding thus helps to explain why the religion clauses and the rights of speech, press, and the like were lumped together into a single amendment. To be sure, there is also truth rooted in conventional wisdom that the free exercise of religion clause flanks the free-speech clause to remind us of the importance of protecting not only political speech (as emphasized by the adjoining assembly and petition clauses) but religious speech, too.[28]

As we shall see, the next two amendments in the Bill also sought to safeguard the foundations of democracy, albeit in a different way.

III

THE SECOND AND THIRD AMENDMENTS

(THE MILITARY AMENDMENTS)

These amendments were included in the Bill to protect the people from the possible tyranny of an aristocratic central government. The Second Amendment, as originally framed, guaranteed the people the right to keep and bear arms, and also prohibited the federal government from drafting citizens into the army in peacetime . . . The Third Amendment prohibits the quartering of soldiers in private homes in peacetime.

THE SECOND AMENDMENT

"A well regulated Militia, being necessary to the security of a free State, the right of the people to keep and bear arms, shall not be infringed."

As with our First Amendment, the text of the Second is broad enough to protect rights of private individuals and discrete minorities; but, as with the First, the Second's principal concerns are the needs of the popular majority and the relationship between the federal and state governments.

POPULAR SOVEREIGNTY IN ACTION

As we have already noted in our discussion of the First Amendment, the rights of the people to petition and assemble in conventions are intimately bound up with the people's right to alter or abolish their government. Whenever self-interested government agents abused their powers or shirked their duties, "the people" could "assemble" in convention and reassert their sovereignty. "Who shall dare to resist the people?" asked Edmund Pendleton with flourish in the Virginia ratifying convention.[1]

Only an armed populace could deter a central government from resisting the sovereignty of the people

To many Antifederalists, the answer to Pendleton's question seemed both obvious and ominous. An aristocratic central government, lacking sympathy with and confidence from ordinary constituents, might dare to resist — especially if that government were propped up by a standing army of mercenaries, vagrants, convicts, aliens, and the like. Only an armed populace could deter such an awful spectacle. Hence the need to bar Congress from disarming freemen. Thus the Second Amendment was closely linked to the textually adjoining First Amendment's guarantees of assembly and petition. One textual tip-off is the use in both amendments of the authoritative phrase "the people" from the Constitution's Preamble, thereby conjuring up the Constitution's grand principle of popular sovereignty and the popular right to alter or abolish the national government. More obvious is the preamble to the Second Amendment itself, and its concern with democratic self-government in a "free State."

History also connected the right to keep and bear arms with the idea of popular sovereignty. In Locke's influential *Second Treatise of Government*, the people's right to alter or abolish tyrannous government invariably required a popular appeal to arms.[2] To Americans in 1789, this was not merely speculative theory. It was the lived experience of their age. Beginning with the shot heard round the world, when British soldiers met armed Massachusetts minutemen at Lexington and Concord, Americans had seen the Lockean words of the Declaration of Independence — affirming "the Right of the People to alter or to abolish" oppressive government — made flesh (and blood) in a Revolution wrought by arms. Thus when Pendleton trumpeted the right of the people to assemble in convention as the answer to any federal misbehavior, Patrick Henry rose

History also connected the right to keep and bear arms with popular sovereignty

up to offer a more bleak assessment: "O sir, we should have fine times, indeed, if, to punish tyrants, it were only sufficient to assemble the people! Your arms, wherewith you could defend yourselves, are gone. . . ."[3]

The distinction between *political* and *civil* rights

In connection with arms-bearing, consider the key nineteenth-century distinction between *political* rights and *civil* rights. Political rights were rights of only certain members of society — call them First-Class Citizens — whereas civil rights belonged to all (free) members of the entire society. Alien men and single white women circa 1800 typically could speak, print, worship, enter into contracts, hold personal property in their own name, sue and be sued, and exercise sundry other civil rights, but typically could not vote, hold public office, or serve on juries. These last three were political rights, reserved for First-Class Citizens. So too, the right to bear arms had long been viewed as a political right, a right of First-Class Citizens. Thus the "people" at the core of the Second Amendment were the same "We the People" who in conventions had "ordain[ed] and establish[ed]" the Constitution and whose right to reassemble in convention was at the core of the First Amendment.

In emphasizing these central concerns of the Second Amendment, we do not deny that the phrase *the people* can be read broadly, and that other interpretations and definitions can placed under the language of the Second Amendment's spacious canopy. (After all, if a citizen is in lawful possession of a firearm in order to be prepared for service in the militia, it might be reasonable to suppose that he might also use it lawfully to pursue game or to defend his homestead.)[4] But to see the original Second Amendment crafted by the Founding Fathers as being primarily concerned with an individual's right to hunt or to protect his home is like viewing the heart of the speech and assembly clauses of the First Amendment as being the right of persons to meet to play bridge or to have sex.[5] In their view, the Second Amendment was first and foremost *a military amendment*. But as we shall see in Part II, the Reconstruction Congress was to radically alter that definition.

Originally, the Second Amendment was a *military amendment*

FEDERALISM

Even if heavily armed, citizens acting individually would face an uphill struggle when confronting a disciplined and professional standing army. In *The Federalist* No. 28, Alexander Hamilton described a typical nonfederal regime: "[I]f the persons intrusted with supreme power become usurpers, the different parcels, subdivisions, or districts of which [the nation] consists, having no distinct government in each, can take no regular measures for defense. The citizens must rush tumultuously to arms, without concert, without system, without resource. . . ."[6] In the federal system of America, however, Article I, section 8, clause 16 of the Constitution explicitly delegated to state governments the power of "Appointment of the officers, and the authority of training the militia according to the discipline prescribed by Congress." In the event of central tyranny, state governments could do precisely what colonial governments had done beginning at Lexington and Concord and Bunker Hill: organize and mobilize their citizens into an effective fighting force capable of besting even a large standing army. Wrote Madison in *The Federalist* No. 46: "[T]he State governments with the people on their side would be able to repel the danger. . . . [A standing army] would be opposed [by] a militia amounting to near half a million of citizens with arms in their hands, officered by men chosen from among themselves, fighting for their common liberties and united and conducted by governments possessing their affections and confidence."[7]

The "military check of federalism" did not quiet Antifederalist fears

Yet the "military check of federalism"[8] built into the original Constitution did not quiet Antifederalist fears. Many pointed a suspicious finger at earlier language in clause 16 of the Constitution empowering Congress "to provide for organizing, arming, and disciplining, the militia." Might Congress try to use the power granted by these words, they asked darkly, to *dis*arm the militia?[9] The Second Amendment was designed to make clear that any such congressional action was off-limits.

The obvious importance of states' rights in the Constitution's original allocation of military power prompts key questions about the relationship between the federal and state governments in interpreting the language of the Second Amendment. Several modern scholars have read the amendment as protecting only arms-bearing in organized "state militias," like SWAT teams and National Guard units.[10] If this reading were accepted, the Second Amendment would be at base a right of state governments rather than citizens.

This reading doesn't quite work. The states'-rights reading puts great weight on the word *militia*, but this word appears only in the amendment's subordinate clause. The ultimate right to keep and bear arms belongs to "the *people*" not the *states*. As we will see later when we examine the language of the Tenth Amendment, these two words are of course not identical: when the Constitution means "states," it says so.[11] Thus, as noted above, "the people" at the core of the Second Amendment are the same people at the heart of the Preamble of the Constitution and the First Amendment. Elbridge Gerry put the point nicely in the First Congress, in language that closely tracked the populist concern about governmental self-dealing at the root of earlier amendments: "This declaration of rights, I take

The ultimate right to keep and bear arms belongs to "the people" not the states

it, is intended to secure *the people* against the
mal-administration of the Government."[12]

**The word
"militia"
had a very
different
meaning
two hun-
dred years
ago**

What's more, the "militia," as used in the Second Amendment and in clause 16 of the Constitution, had a very different meaning two hundred
years ago than in ordinary conversation today.
Nowadays, it is quite common to speak loosely of
the National Guard as "the state militia," but two
hundred years ago, any band of paid, semiprofes-
sional, part-time volunteers, like today's Guard,
would have been called "a *select* corps" or
"*select* militia" — and viewed in many quarters
as little better than a standing army.[13] Indeed, in
1789, when used without any qualifying adjective, "the militia" referred to all First-Class
Citizens capable of bearing arms.[14] The seeming
tension between the dependent and the main
clauses of the Second Amendment thus evapo-
rates on closer inspection — the "militia" is identical to "the people" in the core (First-Class Citizen) sense described above, encompassing adult
male citizens eligible to vote, serve on juries, and
hold public office. Indeed, the version of the Second Amendment that initially passed in the
House, only to be stylistically shortened in the
Senate, explicitly defined the militia as "composed of the body of the People."[15] This is clearly
the sense in which "*the* militia" is used in clause
16 of the Constitution and throughout *The Federalist*,[16] in keeping with standard usage[17] confirmed by contemporaneous dictionaries, legal

and otherwise. As Tench Coxe wrote in a 1788 Pennsylvania essay, "Who are the militia? Are they not ourselves?"[18]

A FEDERAL DRAFT?

The Founders' Constitution, as modified by the Second Amendment, did not authorize the federal government to draft citizens directly into a federal army. Consider first the following clauses in the Constitution's Article I, section 8:

The Congress shall have Power . . .

clause   1 – To lay and collect taxes [and] duties . . .

clause   9 – To constitute tribunals inferior to the Supreme Court:

clause 12 – To raise and support armies . . .

clause 13 – To provide and maintain a navy:

clause 15 – To provide for calling forth the militia to execute the laws of the Union, suppress insurrections and repel invasions:

clause 16 – To provide for organizing, arming, and disciplining the militia . . . reserving to the States respectively, the appointment of the officers, and the authority of training the militia according to the discipline prescribed by Congress.

By itself, the authority to "raise" armies in clause 12 no more naturally grants Congress the power to conscript soldiers than does clause 1's authority to "lay and collect Taxes [and] Duties" grant Congress the power to draft tax collectors and customs officers; nor does clause 9's authority to "constitute tribunals inferior to the Supreme Court" grant Congress the power to conscript judges and bailiffs;[19] nor does clause 13's authority to "provide and maintain a navy" grant it the power to engage in the odious practice of impressment (to compel a person to serve in the mililtary).[20]

In 1789, the word *army* meant a mercenary force

In 1789, the word *army* — as opposed to the word *militia* — meant a mercenary force, as even a casual glance at contemporaneous dictionaries reveals.[21] This was largely why an "army" was feared. It was not composed of a randomly conscripted cross-section of the general militia (all First-Class Citizens capable of bearing arms), but was instead filled with hired guns. These men, full-time soldiers who had sold themselves into virtual bondage to the government, were typically considered the dregs of society — men without land, homes, families, or principles. Full-time service in the army further weakened their ties to a civilized, civilian society, and harsh army discipline increased their servility to the government.

Small wonder, then, that many traditional republicans opposed standing armies, at least in peacetime. (Perhaps in war, with the very survival of the nation at stake, an army was the lesser of two evils — an American army of mercenaries might be marginally less threatening to domestic liberty than an enemy army of mercenaries.) Thus, mainstream republican thought in the late eighteenth century saw a "well regulated *Militia*" as the best "security of a free State."

Of course, clause 15 clearly gave Congress authority in actual emergencies to federalize the militia instead of raising an army — but only under a system of cooperation with the states in order to maintain the integrity of the militia. Furthermore, clause 16 painstakingly prescribed the precise role that state governments had to play in training and organizing the militia and in appointing its officers. These carefully wrought limitations in clause 16 were widely seen in 1789 as indispensable barriers against any congressional attempt to misuse its power over citizen militiamen. Yet these barriers would become trivial if Congress could outflank them by relabeling militiamen as army "soldiers" conscriptable at will, in time of war or peace, under the purported authority of the clause 12 army provision.[22] Seen from another angle, the Constitution's explicit invocation of "the militia" in clause 16, in contradistinction to its use of "armies" in clause 12, makes clear that each word is used in its ordinary-language sense: *army* means enlisted soldiers, and *militia* means citizen conscripts.[23]

The realities of eighteenth-century life confirm this reasoning. The unfortunate individuals who were miserable enough to volunteer as hired guns might deserve whatever treatment that they got at the hands of army officers, but citizens wrenched by conscription from their land, their

Army means enlisted soldiers, and *militia* means citizen conscripts

homes, and their families deserved better. Such individuals were entitled to be placed in units with fellow citizens from their own locality. In fact, "the [militia] muster was almost a family reunion. Fathers and sons, uncles and nephews, brothers, cousins and in-laws often enlisted in the same units."[24] "The Minutemen of the towns were held together less by chains of command than by familial loyalties. . . . Over one-quarter of the Lexington militiamen mustered by Captain John Parker on April 19, 1775, were related to him by blood or marriage."[25] In this system, local militiamen were entitled to be officered by local leaders — men chosen by state governments closest to them and most representative of them, men who were likely to be persons of standing in their communities (indeed, likely to be elected civilian officials), men whom they were likely to know directly or indirectly from civilian society and who were likely to know them.[26] The ordinary harshness of military discipline would be tempered by the many social, economic, and political linkages that predated military service and that would be renewed thereafter. Officers would know that, in a variety of ways, they could be called to account back home after the fighting was over. Men serving alongside their families, friends, neighbors, classmates, and fellow parishioners — in short, their community — would be constantly reminded of civilian norms of conduct.

They were less likely to become uncivilized marauders or mindless brutes. Thus the preeminent constitutional principle of civilian control over the military[27] would be embedded in the everyday mind-set of each militiaman. Adam Smith put the point as follows, in words later quoted by the most important Second Amendment case decided by the Supreme Court in the twentieth century, *United States v. Miller*: "In a militia, the character of the labourer, artificer, or tradesman, predominates over that of the soldier: in a standing army, that of the soldier predominates over every other character; and in this distinction seems to consist the essential difference between those two different species of military force."[28]

In the end, the militia system was carefully designed to protect liberty through localism. Freedom and federalism pulled together. Just as the establishment clause of the First Amendment saw a national establishment of religion as far more likely to oppress than state and local establishments — and in the worst case scenario, it was always easier for one to flee an oppressive locality or state than the nation as a whole — so here, national conscription was far more dangerous than the state and local militia system.

Postconstitutional history supports this analysis. During the War of 1812, various sorts of federal draft bills were introduced, setting the scene

The militia system was carefully designed to protect liberty through localism

for an important congressional debate over the army and militia clauses of Article I and their relationship to the Second Amendment. Opposition to these bills in the House of Representatives was led by none other than Daniel Webster, who argued that any federal draft under the army clause impermissibly evaded the constitutional limitations on federal use of the militia. The plan was an illegitimate attempt to raise "a standing army out of the militia by draft."[29] Webster conjured up a vivid image of the evils of such an evasion of clause 16:

> Where is it written in the Constitution, . . . that you may take children from their parents, and parents from their children . . .[?]
> . . . .
> But this father or this son . . . goes to the camp. With whom do you associate him? With those only who are sober and virtuous and respectable like himself? No, sir. But you propose to find him companions in the worst men of the worst sort. Another bill lies on your table offering a bounty to deserters from your enemy. Whatever is most infamous in his ranks you propose to make your own. . . . In the line of your army, with the true levelling of [Napoleonic] despotism, you propose a promiscuous mixture of the worthy and the worthless, the virtuous and the profligate; the husbandman, the merchant, the mechanic of your own country, with [the dregs of Europe] who possess neither interest, feeling, nor character in common with your own people, and who have no other recommendation . . . than their propensity to crimes.

However, as will be evident when we examine the Reconstruction's Fourteenth Amendment in Part II, by the late 1860s loyal Unionists had a much more sympathetic view of a national army and a much more skeptical view of state-organized militias. This nationalist view was embraced yet again during World War I, when in the *Selective Draft Law Cases*[30] the Supreme Court upheld a federal draft. Though hard to square with the original Founding vision, the Court's approach draws support from post-Founding developments. Over the centuries, circumstances have changed — the Founding Fathers' militia does not really exist today, and their military balance between the central army and local militias was profoundly changed by the Civil War and the Fourteenth Amendment.

THE THIRD AMENDMENT

"No soldier shall, in time of peace be quartered in any house, without the consent of the owner, nor in time of war, but in a manner to be prescribed by law."

Like the Second Amendment, the Third centrally focuses on the issue of protecting civilian values against the threat of an overbearing military. No standing army in peacetime can be allowed to dominate civilian society, either openly or by subtle insinuation. The Second

Amendment's militia could thwart any open military usurpation — say, a siege — but what about more insidious forms of military occupation, featuring federal soldiers cowing civilians by psychological guerrilla warfare, day by day and house by house? Bostonians who had lived under the hated Quartering Act of 1774 knew that this was no wild hypothetical. Hence the Third Amendment was needed to deal with military threats too subtle and stealthy for the Second's "well regulated militia."

It is no accident that the Second and Third Amendments stand back-to-back, for these siblings spring from the same stock: at heart they are *military* amendments. In the English Bill of Rights of 1689, the quartering question locked arms with the more general military issue of standing armies. In the words of the Bill's preamble, James II had subverted the liberties of his subjects by "raising and keeping a standing army within this kingdom in time of peace, without consent of parliament, and quartering soldiers contrary to law."[31]

At heart, the Second and Third Amendments are *military* amendments

Americans learned these lines well and reenacted them in staging their own Glorious Revolution a century later. In the Declaration of Independence, the colonists scolded King George for keeping "among us, in times of peace, Standing Armies without the Consent of our legislatures"; and in the very next clause for affecting "to render the Military independent of and superior to the Civil power"; and in the next clause for approving Parliamentary laws "quartering large bodies of armed troops among us."[32]

Most Revolutionary state constitutions that addressed quartering followed a rather similar pattern, linking together various military issues in an integrated package.[33] These linkages are nicely visible in the remarks of Patrick Henry in Virginia:

> [T]he clause which gives Congress the power of raising armies . . . appears a very alarming power, when unlimited. [Congress] are not only to raise, but to support, armies; and this support is to go to the utmost abilities of the United States. If Congress shall say that the general welfare requires it, they may keep armies continually on foot. There is no control on Congress in raising or stationing them. They may billet them on the people at pleasure. This unlimited authority is a most dangerous power: its principles are despotic. If it be unbounded, it must lead to despotism; for the power of a people in a free government is supposed to be paramount to the existing power.
> . . . Here we may have troops in times of peace. They may be billeted in any manner — to tyrannize, oppress, and crush us.[34]

The Constitution's Article I, section 8, clause 15 limits Congress's power to commandeer local militias to specified national emergencies; the militia may be called out by the federal government to "execute the Laws of the Union, suppress Insurrections and repel Invasions." In similar fashion the Third Amendment limits Congress's quartering power to wartime. (Note also that the English Bill of Rights, the Declaration of Independence, various state constitutions and conventions, and Patrick Henry's above-quoted speech, all sharply distinguished between peacetime and wartime.)[35]

The strict limits in both the militia clause of the Constitution and the Third Amendment derive from the awesome nature of the conscription power. Like a criminal sanction, conscription of a person's body or his place of abode can take over much of his life.

This leads to our final point about the Third Amendment. The Third Amendment requires a special legislative finding before a civilian's house can be conscripted. Military use must be prescribed by national law, and only Congress can pass such a law.[36] Thus the amendment stands as an important reaffirmation of separation of powers and limited executive authority.

Today the separation-of-powers implications of the Third Amendment often go unnoticed

Today, the separation-of-powers implications of the Third Amendment and, in fact, the entire Bill of Rights, often go unnoticed because of our modern-day fixation on individual rights. To put the point a different way, the deep spirit of the Third Amendment cautions extreme skepticism about unilateral executive assertions of military necessity.

To the extent that modern Americans think

about the Third Amendment at all, they are likely to see it as an affirmation of the general right of individual privacy that today is thought to be contained in the Bill of Rights — a right most famously asserted in the modern era by Justice Douglas's opinion of the Court in *Griswold v. Connecticut*.[37] In today's world, lawyers, scholars, and judges therefore tend to link the Third Amendment to the Fourth rather than to the Second, despite the fact that no state constitution or convention paired antiquartering and anti-search clauses. But as we have seen, privacy is not the whole story — indeed perhaps not even the headline. To be sure, there is an important connection between the Third and Fourth Amendments. Both explicitly protect "houses" — above and beyond all other buildings — from needless and dangerous intrusions by governmental officials. But the privacy connections between the Third Amendment and the Fourth Amendment must not be allowed to obscure the originally more significant but typically unmentioned military linkages between the Third Amendment and the Second. With this in mind, let us now turn to the Fourth in its own right.

Today the legal profession tends to link the Third Amendment to the Fourth rather than to the Second

IV

THE FOURTH
AMENDMENT

(SEARCHES, SEIZURES, AND
FIFTH AMENDMENT TAKINGS)

*How the people are protected
from the unreasonable search or
seizure of their persons, houses,
papers and effects . . . That no
warrants shall issue except upon
probable cause . . . That the
determination of the legality of
these issues, originally involving
a jury, has now been placed into
the hands of judges and magistrates . . . The interrelationship
among the First, Fourth, and
Seventh Amendments . . . How
the takings clause of the Fifth
Amendment can be better understood by reading it through the
prism of the Fourth.*

"The right of the people to be secure in their
persons, houses, papers, and effects, against
unreasonable searches shall not be violated, and

> no warrants shall issue, but upon probable
> cause, supported by oath or affirmation, and
> particularly describing the place to be searched,
> and the persons or things to be seized."

So reads our Fourth Amendment. How do its
words and spirit fit with the rest of the Bill?

A RIGHT OF THE PEOPLE?

We have already noted that the First and Second
Amendments' references to "the people" implied
a core *collective right*, echoing the commitment
of the Preamble of the Constitution to the ultimate sovereignty of "We the People of the
United States." The historian Lawrence Cress
has argued that in constitutions in "state after
state, [the phrases] 'the people' or 'the militia'
[were used to connote] the sovereign citizenry,
described collectively." In contrast, "the expression, *'man'* or *'person'* [was typically] used to
describe *individual rights* such as freedom of conscience."[1] The Virginia ratifying convention's
declaration of rights followed a similar pattern,
invoking "the people's" rights to assembly,
instruction, speech, and arms-bearing but using
"every freeman" and "man" in connection with a
variety of individual civil rights involving due-
process and criminal-procedure safeguards. The
Virginia prototype of the Fourth Amendment

similarly used the word "person" to describe an individual right — "every *freeman* has a right to be secure from all unreasonable searches and seizures of his *person*. . . ."[2] Madison was surely aware of this, given his leading role in the Virginia convention, but his initial proposal for the Fourth Amendment instead invoked not "person" but "the people"[3] — language that survived all subsequent congressional modifications.

Was Madison's use of the phrase "the people" simply sloppy draftsmanship, or is there a way of understanding that the original Fourth Amendment was drafted to protect both collective as well as individual rights?

In the Fourth Amendment, as nowhere else in the Constitution, the collective-sounding phrase *the people* is immediately qualified by the use — twice — of the more individualistic language of *persons*. The amendment's text seems to move quickly from the public to the private, from the political to the personal, from "the people" out-of-doors in conventions and suchlike to "persons" very much indoors in their private homes. We should note, too, that the amendment particularly singles out "houses" for special mention above and beyond other buildings included within the catchall word *effects*. *Houses* first appeared alongside a ban on "unreasonable" searches and seizures in the famous Article XIV of the Massachusetts Constitution of 1780, and here it clearly referred to a right of "[e]very subject" to be "secure from all unreasonable searches, and seizures, of *his* person, *his* houses, *his* papers, and all *his* possessions."[4]

Madison's choice of language may well have been influenced by the celebrated 1763 English case of *Wilkes v. Wood*,[5] one of the two or three most important search-and-seizure cases in the law books in 1789. The *Wood* case involved a famous cast of characters — both the target of the government search, John Wilkes, and the author of the opinion, Lord Chief Justice Charles Pratt (soon to become Lord Camden), became folk heroes in the colonies. (Pennsylvania residents named the town of Wilkes-Barre after the plaintiff; North Carolina and Georgia each created a Wilkes County; New Jersey, South Carolina, and Maine each dedicated a city in Camden's honor; and Baltimore, Maryland, named two streets — and later, Camden Yards, home of today's Baltimore Orioles — after the great chief justice.)[6]

No less famous were the facts of the case. Wilkes, a member of the House of Commons and champion of the people, had used the press to communicate with his constituents and criticize George III's ministry and majesty. When the government reacted by breaking into his house and rummaging through his personal papers under the authority of a general warrant, Wilkes brought suit in *Wood* and successfully challenged the legality of such warrants. Wilkes also brought suit to challenge the "seizure" of his "person." (The government had imprisoned him in the Tower of London.)

Wilkes v. Wood illustrated that a government comprised of a small group of self-dealing rulers could threaten the rights of the majority of *the people* collectively by singling out certain *persons* — opposition leaders like John Wilkes, for example — for special abuse. To counter this and other threats, the Fourth Amendment (and the Seventh, as we shall later see) armed civil juries, drawn from "the people," with special weapons to protect both individual persons and the collective people against a possibly unrepresentative and self-serving officialdom.

To understand the Founders' vision, reflect on the fact that the Fourth Amendment actually contains two different commands. First, all government searches must be reasonable. Second, no warrants shall issue without probable cause. The modern Supreme Court has intentionally collapsed and intermingled these two requirements. It treats *all* searches and seizures without a warrant — with some exceptions, such as various types of special, urgent circumstances requiring immediate governmental action — as being per se unreasonable.[7] But the amendment does not say this, nor did the Founding Fathers intend that it should. For the Supreme Court's reasoning to make sense, an additional second sentence would need to be engrafted onto the amendment:

The Fourth Amendment actually contains two different commands

"Absent special circumstances, no search or seizure shall occur without a warrant." But the fact that the amendment does not contain such a sentence should invite us to rethink the Court's assumptions.

Consider the way in which the Founding Fathers intended that Fourth Amendment rights should be enforced. Under common-law principles, since virtually any search or seizure by a federal officer would involve a physical trespass, an aggrieved target could use the common law of trespass to bring suit for damages against the official — just as Wilkes brought a trespass action in *Wood*. If the search or seizure were deemed lawful in court, the defendant government official would prevail; but if, as in *Wood*, the search were found unlawful, the defendant would be held strictly liable.

Given this risk, many government officials would obviously prefer to litigate the lawfulness of a contemplated search or seizure before it occurred — to seek a judicial warrant authorizing the intrusion. Such a warrant, if strictly complied with, would act as a sort of declaratory judgment that would effectively bar a plaintiff from being awarded damages in any later lawsuit. A lawful warrant, in effect, would compel a sort of directed verdict for the defendant government official in any subsequent lawsuit for damages.[8] But note what this means: a warrant issued by a judge or magistrate — a permanent government official on the government payroll — has had the effect of taking a later trespass action away from a jury of ordinary citizens.

Because juries could often be trusted more than judges to protect against government, warrants at the Founding were generally *dis*favored: "*No* warrants shall issue, but. . . ." And warrants had other flaws: they issued from a single person (as opposed to a judge sitting alongside a jury, twelve good men and true); that single decision-maker was an officer of the central government (unlike jurors of the community); the decision occurred after a one-sided (ex parte) hearing, with no notice or opportunity to be heard given to the target of a search; and the warrant proceeding was a secret affair, unlike a civil suit open to the watchful eye of a public. Thus even when issued by a judge, warrants lacked many traditional safeguards of judicial process: notice, presentation of the issues by both parties in an adversarial procedure, publicity, and so on. To make matters even worse, the government could forum shop; if only a single magistrate were lazy or abusive, cynical officers would know where to go to get an easy warrant. Judges and warrants are the heavies, not the heroes, of our Creation story.

The modern Supreme Court's reading of the Fourth Amendment is thus not what the Found-

Judges and warrants are the heavies, not the heroes, of our Creation story

ing Fathers intended. They understood that searches without warrants were not presumptively illegitimate; and that not every search or seizure without a warrant would require probable cause. Rather, they understood that whenever such a search or seizure occurred, a jury, guided by a judge in a public trial and able to hear arguments from both sides of the case, could typically assess the reasonableness of government action in an after-the-fact tort suit. If the jury deemed the search unreasonable, the plain words of the Fourth Amendment would render the search unlawful. The defendant official could thus be held strictly liable and made to pay compensatory as well as (in outrageous cases) punitive damages.

In the Founding Father's view, the ultimate issue of whether the defendant's actions were reasonable or unreasonable was often a classic question of fact for the jury;[9] As they saw it, the Fourth Amendment, in combination with the Seventh (as we shall see), would require the federal government to furnish a jury to any plaintiff-victim who demanded one, and to protect that jury's finding of fact from being overturned by any judge or other government official. The prospect of jury oversight and jury-awarded punitive damages would powerfully deter government officials contemplating unreasonable conduct. (In the Wilkes affair in England, the government

The jury would powerfully deter government officials

ended up paying out an eighteenth-century king's ransom in damages and court expenses — "The expenses incurred were said to be £100,000."[10])

Thus, contrary to the modern approach of the Supreme Court, the words of the Fourth Amendment mean what they say: warrantless searches are not always unconstitutional, and the probable-cause requirement applies only if and when a warrant issues.[11] Put another way, the Court has simply misread the original linkage between the Fourth Amendment's two different commands. It is not that a search or seizure without a warrant was presumptively unreasonable, as the Court has assumed; rather, it is that an overbroad warrant lacking probable cause or specificity — in other words, a general warrant — was per se unreasonable, in part because it unjustifiably displaced the proper role of the jury.

There is an obvious connection between this reasoning and the common-law rule against prior restraint that we noted in the First Amendment context.[12] For just as judges were barred from restraining the press before publication whereas civil and criminal juries after publication could impose sanctions on publishers, so here judges and magistrates acting before a search were much more strictly limited than juries acting afterward. This connection would hardly have been lost on the Fourth Amendment framers. In sixteenth- and seventeenth-century England,

The Supreme Court has misread the original linkage between the Fourth Amendment's two different commands

general warrants were the very devices by which various schemes of prior restraint and printer licensing were enforced.[13]

Why didn't the framers of the Fourth Amendment simply ban all warrants? If warrants were in some ways like prior restraints, why, it might be asked, didn't the framers of the Fourth Amendment simply ban all warrants instead of merely imposing a strict standard of probable cause for every warrant? A good modern-day analogy to explain their reasoning is the temporary restraining order. Sometimes, emergency action must be taken to freeze the status quo and prevent future harm, and so judges may act after hearing only one side of the case (ex parte), without the traditional safeguards of adversarial proceedings. But precisely because of the due-process dangers it poses, an ex parte temporary restraining order is strictly limited to situations where there is a risk of "irreparable injury" and a high likelihood of "success on the merits." At common law, a warrant could likewise issue when there was a high likelihood — "probable cause" — that a particular place contained stolen goods. The whole point of the ex parte warrant was to authorize a search that would bring the stolen goods before the magistrate. To give the owner of the hideaway a heads-up in advance of the surprise search might enable him to whisk the goods away — a kind of irreparable injury to the truth, to the justice system, and to the victim of the theft seeking to recover his goods. The need for a surprise search on these facts is obviously strong, but without the absolute guarantee of immunity provided by a warrant, an officer might hesitate to perform the surprise search for fear of a future lawsuit.

Once extended beyond the limited context of the common-law warrant for stolen goods, however, warrants had the potential for great evil. If general warrants were authorized on less than probable cause, they would give government henchmen absolute power to "round up the usual suspects," rousting political enemies (like Wilkes). In the end, the Fourth Amendment framers accepted some warrants as necessary but imposed strict limits — the requirements of probable cause and particular description — on these dangerous devices. Warrantless searches did not pose the same threat because those searches would be subject to full and open after-the-fact review in civil-trespass cases featuring civil juries.

As with the First Amendment, the central role of the jury in the Fourth Amendment should remind us that the core rights of "the people" were majority rights, rights that the majority was well suited to implement and support through the body of a jury. And here, in focusing on a role for the jury in helping to determine the reasonableness of official action and to levy punitive damages to deter official misconduct, we have an explanation of the inclusion of the words *the right*

The core rights of "the people" were majority rights

of the people in an otherwise individualistic and "person[al]" Fourth Amendment.

THE INTERRELATIONSHIP OF THE FIRST, FOURTH AND SEVENTH AMENDMENTS

There is a subtle triangular relationship interlinking the First, Fourth, and Seventh Amendments. We have already observed how Seventh Amendment civil juries could safeguard First Amendment values in civil libel cases and how such juries could similarly safeguard Fourth Amendment values in civil trespass cases. It now remains to sketch the third leg of our triangle linking the First and Fourth Amendments.

The Fourth Amendment singles out "papers" for special mention and protection above and beyond all other "effects." In England, Lord Camden's famous decision in *Entick v. Carrington* (a companion case to *Wilkes v. Wood*) had suggested that "paper-search[es]" were specially disfavored.[14] As Professors William Stuntz and Eric Schnapper have pointed out, Camden's imposition of direct limitations on paper searches indirectly protected values of free religious and political expression.[15] As Professor Stuntz puts it, *Entick* and *Wilkes* were "classic First Amendment cases in a system with no First Amendment, no vehicle for direct substantive judicial review. Restricting paper searches had the effect of limiting government power" over opposition speakers and expressive activity.[16] Although the Fourth Amendment does not, in so many words, demand special solicitude for expressive "papers," it surely invites it, just as it invites a special sensitivity to searches and seizures of "persons" and "houses" above and beyond all other "effects." Under this amendment, American judges and juries were therefore invited to carry on Lord Camden's tradition by requiring heightened justification and special procedures before deeming searches of expressive "papers" constitutionally "reasonable." The modern Supreme Court has in theory (but not always in practice) embraced just such an approach: "Where the materials sought to be seized may be protected by the First Amendment, the requirements of the Fourth Amendment must be applied with 'scrupulous exactitude.' 'A seizure reasonable as to one type of material in one setting may be unreasonable in a different setting or with respect to another kind of material.'"[17]

Fourth Amendment searches of First Amendment materials must be conducted with 'scrupulous exactitude'

With this picture of the Fourth Amendment in mind, let us now take a quick peek at the next block of amendments — Five, Six, Seven, and Eight. Each of the clauses in this block of amendments can be understood as regulating the structure and procedure of federal courts — each, that is, except for the takings clause of the Fifth Amendment. In a number of ways, this clause doesn't quite fit with its companion clauses in the Fifth Amendment, but it does mesh in several interesting ways with the principles of the Fourth Amendment.

TAKINGS
(FROM THE FIFTH AMENDMENT)

"nor shall private property be taken for public use, without just compensation."

At first reading, this prohibition seems primarily designed to protect individuals and minority groups. (After all, any government action imposing a financial burden on a majority of the populace would look more like a legitimate tax than an unconstitutional taking.) In this respect, the provision might seem to run counter to the dominant majoritarian theme of the First Congress's Bill of Rights. Indeed, the takings clause also seems distinctly modern in proclaiming that limits should be imposed on government action even when government agents are acting on behalf of their constituents rather than pursuing their own self-interest: it requires private compensation even if property is taken for genuinely "public" use.

The concerns underlying the takings clause of the Fifth Amendment were deeply felt by James Madison and the other Federalists seeking to protect the rights of property owners. Both Article I, section 10 of the Constitution (the contracts clause) and Madison's own words in *Federalist* No. 10 indicate a dislike of legislative redistribution of property. Even so, many Antifederalists were suspicious of the "aristocratical" tendencies of Federalists. Notably, only one the original thirteen colonies, Massachusetts, had a takings clause in its state constitution in 1789;[18] and Jefferson's famous Declaration of Independence had spoken of "life, liberty, and *the pursuit of happiness*" not of "life, liberty, and property." Property protection, it seems, was more central to Madison than to some of his contemporaries.

The Fifth Amendment's takings clause, however, did harmonize with the original Bill of Rights' underlying vision of the proper relationship between the federal and state governments. For like all the rest of the Bill of Rights, Madison's takings clause applied only against the *federal* government. This is especially noteworthy given that the clause of the original Constitution that most closely foreshadowed the substance of the takings clause of the Fifth Amendment — the contracts clause of the Constitution's Article I, section 10 — applied against *state* governments. Indeed, in exact contrast to the takings clause of the amendment, the contracts clause of the Constitution applied only against state, and not federal, officials. Professor Michael McConnell has flagged this contrast to argue that the takings clause of the amendment may have been primarily motivated by the Founding Fathers' concerns

The Fifth Amendment's takings clause applied only against the *federal* government

about economic self dealing on the part of remote and self-interested federal officials, especially military officers.[19] McConnell's explanation derives support from St. George Tucker's 1803 writings that the takings clause "was probably intended to restrain the arbitrary and oppressive mode of obtaining supplies for the army, and other public uses, by impressment."[20] In his pathbreaking work on the Fifth Amendment's takings clause, Professor Jed Rubenfeld has likewise linked its origins to the issue of military impressment, and has emphasized, alongside Tucker, a 1778 tract authored by John Jay condemning "the Practice of impressing Horses, Teems [sic], and Carriages by the military, without the Intervention of a civil Magistrate, and without any Authority from the Law of the Land."[21] These sentiments, of course, resonate with the special fears of an immoderate and unaccountable federal military that is audible in the Second and Third Amendments.

The Fifth Amendment's takings clause may have been primarily motivated by a fear of the military

There is also a conspicuous connection between the Fourth Amendment's limitations on "seizures" of "houses" and "effects" and the Fifth's restrictions on "takings" of "private property." In both cases, state law typically defines the property rights given constitutional protection against federal officials. And in both the Fourth Amendment and the takings clause of the Fifth Amendment, civil juries of ordinary people loomed large in providing justice to citizens aggrieved by governmental grabbing — by helping decide which searches were "reasonable," whether punitive damages should be awarded to deter outrageous governmental misconduct, and what kind of compensation would be "just."

As it turns out, juries loomed large in other contexts as well, as a close look at the other clauses of Amendments Five, Six, Seven, and Eight will make clear.

V

THE FIFTH, SIXTH, SEVENTH, AND EIGHTH AMENDMENTS

(THE JURY AMENDMENTS)

The jury amendments were at the center of the original Bill of Rights, providing safeguards against the possibility that government officials might attempt to rule in their own self-interest to deprive the people of their liberty . . . The jury's central role as a representative of local interests, as a school for the public, and as a participant in politics . . . Jury review and waivability . . . The jury's role in the criminal justice system.

THE FIFTH AMENDMENT

"No person shall be held to answer for a capital, or otherwise infamous crime, unless on a presentment or indictment of a Grand Jury, except in cases arising in the land or naval forces, or in the militia, when in actual service in time of war or public danger; nor shall any person be subject for the same offence to be twice put in jeopardy of life or limb, nor shall be compelled in any criminal case to be a witness against himself, nor be deprived of life, liberty, or property, without due process of law; nor shall private property be taken for public use without just compensation".

THE SIXTH AMENDMENT

"In all criminal prosecutions, the accused shall enjoy the right to a speedy and public trial, by an impartial jury of the State and district wherein the crime shall have been committed, which district shall have been previously ascertained by law, and to be informed of the nature and cause of the accusation; to be confronted with the witnesses against him; to have compulsory process for obtaining witnesses in his favor, and to have the assistance of counsel for his defence."

THE SEVENTH AMENDMENT

"In suits at common law, where the value in controversy shall exceed twenty dollars, the right of trial by jury shall be preserved, and no fact tried by a jury shall be otherwise reexamined in any Court of the United States, than according to the rules of the common law."

THE EIGHTH AMENDMENT

"Excessive bail shall not be required, nor excessive fines imposed, nor cruel and unusual punishments inflicted."

Juries — grand juries, criminal trial juries, and civil juries — stood at the center of the original Bill of Rights, but today they sit on the periphery. To some extent, the overriding importance the Founding Fathers placed upon the jury may have reflected a mild ideological time lag. Each generation seeks lessons from the past, and for many well-educated eighteenth-century Americans, abiding lessons of liberty lay in the history of seventeenth-century England. Judges acting without juries could do outrageous deeds — this, for Americans, was the lesson of the Star Chamber.[*] **The lesson of the Star Chamber**

Also lingering on in the American consciousness was the distrust of colonial judges who were subject to royal influence, and who at times proved too willing to dance the king's tune (especially when acting without juries in vice-admiralty courts).[1] Thus the Declaration of Independence thundered against the king for making "judges dependent on his will alone, for the

[*]Star Chamber was an infamous English court of law during the sixteenth and seventeenth centuries that tried defendents in secret juryless proceedings.

tenure of their offices, and the amount and payment of their salaries."[2]

Nor could Americans take solace from the existence of the Parliament in England. They could not vote for Parliament, and that body could trump the acts adopted by the colonial legislatures they *could* vote for. This was another large theme of the Declaration of Independence, which denounced Parliament's "pretended legislation" and assertions of "unwarrantable jurisdiction."[3] Lacking tight control over English Parliaments and royal judges, Americans in the pre-Revolution period instinctively turned to one institution they could and did control: the good old jury of the vicinage (the neighborhood). This emphasis on juries made all the more sense in a world where few American judges were deeply and distinctively learned in law, where common law was relatively simple rather than intricately regulatory, and where ordinary yeomen were remarkably literate and rights conscious — Blackstone's *Commentaries* was a runaway best-seller in the colonies. In response, the British, who well understood the nullifying possibilities of colonial juries, tried to channel as much judicial business as possible into juryless vice-admiralty courts.[4] Americans resisted, and the battle lines of liberty were clearly drawn.

In theory, the success of the American Revolution and the adoption of the new federal Constitution could have triggered a complete

In the pre-Revolution period, the jury was one institution that Americans controlled

rethinking of the role of the jury. Once American legislatures had wrested control from Parliament and federal judges had won life tenure and other attributes of independence, perhaps juries would not need to carry all the load they had borne during colonial times.

But could Americans in 1789 be sure that a small and newfangled Congress would never become as aloof and distant as Parliament had been, or that federal judges seeking power and promotions would never abet a grasping executive?[5] Abiding ideologies of liberty and ingrained patterns of thought and action do not die overnight. Thus when Federalists proposed to summon up a new and awesome imperial government to stand in the shoes of the ousted British king, many suspicious Antifederalists instinctively reached for their trusty ideological weapons, including, of course, the jury.

Most provisions of Amendments V-VIII were centrally concerned with the Antifederalists' recurring nightmare, to which we have referred many times, that government officials might attempt to rule in their own self-interest at the expense of their constituents' sentiments and liberty. Consider, for example, the special historical tie that linked the First Amendment's guarantees of free speech and religion and the Eighth Amendment's prohibition against cruel and unusual punishments.

The most grisly punishments in England had

The Antifederalists' recurring nightmare

typically been inflicted on those who spoke out against the government. Justice Hugo Black noted one example: the case of the English lawyer William Prynne, who was tried in the 1630s by judges of the infamous Star Chamber. For the crimes of "writing books and pamphlets," Prynne's "ears were first cut off by court order and . . . subsequently, by another court order, . . . his remaining ear stumps [were] gouged out while he was on a pillory."[6] Even more gruesome was the typical sentence heaped upon a political dissenter in a treason trial:

> You are to be drawn upon a hurdle to the place of execution, and there you are to be hanged by the neck, and being alive cut down, and your privy-members to be cut off, and your bowels to be taken out of your belly and there burned, you being alive; and your head to be cut off, and your body to be divided into four quarters, and that your head and quarters be disposed of where his majesty shall think fit.[7]

Similarly, the English origins of the Fifth Amendment's right against compelled self-incrimination, according to a leading scholar, were "most closely linked to freedom of religion and speech" — that is, freedom to challenge the official government ideology and the official government hierarchy, political or religious.[8] (In a country like England with an officially established church, criticism of religious orthodoxy was not simply religious speech but inescapably political speech as well.)[9]

The dominant strategy to keep agents of the central government under control was to use the populist and local institution of the jury.

THE JURY'S LEADING ROLE

If we seek a vivid illustration of the main ideas of the original Bill of Rights, we cannot go far wrong in picking the jury. Juries, guaranteed in no fewer than three amendments, were both literally and figuratively at the center of the original Bill of Rights. The Fifth Amendment safeguarded the role of the grand jury; the Sixth, the criminal trial jury; and the Seventh, the civil jury. The jury also influenced the judge-restricting doctrines underlying the First, Fourth, and Eighth Amendments. What's more, trial by jury in all federal criminal cases had earlier been mandated by the clear words of Article III of the Constitution: "The Trial of all Crimes, except in Cases of Impeachment, shall be by Jury." Indeed, the entire debate at the Philadelphia convention over whether to add a Bill of Rights was triggered when George Mason picked up on a casual comment from another delegate that "no provision was yet made for juries in civil cases."[10] Between

Juries were literally and figuratively at the center of the Bill of Rights

the close of the Philadelphia convention and the opening of the First Congress, five of the six state ratifying conventions that called for amendments put forth two or more jury-related proposals.[11] State constitutions further confirm the central role of the jury. The only right secured in all state constitutions penned between 1776 and 1787 was the right of jury trial in criminal cases.[12] We should also note the emphatic words of the Declaration of Independence, condemning George III and Parliament "[f]or depriving us, in many cases, of the benefits of trial by jury."[13]

Spanning both civil and criminal proceedings, the jury played a leading role in protecting ordinary individuals against governmental overreaching. Jurors would be drawn from the community; like the militia they were ordinary citizens, not permanent government officials on the government payroll. Just as the militia could check a paid professional standing army, the jury could thwart overreaching by powerful and ambitious prosecutors and judges. In the words of one Antifederalist pamphlet, "Judges, unincumbered by juries, have been ever found much better friends to government than to the people. Such judges will always be more desireable than juries to [would-be tyrants,] upon the same principle that a large standing army . . . is ever desireable to those who wish to enslave the people."[14] Thus Madison proposed a jury amendment in language

"Judges have been ever found much better friends to government than to the people"

reminiscent of the Second Amendment's ode to the militia: "the trial by jury, as one of the best securities to the rights of the people, ought to remain inviolate." And a leading Antifederalist described jurors as "centinels and guardians" of "the people."[15]

THE GRAND JURY

The grand jury provided for in the Fifth Amendment could thwart any prosecution that it deemed unfounded or malicious, especially if it suspected that the executive was trying to use the powers of incumbency illegitimately to entrench itself in office by prosecuting its political critics. Before government officials can force a defendant to suffer the physical and financial ordeal of a serious criminal prosecution, they must first win the consent of a large ("grand") panel of ordinary Americans — twenty-three citizens, good and true, acting by majority rule.

Colonial grand juries had already flexed their muscles to resist unpopular prosecutions. In the 1730s, two successive New York grand juries had refused to indict the popular publisher John Peter Zenger for seditious libel — and when the government instead proceeded by "information" (a highhanded procedural device by which prosecutors sidestepped the grand jury), the trial jury famously acquitted.[16] Similarly, in the 1760s and

Colonial grand juries resisted unpopular prosecutions

1770s various grand juries refused to indict leaders of the Stamp Act protests and other patriot publishers and speakers.[17]

More broadly, the grand jury had sweeping proactive and inquisitorial powers to investigate suspected wrongdoing or cover-ups by government officials and to make its findings known through the legal device of "presentment" — a public document stating its accusations. The grand jury's role thus went far beyond oversight of a prosecutor's proposed indictments. Through presentments and other customary reports, the American grand jury in effect enjoyed a roving commission to ferret out official malfeasance or self-dealing of any sort and bring it to the attention of the public at large.

The grand jury enjoyed a roving commission to ferret out official malfeasance

THE CRIMINAL TRIAL JURY

Though not as proactive as its "grand" counterpart, the Sixth Amendment's criminal trial jury (also known as a "petit" — i.e., small — jury) could likewise interpose itself on behalf of the people's rights by refusing to convict when the government sought to trump up charges against its political critics (as in the Zenger case). Once again, more than a permanent government official — even an independent federal judge — was required to safeguard liberty.

OTHER JURY CLAUSES

In those aspects of a criminal case that might involve a judge acting without a jury — issuing arrest warrants, setting bail, and sentencing, for example — additional restrictions came into play via the Fourth Amendment's warrant clause and the Eighth Amendment. The language of both the Massachusetts and New Hampshire state constitutions is revealing here: "No *magistrate or court of law* shall demand excessive bail or sureties, impose excessive fines, or inflict cruel or unusual punishments."[18] Indeed, in the late eighteenth century, every schoolboy in America was aware that the English Bill of Rights' 1689 ban on excessive bail, excessive fines, and cruel and unusual punishment — a ban repeated virtually verbatim in the Eighth Amendment — arose in response to the misbehavior of certain infamous judges.[19]

Another provision implicating the jury was the double-jeopardy clause of the Fifth Amendment, which makes no explicit mention of juries, but which dovetails with the Sixth Amendment jury right. When a defendant is put on trial and is at risk of conviction and punishment, it is said that "jeopardy attaches," so that, in Blackstone's words, "[if] the jury therefore find the prisoner not guilty, he is then and forever quit and dis-

The double-jeopardy clause

charged of the accusation."[20] At the hard core of the double-jeopardy clause was the absolute, unquestionable finality of a properly instructed jury's verdict of acquittal, even if this verdict was grossly erroneous in the eyes of a judge. If a properly instructed jury voted to convict, a judge could set aside the conviction, but if that jury voted to acquit, reexamination was barred.

The Fifth Amendment due-process clause concerned the jury even more directly, for its core meaning was that a criminal defendant could typically be brought to trial only by means of a lawful indictment or presentment by a grand jury.[21] And even those amendments that at first seem rather far afield appear on closer inspection to link up with the values underlying the central role of the jury. For example, we have glimpsed important parallels between the jury and the Second Amendment's vaunted "well regulated militia." The jury summed up — indeed embodied — the ideals of federalism, populism and civic virtue that were the essence of the original Bill of Rights.

The jury summed up the ideals of federaism, populism, and civic virtue

JURORS AS PROVINCIALS

Juries were local. The Sixth Amendment explicitly guaranteed a jury "of the State *and district* wherein the crime shall have been committed," going a step beyond the language of Article III of the Constitution, which required only that jury trials be held somewhere within the state where the crime occurred. Just as state legislators could in various ways protect their constituents against national oppression, local grand and petit jurors could exercise their powers to interpose themselves against central tyranny through the devices of presentments, nonindictments, and general verdicts of acquittal. As with the militia, the jury would be composed of citizens from the same community, and its actions were expected to be informed by community values.

JURORS AS PUPILS

The jury was also to be informed by judges — most obviously in the judges' instructions. As Ralph Lerner has shown in his essay on "Republican Schoolmasters," judges often seized the occasion to educate jurors about legal and political values ranging well beyond the narrow issues before them.[22] Like the church and the militia, the jury was in part an intermediate institution situated between the government and the people designed to educate and socialize its members into virtuous thinking and conduct. Churches stressed religious and moral virtues; militias struck a proper balance between civilian and martial virtues; and juries instilled republican legal and political virtues. In the words of the

Juries were intended to instill republican legal and political virtues

leading Antifederalist essayist of the ratification
period, the Federal Farmer, "jury trial brings
with it an open and public discussion of all causes
. . . [and this is] the means by which the people
are let into the knowledge of public affairs."[23]

No one understood all this better than Alexis
de Tocqueville, a keen student of American constitutional law and the leading theorist on the
importance of intermediate institutions:

> The jury, and more especially the civil jury,
> serves to communicate the spirit of the judges to
> the minds of all the citizens; and this spirit, with
> the habits which attend it, is the soundest prepa-
> ration for free institutions. It imbues all classes
> with a respect for the thing judged and with the
> notion of right. . . . It teaches men to practice
> equity; every man learns to judge his neighbor as
> he would himself be judged. . . .
>   . . . *It may be regarded as a gratuitous pub-
> lic school*, ever open, in which every juror learns
> his rights, enters into daily communication with
> the most learned and enlightened members of
> the upper classes, and becomes practically ac-
> quainted with the laws, which are brought within
> the reach of his capacity by the efforts of the bar,
> the advice of the judge, and even the passions of
> the parties. . . .
>   . . . I look upon [the jury] as one of the
> most efficacious means for the education of the
> people which society can employ.[24]

Through the jury, citizens would learn self-
government by doing self-government. In Tocqueville's memorable phrase, "the jury, which is

the most energetic means of making the people rule, is also the most efficacious means of teaching it how to rule well."[25]

JURORS AS POLITICAL PARTICIPANTS

While ordinary citizens could not realistically expect to serve in the Founders' small House of Representatives or the even more aristocratic Senate, they could nevertheless participate in the application of national law through their service on juries.[26] In the words of the Federal Farmer, through juries "frequently drawn from the body of the people . . . we secure to the people at large, their just and rightful controul in the judicial department."[27]

Analogies between legislatures and juries also abounded. Wrote the Federal Farmer:

Analogies between legislatures and juries abounded

> It is essential in every free country, that common people should have a part and share of influence, in the judicial as well as in the legislative department.
> . . . The trial by jury in the judicial department, and the collection of the people by their representatives in the legislature . . . have procured for them, in this country, their true proportion of influence, and the wisest and most fit means of protecting themselves in the community. Their situation, as jurors and representatives, enables them to acquire information and knowledge in the affairs and government of the

society; and to come forward, in turn, as the centinels and guardians of each other.[28]

Similarly, Jefferson declared in 1789 that "it
is necessary to introduce the people into every
department of government. . . . Were I called
upon to decide whether the people had best be
omitted in the Legislative or Judicial department,
I would say it is better to leave them out of the
Legislative."[29] Tocqueville later made much the
same point: "The jury is, above all, a political
[and not a mere judicial] institution. . . . The jury
is that portion of the nation to which the execution of the laws is entrusted, as the legislature is
that part of the nation which makes the laws; and
in order that society may be governed in a fixed
and uniform manner, the list of citizens qualified
to serve on juries must increase and diminish
with the list of electors."[30]

Even more elaborate was the vision of the jury
conjured up by John Taylor of Caroline, one of
the early republic's leading constitutional theorists. The jury, wrote Taylor, was the "lower judicial bench" in a bicameral judiciary.[31] The judicial structure mirrored that of the legislature,
with an upper house of greater stability and experience and a lower house to represent popular
sentiment more directly. Thus the essayist Maryland Farmer defined the jury as "the democratic
branch of the judiciary power — more necessary
than representatives in the legislature."[32]

The jury is "the democratic branch of the judiciary power"

Tocqueville explicitly defined the jury as "a certain number of citizens chosen by lot and invested with a temporary" commission[33] — the analogy to militias suggests itself once again — and the Federal Farmer also seemed to stress the rotating quality of jury service, as evidenced by his reference to citizens coming forward "in turn."[34] The idea of mandatory rotation also illustrates the connections between juries and legislators, for many Antifederalists wanted compulsory rotation in the legislature as well.[35] Indeed, Thomas Jefferson's two biggest objections to the original Constitution were its lack of a bill of rights and its abandonment of the republican principle of mandatory rotation.[36] At the New York ratifying convention Gilbert Livingston criticized the lack of mandatory rotation in the legislature, but his comments fit the jury context as well: "[Rotation] will afford opportunity to bring forward the genius and information of the states, and will be a stimulus to acquire political abilities. It will be the means of diffusing a more general knowledge of the measures and spirit of the administration. These things will confirm the people's confidence in government."[37] Like so many other ideas that we have encountered in examining the First Congress's Bill of Rights, the mandatory rotation principle drew its strength from the Founding Fathers' concern about the character and manner in which a majority of the people were to be represented in their new gov-

Jefferson's objections to the original Constitution

ernment, rather than elaborate ideas about minority rights.

JURY REVIEW

The present-day jury is a shadow of its former self

If our description of the role of the jury seems strange to the modern reader perhaps the reason is that the present-day jury is only a shadow of its former self. First Amendment doctrine has evolved beyond the prohibition against prior restraint, while the judge-created and judge-enforced exclusionary rule (that evidence obtained in violation of a person's constitutional rights must generally be excluded from consideration at his criminal trial) has displaced the jury trial for damages as the central enforcement mechanism of the Fourth Amendment — in part because of judge-created doctrines that grant government officials immunity from damages.[38] As we shall now see, even the core role of the jury in criminal trials has seriously eroded over the past two centuries.

Consider the question of "jury review": may a jury refuse to follow a law if it deems that law unconstitutional?[39] The concept is exactly analogous — the precise bicameral counterpart — to the idea of judicial review, as traditionally understood. Judges may not ignore a law simply because they think it wrong, or unjust, or silly; but they may — indeed must — do so if they deem it unconstitutional. The precise question is not whether a jury has the raw power of review by entering a general verdict (of "guilty" or "not guilty") and getting away with it. Rather, the question is whether and to what extent a jury has the legal right — perhaps even the duty — to refuse to follow a law it deems unconstitutional. As a practical matter, the issue often boils down to whether an attorney should be allowed to argue the unconstitutionality of a law, typically as a defense, to a jury.[40]

May a defense attorney argue the unconstitutionality of a law to the jury?

This is exactly how the issue arose in perhaps the most famous of all federal Sedition Act prosecutions, *United States v. Callender*,[41] tried in 1800 in a federal Circuit Court. When the publisher James Callender's attorney, William Wirt, tried to argue to the jury that the infamous 1798 Sedition Act (part of the notorious Alien and Sedition Acts of that year) was unconstitutional, he was cut off by presiding Circuit Justice Samuel Chase. Chase was later impeached for his overall handling of *Callender* and for refusing to allow defense counsel in another criminal case to argue law to the jury. About half of the Senate voted to convict Chase, several votes short of the two-thirds required by the Constitution.[42] Wirt, by contrast, went on to become "one of the greatest Supreme Court advocates of all time and the man who holds the record for years of service as Attorney General."[43] Here is an edited transcript of the Chase-Wirt exchange:

Here CHASE, Circuit Justice — Take your seat, sir, if you please. If I understand you rightly, you offer an argument to the petit jury, to convince them that the . . . Sedition Law[] is contrary to the constitution of the United States and, therefore, void. Now I tell you that this irregular and inadmissible; it is not competent to the jury to decide on this point. . . .

. . . [W]e all know that juries have the right to decide the law, as well as the fact — and the constitution is the supreme law of the land, which controls all laws which are repugnant to it.

Mr. Wirt. — Since, then, the jury have a right to consider the law, and since the constitution is law, the conclusion is certainly syllogistic [i.e., logical], that the jury have a right to consider the constitution.

CHASE, Circuit Justice. — A non sequitur [i.e., an illogical inference], sir.

Here Mr. Wirt sat down.[44]

Chase went on to try to explain his ruling, but if anything, it is his arguments that border on non sequitur. At times he seemed to say that if the jury could consider constitutionality, it would necessarily follow that judges could not. But nothing in the idea of judicial review requires that *only* judges consider constitutionality.[45] Surely, for example, President Jefferson was within his constitutional rights — perhaps duties — when he pardoned those convicted under the Sedition Act because he deemed the act unconstitutional, notwithstanding that Circuit Courts had held to the contrary in cases involving the very convicts

Nothing in the idea of judicial review requires that *only* judges consider constitutionality

in question. Judges took oaths to uphold the Constitution, but so did presidents and so could jurors.

And as the Antifederalist essayist Maryland Farmer pointed out, juries can be seen as part of the judicial department — the lower (and if anything, presumptively more legitimate, because more popular) house.[46] Just as both House and Senate had to agree the Sedition Bill was constitutional before it became law, why shouldn't both judge and jury be required to agree on its constitutionality before Callender was sent to jail? In language borrowing from vocabulary about legislative checks and balances, the Federal Farmer had declared that if judges tried to "subvert the laws, and change the forms of government," jurors would "check them, by deciding against their opinions and determinations."[47]

Chase's final argument simply asserted the jury's lack of "competence" to decide the Sedition Act's (un)constitutionality: judges were learned in law, and juries were not. But even if juries generally lacked competence to adjudicate intricate and technical "lawyer's law," didn't they possess the ability to understand the Constitution? After all, the Constitution was not supposed to be a lengthy and detailed code. *It was the people's law.* It had been made, and could be unmade at will, by We the People of the United States — citizens acting in special single-issue assemblies (ratifying conventions), asked to lis-

Didn't jurors possess the ability to understand the Constitution?

ten, deliberate, and then vote yea or nay. How, it might be asked, were juries different from conventions in this regard? If ordinary citizens were competent to make constitutional judgments when signing petitions or assembling in conventions, why not in juries, too? In the words of the Federal Farmer, "the freemen of a country are not always minutely skilled in the laws, but they have common sense in its purity, which seldom or never errs in making and applying laws to the condition of the people, or in determining judicial causes."[48]

The Founding Fathers' argument for jury review was not airtight, but it was nonetheless substantial. Yet jury review and many other powers of the jury that were strongly or weakly **Jury review and other powers of the jury have seriously eroded over time** implied by the Founding Fathers in Amendments V-VIII have seriously eroded over time. Of course, no one knows how strikingly powerful the jury might have become had American history after the 1790s unfolded differently. As we will see, the Civil War and the subsequent adoption of the Fourteenth Amendment had the effect of radically transforming the fundamentally populist and localist philosophy of the original Bill of Rights, including whatever power of jury review the Founders may have envisioned.

But even today, remnants of the Founding Fathers' pro-jury vision remain — for example, in rules preventing judges from ordering criminal

trial juries to find defendants guilty; and rules
barring trial judges from reversing, and appellate
courts from reviewing, criminal jury acquittals.
In logic, each of these doctrines seems to bow to
the criminal jury's right to go beyond merely
deciding the facts.[49]

WAIVABILITY OF JURY TRIAL

For whose benefit did the Sixth Amendment's
right to criminal jury trial exist? To Tocqueville,
the answer was easy — the core interest was that
of the citizen jurors, rather than the parties: "I do
not know whether the jury is useful to those who
have lawsuits, but I am certain it is highly bene-
ficial to those who judge them. . . ."[50] More
recently, Justice Blackmun has written that the
public has interests, independent of a criminal
defendant, in monitoring judges, police, and prosecutors, and in being "educat[ed]" about "the
manner in which criminal justice is adminis-
tered."[51] Though he was speaking of the gallery's
right to a "public" trial within the meaning of the
Sixth Amendment, Justice Blackmun's insight
would seem to apply even more to the jury's
right, for every trial in which a jury sits is to that
extent a public trial, of and by the people, and not
just for them.

Nevertheless, in 1930 the Supreme Court
held in *Patton v. United States* that the criminal

jury trial right was the defendant's alone, to waive if he pleased. The Court explicitly framed the question as whether jury trial was "only [a] guaranty to the accused" instead of a component of the structure of "a tribunal as a part of the frame of government."[52] But having asked the right question, *Patton* proceeded to give the wrong answer: none of the arguments in *Patton* survives close scrutiny. Predictably, the Court stressed the words of the Sixth Amendment guaranteeing to "the accused" the right of jury trial. But this ignores the clear words of Article III of the Constitution mandating that "the trial of *all* Crimes . . . *shall* be by Jury," a command no less mandatory than its companion commands that the judicial power of the United States "*shall* be vested in" federal courts, whose judges "*shall*" have life tenure and undiminished salaries, and whose jurisdiction "*shall* extend to *all*" cases in certain categories.[53] The words in the Article III jury clause were plainly understood during the ratification period as words of obligation.[54] Nothing in the Sixth Amendment repeals those words.

Indeed, it would be perverse to read the Sixth Amendment, a provision designed to strengthen the Article III jury trial, as somehow weakening it. Had this been the intended or even a plausible reading in 1789, there would have been howls of protest from Antifederalists like the Federal Farmer. Instead, there is not a scrap of evidence that anyone thought that the Article III mandate

The Supreme Court's error in *Patton v. United States*

could be slyly undone by the Sixth Amendment, which gave the accused a right to a *local* trial while leaving intact the basic Article III jury trial requirement.

Ignorance is indeed a great law reformer, but surely there are limits. *Patton* claimed that none of the Founding Fathers viewed jury trial as going beyond the protection of the accused — a statement that ignores the writings of the Federal Farmer, the Maryland Farmer, Jefferson, and many others.[55]

Nevertheless, it would be a mistake to put all the blame for the vanishing significance of the jury on the shoulders of the *Patton* Court. The issue in *Patton* was a rather narrow one: could a defendant who pleaded not guilty be tried without a (twelve-person) jury? Even had *Patton* said no, backdoor evasion of jury trial was possible through the device of the guilty plea. Historically, the petit jury had a role only at trial; a guilty plea occurred prior to, and precluded, any trial (although even a guilty plea could occur only after a different jury — the grand jury — had authorized the charge).[56] As a practical matter, the back door opened by guilty pleas was of little significance two hundred years ago, for as Professor Albert Alschuler has shown, such pleas were then highly atypical, and plea bargaining was generally viewed with suspicion, if not hostility.[57] Today, by contrast, roughly 90 percent of criminal defendants convicted in American courts

Ignorance is indeed a great law reformer, but surely there are limits

Two hundred years ago, plea bargaining was viewed with suspicion and hostility

plead guilty, and plea-bargaining has the blessing of the Supreme Court.[58]

BEYOND JURIES

The jury was the dominant concept of Amendments V-VIII, but not the only one. Throughout these amendments there are other subtle themes at work, implicating the values of publicity, truth seeking, and fairness.

THE VIRTUES OF A PUBLIC TRIAL

Consider, for example, the Sixth Amendment guarantee that "the accused shall enjoy the right to . . . a . . . public trial." At seems obvious at first glance that this is a right of the defendant, and thus waivable by him. But as we have seen in analyzing the Sixth Amendment's right of "the accused" to a jury trial, things may not be quite what they seem at first glance. Perhaps the public trial was also a right of, well, the public, and was as such not waivable.

Nowhere does the Sixth Amendment say that "the accused" shall enjoy the right to a secret trial

Begin with the text. Although the amendment says that "the accused" shall enjoy the right to a public trial, it nowhere says that he has the right to a *secret* trial.

Historically, virtually all criminal trials in England and America have been trials open to the public.[59] In his influential law book, *Insti-*

tutes, Sir Edward Coke declared that the very word *court* implied public access: "[A]ll Causes ought to be heard, ordered, and determined before the judges of the kings courts openly in the kings courts, *wither all persons may resort*; and in no chambers, or other private places: for judges are not judges of *chambers*, but of *courts*, and therefore *in open court*. . . ."[60] Coke's contrast of *courts* with *chambers* had special meaning for eighteenth-century Americans; one of the defining characteristics of the Star Chamber that they had been taught to despise was that this (juryless) body interrogated suspects in private, not in public.[61] Joseph Story echoed Coke's ode to openness in his *Commentaries on the Constitution*, where he wrote that the Sixth Amendment "does but follow out the established course of the common law in all trials for crimes. The trial is always public."[62]

There were several important purposes served by public trials in America. The phrase *the people* appears in no fewer than five of the ten amendments that make up our Bill of Rights;[63] and so we would do well to take seriously the republican and populist overtones of a word closely related to the word *people* in a sixth — the Sixth — Amendment: the word *public* in the amendment's phrase *the right to a speedy and public trial*. The framers crafted a system of *republican* governments, state and federal — governments of, by, and for the people.[64] (Note

The important purposes of public trial in America

the root word "public" in the word "republican.")
Here, the people would rule — not day to day,
but ultimately, in the long run. All governmental
policy and governmental policymakers could, in
time, be lawfully replaced by the sovereign people via constitutional conventions and ordinary
elections. And this ultimate right of the public to
change policy and policymakers called for a
strong presumption that courts would be open to
Courts the public.[65] If citizens did not like what they saw
would be their government agents doing in open court, the
open to people could throw the rascals out at the next
the public election, or could petition and agitate to change
the law.

The people, however, would not need to wait
until election day to make a difference; their very
presence in the courtroom could discourage judicial misbehavior. In the words of Sir Matthew
Hale's widely influential treatise, "if the judge be
PARTIAL, his partiality and injustice will be evident to all by-standers."[66] Sir William Blackstone
concurred in his even more widely influential
treatise: "[Objections to evidence] are publicly
stated, and by the judge are openly and publicly
allowed or disallowed, in the face of the country;
which must curb any secret bias or partiality,
Public that might arise in his own breast."[67] The ability
scrutiny of the public to judge the judge would tend to
was bad protect innocent defendants from judicial corrup-
news for tion or oppression, but public scrutiny was bad
many a
guilty
defendant news for many a guilty defendant, who might

prefer an incompetent judge or one "partial" to the defendant's cause — an old political friend, perhaps, or a new financial one.

So too, the public right to monitor witnesses at trial was designed to help the truth come out, and truth would as a rule help innocent defendants more than guilty ones. If, at trial, a bystander happened to have relevant information bearing on a key point, he could bring the matter to the attention of court and counsel. In part because of this, witnesses who testified would be less likely to perjure themselves in front of a public gallery — or at least this was the theory underlying the common law's commitment to public trials. In 1685, Solicitor General John Hawles put the point as follows: "[T]he reason that all trials are public, is, that any person may inform in point of fact, though not subpoena'd, that truth may be discovered in civil as well as criminal matters. There is an invitation to all persons, who can inform the court concerning the matter to be tried, to come into the court, and they shall be heard."[68] Truth was also Blackstone's theme: "This open examination of witnesses *viva voce* [orally], in the presence of all mankind, is much more conducive to the clearing up of truth, than [a] private and secret examination. . . . [A] witness may frequently depose that in private, which he will be ashamed to testify in a public and solemn tribunal."[69]

In short, the public trial was designed to infuse

Witnesses would be less likely to perjure themselves in front of a public gallery public knowledge into the trial itself, and, in turn, to satisfy the public that truth had prevailed at trial. A public trial would protect innocence while making life more difficult for the guilty. When government officials or friends of judges misbehaved, only a public trial could assure the people that judges were not on the take or playing favorites. Thus, even if a defendant might prefer a closed proceeding, the republican ideology underlying the public-trial clause overrode that preference in the name of democratic openness and education, public confidence, anticorruption, and truth seeking.

The Sixth Amendment's vision of the gallery box blended nicely with its vision of the jury box. **The Sixth Amendment's vision of the public in the gallery box and the jury panel in the jury box** The public sitting in the gallery box and the jury panel sitting in the jury box both would be educated in their rights and duties and in the workings of the criminal justice system that operated in their name. The many heads in the gallery box could improve fact-finding by bringing information to light, and the twelve heads in a jury box would be more reliable and less biased fact finders than a single judge. Also, the very presence of the people in both boxes could deter judicial corruption. A guilty defendant or a malicious prosecutor would have a harder time bribing a judge whose every move was monitored by the gallery; likewise, even Alexander Hamilton — hardly a jury worshiper — emphasized in *The Federalist* that juries made bribery more difficult. "As there is always more time and better opportunity to tamper with a standing body of magistrates than with a jury summoned for the occasion," judges acting alone would face more "temptations to prostitution" and offer less "security against   corruption."[70]

AN AFFIRMATION OF THE RIGHTS OF THE ACCUSED

Consider next the Sixth Amendment's clustered rights of confrontation of witnesses, compulsory process of witnesses, and the right to counsel. Here too the amendment does not explicitly confer upon the accused a constitutional right of waiver, or an explicit right to the opposite thing — the right *not* to cross-examine, or subpoena, or use a lawyer. But the right to counsel clause does say that counsel's job is to "assist[]" the accused in making "his" — the accused's — defense, and it is hard to see how the accused would still be in control of his defense if some government-imposed agent took it over against his will; the assistant would be usurping the place of the master. More generally, in practice it would be exceedingly hard to force a lawyer upon a defendant of sound mind who said no; or to oblige an unwilling defendant to subpoena witness X, or to cross-examine witness Y. And so, with this cluster at least, we see a genuine affirmation of rights of the accused and only the accused, rights of a single person standing alone against the world. What ideas underlay this cluster?

One idea was autonomy. The accused, after all, was the one on trial, with his embodied "person" being "held," his "life or limb" on the line, in the graphic words of the Fifth Amendment.

The Sixth Amendment gave the accused some freedom

And so the Sixth Amendment gave the accused some freedom, some autonomy, in controlling the shape of "his defence": whom to cross-examine, whom to subpoena, whom (if anyone) to hire as a lawyer. The Founding Fathers' vision of defendant autonomy, however, was hardly a robust one by modern standards. In seeking to make "his defence" an innocent accused might well wish to testify under oath and tell his story to the jury and the public; but the Sixth Amendment nowhere explicitly guaranteed this (to us) basic right.[71] On the contrary, throughout the colonial

Before the Civil War, criminal defendants could not testify in their defense

and antebellum eras, no American court, state or federal, allowed defendants to take the stand.[72] Not until the Civil War era did the rule begin to change, a change that, as we shall see in Part II, fits well with the increased emphasis on individual autonomy and freedom represented by that era's Fourteenth Amendment.

TRUTH SEEKING

Truth seeking also explains the rights clustered in the Sixth Amendment — confrontation of witnesses, compulsory process of witnesses, and the

right to counsel. As with a public trial, confrontation would deter perjury and promote the truth.
Blackstone discussed these ideas together:

> The oath administered to the witness is not
> only that what he deposes shall be true, but that
> he shall also depose the whole truth. . . .
>   And all this evidence is to be given in open
> court, in the presence of the parties, their attor-
> neys, the counsel, and all by-standers; and
> before the judge and jury. . . .
>   This open examination of witnesses viva voce
> [orally], in the presence of all mankind, is . . .
> conducive to the clearing up of truth. . . .
> Besides[,] the occasional questions of the judge,
> the jury, and the counsel, propounded to the wit-
> nesses on a sudden, will sift out the truth much
> better than a formal set of interrogatories previ-
> ously penned and settled: and the confronting of
> adverse witnesses is also another opportunity of
> obtaining a clear discovery, which can never be
> had upon any other method of trial.[73]

Similarly, the compulsory-process clause — a
fraternal twin of the confrontation clause —
would enable the defendant to present his own
witnesses to tell the jury and the gallery what the
prosecutor's witnesses had left out. And, since
even an intelligent and knowledgeable defendant
might not be particularly skilled at courtroom
procedure and rules of evidence, he had the right
to seek the "assistance" of a legally trained
"counsel" to help him present the whole truth in
the courtroom.

BASIC FAIRNESS AND SYMMETRY

Notions of basic fairness and symmetry were also at work in the Sixth Amendment. If the prosecuting government could have a lawyer, why not the defendant? If the government could put witness X on the stand and ask him questions, why shouldn't the defendant be allowed to ask questions? If the government could use subpoenas to force unwilling witnesses to testify, why couldn't the defendant? In formulating the precise wording of the compulsory-process clause, Madison seems to have borrowed from Blackstone's *Commentaries*, which also explicitly embraced the symmetry principle: the accused must enjoy "the *same* compulsive process to bring in his witnesses for him, as was usual to compel their appearance against him."[74]

Symmetry also helps make sense of two of the criminal-process clauses of the Fifth Amendment Symmetry also helps make sense of two of the criminal-process clauses of the Fifth Amendment. If the government won a fair and suitably error-free criminal trial, it would not give the defendant a right to ignore the verdict and demand a new trial on a clean slate. Why should a defendant be placed in a lesser position if *he* won? Hence the double-jeopardy clause banning any government effort to say "heads we win, tails let's play again until you lose."

And, if a defendant was not able to take the stand to testify in favor of himself, why should the government be able to oblige him to testify against himself? Hence the rule of the self-incrimination clause — a clause that also protected the innocent but inarticulate defendant, who might be made to look guilty if subject to crafty questioning from a trained inquisitor.[75]

In championing the ideas of basic fairness and symmetry, the Founding Fathers had in mind notorious historical examples of unfairness that they wished to avoid. Sir Walter Raleigh, for instance, had been convicted of treason in a 1603 trial where the government procured an ex parte affidavit from one Cobham, a witness of dubious reliability, but refused to let Raleigh meet his alleged accuser face to face, or cross-examine him, or subpoena him. Raleigh objected vigorously: "The Proof of the Common Law is by witness and jury; let Cobham be here, let him speak it. Call my accuser before my face. . . ."[76]

As Raleigh's and countless other cases made clear to late eighteenth-century Americans, treason law was an area where the danger of government self-dealing was especially acute. English history was littered with examples of officials seeking to entrench themselves by criminalizing political opposition, and imprisoning (or worse) political rivals.[77] The Founding Fathers therefore devoted special care to the treason issue in a pair of clauses in Article III of the Constitution. Article III declared that "Treason against the United States, shall consist only in levying War against them, or in adhering to their Enemies, giving them Aid and Comfort." Mere political opposition to the government or the executive — "constructive treason" — was thus shielded from criminal prosecution. Article III also specified that "No Person shall be convicted of Treason unless on the Testimony of two Witnesses to the same overt Act, or on Confession in open Court." The requirement of a confession in *open* court was generalized by the subsequent Sixth Amendment public-trial clause — no Star Chamber nonsense in America! Also, the "witness" clauses of Article III and the Sixth Amendment intermeshed. Lest the government seek to evade the two-witness rule of Article III by fabricating some trumped-up affidavit, à la Raleigh, the Sixth Amendment confrontation clause forbade such ex parte affidavits, and the compulsory-process clause empowered a future Raleigh to subpoena his alleged accuser on his own. Here again, in three clauses featuring the word *witness*, we see linkages between the original Constitution and the Bill of Rights.

The last two amendments of the Bill of Rights also featured an important textual linkage to the original Constitution, as we shall see in the next chapter.

VI

THE NINTH AND TENTH AMENDMENTS
(THE POPULAR-SOVEREIGNTY AMENDMENTS)

How the Ninth and Tenth Amendments and the Preamble to the Constitution are complementary and interrelated affirmations of the right of "We the People" to alter or abolish our government.

THE NINTH AMENDMENT

"The enumeration in the Constitution, of certain rights, shall not be construed to deny or disparage others retained by the people."

THE TENTH AMENDMENT

"The powers not delegated to the United States by the Constitution, nor prohibited by it to the States, are reserved to the States respectively or to the people."

TAKING THE PEOPLE
SERIOUSLY

The key theme of the Bill of Rights' conclud-
ing Amendments is popular sovereignty —
the supreme power of the people. We the People,
acting collectively, have delegated some powers
to the federal government, have allowed others to
be exercised by state governments, and have
withheld some things from all governments. The
Preamble to the Constitution, beginning with
"We, the people . . . ," and the Tenth Amendment, ending with ". . . to the people," are thus
perfect bookends, fittingly the alpha and omega
of the Founding Fathers' (revised) Constitution.

The conspicuously collective meaning of "the
people" in the Tenth Amendment (and elsewhere) should alert us that its core meaning in
the Ninth is similarly collective. Indeed, the most
obvious and inalienable right underlying the
The col- Ninth Amendment is the collective right of
lective We the People to alter or abolish government,
right of
the people through the distinctly American device of consti-
to alter or tutional convention. In *The Federalist* No. 84
abolish
govern- Alexander Hamilton explained the Preamble to
ment the Constitution in language that perfectly foreshadowed the wording of the Ninth and Tenth
Amendments that were to be drafted later: "[Our
Constitution is] professedly founded upon the
power of *the people*. . . . Here, in strictness, *the*

people surrender nothing; and as they *retain* everything they have no need of particular *reservations*. 'WE, THE PEOPLE of the United States, to secure the blessings of liberty to ourselves and our posterity, do ordain and establish this Constitution for the United States of America.' Here is a [clear] recognition of *popular rights*. . . . "[1]

In words that anticipated Hamilton's *Federalist* No. 84, the great Federalist leader James Wilson reminded the Pennsylvania ratifying convention that "supreme . . . power *remains* in the people" — a point he then formulated as follows: The people "never part with the whole" of their "original power" and "they *retain* the right of recalling what they part with. . . . [T]he citizens of the United States may always say, WE *reserve* the right to do what we please."[2] Note how Wilson's emphatic WE tied back to the Preamble, while his other language foreshadowed the Ninth and Tenth Amendments.

Today many constitutional scholars miss the close triangular interrelation among the Constitution's Preamble and the Ninth and Tenth Amendments. According to conventional wisdom, the Ninth is about unenumerated individual rights, like personal privacy (even though it speaks of the collective "people" rather than individual "persons"); the Tenth is only about federalism (even though it too invokes "the people"); and the Constitution's Preamble is about some-

Many scholars miss the interrelation among the Constitution's Preamble and the Ninth and Tenth Amendments

thing else entirely. But look again at these texts. All are at their core about popular sovereignty. All explicitly invoke "the people." In the Constitution's Preamble, "We the people . . . *do*" exercise our right and power of popular sovereignty, and in the Ninth and Tenth "the people" expressly "retain" and "reserve" our "right" and "power" to do it again.

These concepts were famously featured in the language of the 1776 Declaration of Independence, which spotlighted the phrase "the Right of the People" in its most celebrated passage: "[W]henever any Form of Government becomes destructive of [its] ends, it is the Right of the People to alter or to abolish it, and to institute new Government."[3] Alexander Hamilton did not always agree with Thomas Jefferson, but he agreed with him on this, as his own use of the phrase "the right of the people" in *The Federalist* No. 78 made clear: "I trust the friends of the proposed Constitution will never concur with its enemies in questioning that fundamental principle of republican government which admits *the right of the people* to alter or abolish the established Constitution whenever they find it inconsistent with their happiness. . . ."[4] The rights of "the people" affirmed in the Ninth and Tenth Amendments may well mean more than the right to alter or abolish, but at their core they surely mean at least this much.

Hamilton agreed with Jefferson about the sovereignty of the people

TAKING THE STATES
SERIOUSLY

Let's consider next how the Ninth and Tenth
Amendments elegantly integrate popular sovereignty with federalism.[5] All government power,
both federal and state, derives from the people,
but these grants of power are limited. In the language of the Tenth Amendment, the federal
government has only powers "delegated" to it,
expressly or by implication, and certain "prohibit[ions]" are imposed on state governments.
How are these federal agents to be kept within
these limits? In part by mutual jealousy and monitoring. State legislatures could alert the people to
any perceived usurpations by federal agents;
state militias could thwart and thus deter a tyrannical standing army; and state common law of
trespass could help vindicate a person's rights
protected by the Fourth Amendment and the
takings clause of the Fifth. For the Founders, **For the**
populism and federalism — liberty and localism **Founders,**
— worked together; We the People would con- **liberty and**
quer government power by dividing it between **localism**
the two rival governments, state and federal, a **worked**
together
structural scheme textually reaffirmed by the
Tenth Amendment. In this sense, the Tenth
Amendment beautifully sums up many of the
themes of prior amendments. It is wholly unsurprising, therefore, that alone among the amend-

ments that were successfully ratified, the Tenth was the only one proposed by every one of the state ratifying conventions that proposed amendments.[6]

The Ninth Amendment explicitly seeks to protect liberty

The Ninth Amendment is also concerned in part with federalism. As with our First and Tenth Amendments, the Ninth explicitly seeks to protect liberty by preventing Congress from going beyond its enumerated powers in Article I, section 8, and elsewhere in the Constitution.

The Ninth and Tenth fit together snugly, as their words make clear; but each amendment complements the other without duplicating it. The Tenth says that Congress must point to some explicit or implicit enumerated power before it can act. The Ninth addresses the closely related but distinct question of whether such express or implied enumerated power in fact exists. In particular, the Ninth warns readers not to infer from the mere enumeration of a right in the Bill of Rights that implicit federal power in fact exists in a given area. Thus, for example, we must not infer from our First Amendment that Congress was ever given Article I legislative power in the first place to regulate religion in the states, or to censor speech.

VII

THE BILL OF RIGHTS
AS A CONSTITUTION

*How the Bill of Rights may be
regarded as a constitution . . .
How it focuses on the structure
of government and protects
the people from the self-dealing
of elected officials . . . How it
operates as a device to educate
ordinary citizens.*

Let us step back and see what larger lessons may be pieced together from the story thus far. In the preceding pages, we have tried to suggest how much is lost by the conventional clausebound approach to studying the Bill of Rights that is favored today by many constitutional scholars. Such a clausebound approach misses the ways in which rights interrelate with structural issues of representation, federalism, separation of powers, bicameralism, and the amendment process. It misses interesting questions within amendments, like "why are the press and religion clauses yoked together in a single amendment?" and "why are the various provisions of the Sixth Amendment bundled together?" It misses thematic continuities across different amendments, like the popular-sovereignty theme sounded by repeated invocations of "the people," and the ways in which jury trial issues reflected the thinking behind the First, Fourth, and Eighth Amendments, and the Fifth Amendment double-jeopardy clause. It misses the many linkages between the original Constitution and the Bill of Rights — the importance of earlier invocations of "the people" in the Preamble and Article I of the Constitution; the harmonies between the original Constitution's language that "Congress shall have power . . . to make all laws" of a certain sort, and the First Amendment's wording that "Congress shall make no law" in various domains; the subtle interplay between the militia and army clauses of Article I and the Second and Third Amendments; the implications of the Constitution's Article III jury-trial command for the Sixth Amendment; and so on.

Our Constitution is not a jumble of disconnected clauses

How could we forget that our Constitution is a single document, and not a jumble of disconnected clauses — that it is a *Constitution* we are expounding?

Today, the very phrase *Bill of Rights* is widely regarded as affirming not majority rights or states' rights, but only personal rights of individuals and minorities. But it is important to remember that two hundred years ago the Bill was understood to mean something quite different. The virulent Antifederalist Luther Martin, for example, argued during 1788 for "a bill of rights" that would encompass "a stipulation in favour of the rights both of states and of men."[1] George Mason, the leading proponent of a bill of rights at the Philadelphia convention, also linked the project to an express reservation of states' rights.[2] Another leading Antifederalist urged a "declaration in favour of the rights of states and of citizens."[3] In the New York ratifying convention, Thomas Tredwell lamented: "Here we find no security for the rights of individuals, no security for the existence of our state governments; here is no bill of rights. . . ."[4] In proposing provisions to be included in such a Bill, Tredwell emphasized populist provisions: "freedom of election, a sufficient and responsible representation, the freedom of the press, and the trial by jury both in civil and criminal cases."[5] In a similar populist spirit, Thomas Jefferson wrote that "a bill of rights is what *the people* are entitled to against every *government* on earth."[6]

"A bill of rights is what the *people* are entitled to"

Gordon Wood sums up this Antifederalist spirit well:

> [T]he Antifederalists' lack of faith was not in the people themselves, but only in the [regular government] organizations and institutions that presumed to speak for the people. . . . [E]nhancing the people out-of-doors as it correspondingly

disparaged their elected officials, [Antifederalist thought] can never be considered un-democratic. [Antifederalists] were "localists," fearful of distant governmental, even representational, authority for very significant political and social reasons that in the final analysis must be called democratic.[7]

Calls for a bill of rights were largely driven by populist and localist concerns

The Federalists understood that calls for a bill of rights were largely driven by populist and localist concerns. In 1788, Madison wrote Jefferson that proponents of a bill of rights sought "further guards to public liberty & individual rights."[8] In *The Federalist* No. 38, he noted that some critics "concur[red] in the absolute necessity of a bill of rights, but contend[ed] that it ought to be declaratory, not of the personal rights of individuals, but of the rights reserved to the States in their political capacity."[9] And in *The Federalist* No. 84, Hamilton stressed that "one object of a bill of rights [is] to declare and specify the *political* privileges of the citizens in the *structure* and *administration* of the government."[10]

Hamilton's answer to the drumbeat for a bill of rights was to stress the ways in which the original Constitution fit the bill, so to speak. For Hamilton and many others, the Philadelphia Constitution was "itself, in every rational sense, and to every useful purpose, A BILL OF RIGHTS."[11] But this point can be flipped around. As we have tried to show throughout, the original Bill of Rights can itself be seen as a *con-*

stitution of sorts — that is, as a document attentive to the structure and organization of government, focused on the problem of government officials pursuing their personal interests at the expense of the people, and rooted in the sovereignty of We the People of the United States.

ITS ATTENTION TO THE STRUCTURE AND ORGANIZATION OF GOVERNMENT

Like the original Constitution, the original Bill of Rights was webbed with structural and organizational ideas. Federalism, separation of powers, bicameralism, representation, republican government, amendment — these issues were understood as central to the preservation of liberty. Our point is not that substantive rights are unimportant, but that these rights were intimately intertwined with structural considerations. The most obvious prototype for an American Bill of Rights in the late eighteenth century was the English Bill of Rights of the late seventeenth century; and that Bill, too, dovetailed individual rights with structural issues — reining in executive authority, shielding legislative speech and debate, endorsing frequent Parliaments, limiting standing armies, and so on. Surely it would not be stretching things to call the English Bill of Rights a constitution of sorts. The same is true, we suggest, of the original American Bill of Rights.

The prototype for the American Bill of Rights was the English Bill of Rights

ITS FOCUS ON THE PROBLEM OF GOVERNMENT OFFICIALS PURSUING THEIR PERSONAL INTERESTS AT THE EXPENSE OF THE PEOPLE

Permanent government officials, even judges, may at times pursue self-interested policies that fail to reflect the views and protect the liberties of ordinary Americans. As the Fourth Amendment warrant clause and the Eighth Amendment make clear, professional judges acting without citizen juries can sometimes be part of the problem rather than the solution.

Today it is commonplace to stress judicial review as the most natural enforcement mechanism of the Bill of Rights. But consider again the two historical quotations typically invoked for this idea. First, there is Madison's speech before the First Congress: "If [rights] are incorporated into the constitution, independent tribunals of justice will consider themselves in a peculiar manner the guardians of those rights; they will be an impenetrable bulwark against every assumption of power in the legislative or executive [department]. . . ."[12]

Madison surely had the Constitution's Article III judicial review in mind here, but he may also have been thinking of juries. He speaks not of judges but "tribunals," which from one perspective can be seen as encompassing both the upper house of the judge and the lower house of the jury. If "independen[ce]" be the key to Madison's remarks, we must remember that juries were in some ways even more independent of the executive and legislative branches of government, since (unlike judges) jurors had never been appointed by these branches and did not draw any permanent salary from them. Emphasis on the populist and localist jury would fit perfectly with other things Madison said in this speech. In the sentence immediately after his mention of "independent tribunals," for example, he stressed populist and localist legislatures as constitutional watchdogs: "Besides this security, there is a great probability that such a declaration in the federal system would be enforced; because the State Legislatures will jealously and closely watch the operations of this Government, and be able to resist with more effect every assumption of power, than any other power on earth can do; and the greatest opponents to a Federal Government admit the State Legislatures to be sure guardians of the people's liberty."[13]

Populist and localist legislatures would be constitutional watchdogs

Now turn to Jefferson's comment that a bill of rights would put a "legal check . . . into the hands of the judiciary. This is a body, which if rendered independent, and kept strictly to their own department merits great confidence for their learning and integrity."[14] Here, too, Jefferson plainly has in mind judicial review by judges. But elsewhere he made clear that he viewed juries as part of the "judiciary." Indeed, only three months after his approving comments about judges and judicial review, Jefferson argued that ordinary citizen jurors, where they suspected self-dealing or other agency bias on the bench, could constitute themselves as judges of both fact and law: "But we all know that permanent judges acquire an Esprit de corps, that being known they are liable to be tempted by bribery, that they are misled by favor, by relationship, by a spirit of party, by a devotion to the Executive or Legislative. . . . It is left therefore to the juries, if they think the permanent judges are under any bias whatever in any cause, to take upon themselves to judge the law as well as the fact. They never exercise this power but when they suspect partiality in the judges. . . ."[15]

ITS USEFULNESS AS A DEVICE FOR EDUCATING ORDINARY CITIZENS ABOUT THEIR RIGHTS AND DUTIES

Beyond juries, both Madison and Jefferson emphasized public education as the remedy for, and deterrent to, unconstitutional conduct. Wrote Jefferson, "Written constitutions may be violated in moments of passion or delusion, yet they furnish a text to which those who are watchful may again rally and recall *the people*; they fix too for *the people* the principles of their political creed."[16] The words of the Bill of Rights would themselves educate Americans; hence the appropriateness of such nonlegalistic phrases as "a well regulated Militia [is] necessary to the security of a free State."[17] Such maxims were the heart and soul of early state constitutions.[18] Virginia's famous 1776 Declaration of Rights even featured a maxim about the need for maxims: "[N]o free government, or the blessings of liberty, can be preserved to any people, but by . . . virtue, and by frequent recurrence to fundamental principles."[19] A bill of rights would crystallize these principles so that they could be memorized and internalized — much like Scripture — by ordinary citizens.[20] In the words of one 1788 commentator, a bill of rights "will be the first lesson of the young citizens."[21] Patrick Henry and John Marshall agreed on very little in the Virginia ratifying convention, but when Henry declared that "[t]here are certain maxims by which every wise and enlightened people will regulate their conduct, [and] our [Virginia] bill of rights contains those admirable maxims," Marshall went out of his way to agree that such maxims "are necessary in any government, but more essential to a democracy than to any other.[22]

Maxims were the heart and soul of early state constitutions

Madison, too, stressed popular education and popular enforcement: "What use then it may be asked can a bill of rights serve in popular Governments? . . . 1. The political truths declared in that solemn manner acquire by degrees the character of fundamental maxims of free Government, and as they become incorporated with the national sentiment, counteract the impulses of interest and passion. 2. [Whenever] usurped acts of the Government [occur], a bill of rights will be a good ground for an appeal to the sense of the community."[23] In 1792, Madison — the great champion of internal checks and balances — noted that such checks "are neither the sole nor the chief palladium [safeguard] of constitutional liberty. The people who are the authors of this blessing, must also be its guardians."[24]

Although their personal labors in founding the University of Virginia signaled the special depth of their commitment, Madison and Jefferson were not alone in seeing the centrality of public education. In 1775, for example, Moses Mather declared that "[t]he strength and spring of every free government is the virtue of the people; virtue grows on knowledge, and knowledge on education."[25] After quoting Mather, Gordon Wood sums up the ethos of the era in his own words: "And education, it was believed, was the responsibility and agency of a republican government.

Madison and Jefferson were not alone in seeing the centrality of public education

So the circle went."[26] As Wood later observes, "The most obvious republican instrument for . . . inculcating virtue in a people was education."[27] We should not be surprised, then, that each of the first six presidents of the United States urged the formation of a national university. Nor should we be surprised at this language of the Massachusetts Constitution of 1780: "Wisdom and knowledge, as well as virtue, diffused generally among the body of the people, being necessary for the preservation of their rights and liberties; and as these depend on spreading the opportunities and advantages of education . . . it shall be the duty of legislatures and magistrates . . . to encourage [these ends]."[28]

The idea of popular education resurfaces over and over in the Bill of Rights. As we have seen, each of the three key institutions it safeguards — church, militia, and jury — was understood to be a device for educating ordinary citizens about their rights and duties. An uneducated populace cannot be a truly sovereign populace.

Yet it is exactly such a sovereign people who constitute the rock on which our Constitution is built. The opening words of the Preamble to the Constitution, of course, dramatize this truth; but so do the words of the Bill of Rights. For we hope it has not escaped notice that no phrase appears in more of the first ten amendments than "the people."

WHAT IS TO HAPPEN NEXT TO THE GRAND IDEA OF THE BILL OF RIGHTS?

It remains, of course, to see what happens when the grand idea of the original Bill of Rights — the rights of the people — meets the grand idea of the Fourteenth Amendment — the privileges and immunities of citizens of the United States. The phrases are similar, yet different. The first idea was centrally directed at the federal government; the second, at the states. The first arose mainly to address the problem of government officials operating in their self interest at the expense of the public, whereas the second arose to address as well the distinct problem of minority rights. The first seems largely republican and collective, addressing mainly political rights — the public liberty of the ancients. The second seems more liberal and individualistic, addressing mainly civil rights — the private liberty of the moderns. How are these two grand ideas to be synthesized? How, in other words, is the original Bill of Rights to be reconstructed by the Fourteenth Amendment? These are the questions of Part II.

II

Reconstruction

VIII

ANTEBELLUM IDEAS

In the antebellum period, lawyers began to develop theories of natural rights, individual liberty, and higher law — theories compatible with the spirit of the common law and their conviction that the Bill of Rights was primarily a declaration of rights and should be applicable to the states.

During the years between the Founding and the Civil War (popularly known as the antebellum period of American history), questions began to arise regarding the possible applicability of the provisions of the Bill of Rights to the states.

Perhaps the best place to begin analysis of this debate is to examine a lawsuit that occurred midway through the period, *Barron v. Baltimore*.[1]

BARRON

In 1833, the U. S. Supreme Court in *Barron* confronted for the first time the argument that a state government had violated one of the provisions of the Bill of Rights. Narrowly framed, the issue raised by *Barron* was whether the Fifth Amendment's takings clause ("nor shall private property be taken for public use without just compensation") limited not just the federal government but states and municipalities as well. But the Court saw that the reasoning behind John Barron's lawsuit radiated much further: it clearly would require state compliance with a vast number of other provisions contained in the Bill of Rights whose general language and logic made them indistinguishable from the Fifth Amendment's takings clause. If the words of the takings clause limited states, so, too, it would seem, would the Fourth Amendment's words, "no warrants shall issue, but upon probable cause," the Eighth Amendment's words, "excessive bail shall not be required," etc. *Barron* thus presented a question "of great importance," as Chief Justice Marshall acknowledged at the outset of his opinion for the Court.[2] However, Marshall immediately added that the question was "not of much difficulty," and went on to dismiss John Barron's lawsuit in less than five pages.

Barron presented a question "of great importance"

The core of Marshall's argument is compelling. Although the takings clause nowhere explicitly says that it ties the hands of only the federal government and not the states, state governments were already in place in the 1780s. In Marshall's view, the dominant purpose of the Constitution was to create, yet limit, a new *cen-*

tral government. "[L]imitations on power, if expressed in general terms, are naturally, and, we think, necessarily applicable to the government created by the instrument" — that is, the federal government.[3] From a strictly legal standpoint, this argument is hard to beat.

Most decisive is what Marshall called the "universally understood" historical background of the Bill of Rights.[4] In state convention after state convention in 1787-88, Antifederalists voiced loud concerns about a new, distant, aristocratic, central government that was being summoned into existence.[5] Many ultimately voted for the Constitution only because Federalists like Madison promised to consider a bill of rights soon after ratification. Madison kept his word; he knew that if he did not, states' rightists might call a second constitutional convention to repudiate the basic structure of the Constitution that he had worked so hard to build.[6] In short, without the goodwill of many moderate Antifederalists, prospects for the new Constitution looked bleak in 1787-88; and a bill of rights was the explicit price of that goodwill. But as we have seen, the bill of rights that Antifederalists sought was a bill to limit the federal government — not just for the sake of individual liberty but also to serve the cause of states' rights. Madison and his fellow Federalists could hardly have placated critics or won over skeptics by sneaking massive new restrictions on states into apparently innocuous general lan-

A bill of rights was the explicit price of the Antifederalists' goodwill

guage. Nor would Antifederalists in Congress or in states have knowingly allowed such a Trojan horse through the gates.

Barron's holding thus kept faith with both the letter and the spirit of the original Bill of Rights. We should not be surprised, then, that the decision in *Barron* was unanimous, or that the Court repeatedly and unanimously reaffirmed *Barron's* rule over the next thirty-three years in cases involving the First, Fourth, Fifth, Seventh, and Eighth Amendments.[7]

A CONTRARY VIEW OF *BARRON*

Some lawyers believed that various provisions of the Bill of Rights did limit states

In the fifteen years before *Barron*, a considerable number of considerable lawyers implied in passing or stated explicitly that various provisions in the Bill of Rights did limit states. Writing for the U.S. Supreme Court in 1819, Justice William Johnson obliquely suggested that the Seventh Amendment's guarantee of civil juries applied to states;[8] and the following year he proclaimed that the Fifth Amendment's double-jeopardy clause "operates equally upon both [state and federal] governments."[9] That same year the New York Supreme Court stated that the double-jeopardy clause "operates upon state courts," and in 1823 the Mississippi Supreme Court appeared to agree.[10] The following year William Rawle published a widely read treatise on the Constitution in which he argued at length that virtually all the general provisions of the Bill of Rights bound states.[11]

What were these lawyers and judges thinking? Some simply may not have given much thought to the *Barron* issue, especially where the case at hand was disposed of on other grounds. And a merely casual look at, say, the Fifth Amendment's double-jeopardy clause might lead a judge to assume it applied to states as well; for as New York Chief Justice Ambrose Spencer noted, the language of the clause was "general in its nature, and unrestricted in its terms."[12]

What were they thinking?

Barron, therefore, was hardly the last word, and views contrary to its holding persisted over the next thirty-three years. At times it appears that lawyers who had simply never heard of *Barron* casually assumed, along with Spencer or Rawle, that the general language of various provisions in the Bill of Rights made their application to states obvious. Thus in 1845, the Illinois Supreme Court noted in passing that the Fifth Amendment's due-process clause limited state action,[13] and two years later Ohio Attorney General Henry Stanbery glibly conceded in oral argument before the U.S. Supreme Court that double jeopardy was "forbidden, as well to the States as to the general government, by the fifth . . . amendment[ ]"[14]

In considering the views of these lawyers, we must keep in mind that at that time modern academic law schools did not exist. Supreme Court reports were not as widely available as nowadays. Constitutional law took a back seat to the common law in its importance to everyday legal practice. Would-be lawyers began their training with Blackstone's *Commentaries*, not *United States Reports*.

The enormous influence of Blackstone and the common law

Once we remember the enormous influence of Blackstone and the English common law upon American lawyers, we can see the *Barron* issue in a new light. For the common-law method in mid-nineteenth-century America involved careful examination of English and colonial codes, charters, statutes, and the like in an effort to distill their animating principles — the spirit of the common law. Judges did not simply make up common law; they found it. Thus, even if the federal Bill of Rights did not, strictly speaking, bind the states of its own legislative force, was it not at least declaratory of certain fundamental common-law rights? And should not these declarations by We the People tend to influence a state judge's analysis?

Three cases at mid-century illustrate this philosophy. In the 1840 case of *Holmes v. Jennison*, former New Hampshire Governor C. P. Van Ness politely but boldly attacked *Barron* in his oral argument before the Supreme Court: "With the utmost deference I beg leave to observe, that in my humble judgment, an error was committed by the Court. . . ."[15] After going out of his way to remind the justices that the original amendments to the Constitution were "commonly called the bill of rights," he distinguished between certain provisions that were merely "limitations of power" and others that "are to be understood as declarations of rights."[16] This latter category, argued Van Ness, encompassed "absolute rights, inherent in the people, and of which no power can legally deprive them," "principles which lie at the very foundation of civil liberty, and are most intimately connected with the dearest rights of the people[,]. . . . [p]rinciples which . . . deserve to be diligently taught to our children, and to be written upon the posts of the houses, and upon the gates."[17]

Far more elaborate were various opinions of the Supreme Court of Georgia, two of which were authored by Chief Justice Joseph Henry Lumpkin. In the first, the 1840 case of *Nunn v. Georgia*, Lumpkin wrote that he was "aware" of contrary rulings (presumably including *Barron*) but nevertheless invoked the Second Amendment to void a state statute.[18] Lumpkin began by emphasizing English common-law rights that preexisted state and federal constitutions. For him, state constitutions "confer no new rights on the people which did not belong to them before."[19] The federal Bill of Rights, "in declaring that the right of the people to keep and bear arms, should not be infringed, only reiterated a truth announced a

It was emphasized that common-law rights preexisted state and federal-constitutions

century before, in the [English Bill of Rights] of
1689."[20] The people, wrote Lumpkin, adopted
the Bill "as beacon-lights to guide and control the
action of [state] legislatures, as well as that of
Congress. If a well-regulated militia is necessary
to the security of the State of Georgia and of the
United States, is it competent for the [Georgia]
General Assembly to take away this security, by
disarming the People?"[21] In asking the question
whether arms-bearing was "a right reserved to
the States or to themselves [that is, the peo-
ple],"[22] Lumpkin found that the language of the
Second Amendment declaring a "right of the people" was controlling.

**Arms-
bearing
was a
right of
the
people**

Lumpkin reiterated and elaborated these
themes in the 1852 case of *Campbell v. Georgia,*
in which he explicitly cited *Barron* but once again
held that the provisions of the Bill of Rights generally bound states.[23] Unlike Marshall in *Barron*,
Lumpkin began not with the framing of the federal Bill of Rights but with the ancient landmarks
of the common law: Magna Carta, the Petition of
Rights, the [English] Bill of Rights [of 1689], and
other revered documents.[24] By emphasizing this
common-law background, Lumpkin could plausi-
bly portray the federal Bill of Rights as added
"out of abundant caution" to clarify preexisting
legal rights.[25] This declaratory purpose, Lumpkin
argued, clearly justified application of the Bill to
states, as emphasized by his own italics: The Bill

of Rights' purpose "was to *declare* to the world the fixed and unalterable determination of our people, that these invaluable rights . . . should never be disturbed by *any* government." The Bill was *"our American Magna Charta."*[26]

HOW CHANGES IN ANTEBELLUM AMERICA UNDERMINED THE *BARRON* DECISION

In their belief that *Barron* had been wrongly decided, men like Van Ness and Lumpkin found themselves in a distinct minority among antebellum lawyers, but time was on their side. As the years wore on, changes were occurring in America that made major premises of the original Bill of Rights — premises faithfully followed by Chief Justice Marshall in *Barron* — more and more problematic. Regardless of whether the original Bill was intended to apply against states, it became increasingly plausible to think that the Constitution should be amended to overrule *Barron*, especially in view of the significant changes that were taking place in America in the first half of the nineteenth century.

Significant changes were taking place in America

ADVANCES IN TECHNOLOGY

Consider first broad technological changes. In the 1780s, Antifederalists had feared that national lawmakers would be literally too far removed from their constituents for mutual confidence to develop between them. Congressmen would lack current information about constituent desires, and citizens would find it difficult to monitor their federal representatives. Hence, special constitutional restrictions on Congress made sense. But over the next eighty years, improved roads, new canals, and the invention of the railroad and the telegraph revolutionized transportation and communication, diminishing the feeling that national lawmakers were qualitatively more distant than state ones.

GEOGRAPHIC EXPANSION

Geographic expansion also altered Americans' self-image. In the 1780s, state governments had distinguished pedigrees dating back to their respective colonial foundings (as early as 1606 in Virginia, for example), while the national government proposed by Madison and his fellow Federalists was something strikingly new.[27] Prudence, if nothing else, dictated special skepticism about the new government, and special restrictions on it. By contrast, in the antebellum era, the federal government was well established, while various new states were springing to life as the nation pushed inexorably westward (an expansion spurred on, of course, by the technological

State governments had pedigrees dating back to the 1600s

advances we have just noted). But this territorial **Territorial** expansion gave rise to several puzzles. Since the **expansions** legislatures of the new territories were *federal* — **sions** agents of Congress — they were presumably **gave rise** bound by the provisions of the federal Bill of **to several** Rights. But why should they be bound when **puzzles** neighboring state governments were not? Moreover, did it make any sense that immediately upon admission to statehood, a territory could ignore all sorts of valuable restraints in the Bill that had previously applied to it? Congressman John Bingham apparently thought not, for in considering Oregon's proposed admission to the Union in 1859, he declared:

> In my judgment, sir, this constitution, framed by the people of Oregon, is repugnant to the Federal Constitution, and violative of the rights of citizens of the United States. I know, sir, that some gentlemen have a short and easy method of disposing of such objections as these, by assuming that the people of the State, after admission, may, by changing their constitution, insert therein every objectionable feature which, before admission, they were constrained to omit. . . .

> [But I deny] that the States are not limited by the Constitution of the United States, in respect of the personal or political rights of citizens of the United States. . . .

> [W]henever the Constitution guaranties to its citizens a right, either natural or conven-

tional, such guarantee is in itself a limitation upon the States. . . .[28]

THE GENERATION GAP

Contrast the lived experiences of the generation of James Madison, Thomas Jefferson, and Patrick Henry — whose labors helped birth the Bill of Rights — with the biography of John Bingham, father of the Bill of Rights' rebirth in the Fourteenth Amendment during the Reconstruction period. As white, male, propertied Virginians, Madison, Jefferson, and Henry belonged to an ongoing republic that had been practicing self-government for 150 years before the Constitution came along. Thus the Virginia House of Burgesses was already older for them than the Fourteenth Amendment is for us today. Likewise, the 1776 Virginia Declaration of Rights had predated the federal Bill of Rights. For eighteenth-century Virginians, Virginia came first, before the Union, chronologically and perhaps emotionally. But not for Bingham, or for an entire generation of later Americans growing up in places like Ohio. Before Ohio was even a state, it was a federal territory, governed by the Union's Northwest Ordinance, the federal Constitution and the federal Bill of Rights. For Bingham, *these* documents came first.

In the years immediately preceding the Founding, the American Revolution had featured

Virginians had been practicing self-government for 150 years

local colonies fighting an imperial British center. In light of their experience with imperial arrogance and oppression on the one hand, and the heroic roles played by local governments in resisting oppression on the other, the Founding Fathers associated a strong central government with tyranny and a strong state government with freedom. But in the middle decades of the nineteenth century, there was little evidence that the well-established federal government acted more repressively than local ones. Why, then, men like Bingham asked, should America be required to abide by the *Barron* double standard exempting the states from rights that sensibly limited the federal government?

SLAVERY AND ABOLITIONISM

But surely, to talk about the changes in technology, geography, and ideology that were taking place in antebellum America is to rehearse Hamlet without the prince, for we have yet to confront the issue that shattered the Founding Fathers Union: slavery. As important as canals, railroads, and telegraph lines were, none of these innovations was more significant than the cotton gin, which killed any chance that slavery might prove so unprofitable that it could be abolished without great economic dislocation. And no issues of geographic expansion posed by the new territories were as explosive as slavery and race — the sub-

The issue that shattered the Union

jects, indeed, of Bingham's specific objections to the Oregon Constitution.

Slavery was a creature of state law

Moreover, slavery was almost exclusively a creature of state law. The peculiar institution of slavery led slave states to violate virtually every right and freedom declared in the Bill of Rights — not just the rights and freedoms of slaves, but of free men and women too.[29] Slavery bred repression.[30] Speech and writing critical of slavery, even if plainly religious or political in inspiration, was incendiary and had to be suppressed in southern states, lest slaves overhear and get ideas.[31] In 1859, a Virginia postmaster even banned the *New York Tribune*, a leading Republican newspaper, under a sweeping state censorship statute; twenty years earlier, the state had tried to prosecute citizens for circulating an antislavery petition to Congress.[32] Teaching slaves to read (even the Bible) was a criminal offense punished severely in some states;[33] and in at least one state, writing, printing, publishing, or distributing abolitionist literature was punishable by death.[34] In a society that saw itself under siege after Nat Turner's rebellion,[35] access to firearms had to be carefully restricted, especially for free blacks.[36] The problem of fugitive slaves put further pressure on civil liberties, triggering rules that made life treacherous indeed for free blacks. Typically, all southern blacks were legally presumed to be slaves, subject to arbitrary "seizures" of their "persons," triable as fugitives with-

out juries in proceedings lacking the basic rudi-
ments of due process and, if adjudged to be
escaped slaves, subject to great cruelty as a warning to others.[37] To prevent the dissemination of
abolitionist literature, slave states allowed sweeping searches of mail and of suspicious travelers,
and even issued search warrants for books in
clear contravention of Lord Camden's famous
rulings in the 1760s.[38]

To counter this regime of repression, abolitionist and antislavery lawyers could not simply
rely on positive law as typified by the technical
legalism of *Barron*, for slavery itself was deeply
embedded in positive law. Therefore, beginning in the 1830s, abolitionist lawyers developed
in-creasingly elaborate theories of natural rights,
individual liberty, and higher law, theories far
more compatible with the idea that the Bill of
Rights was primarily a declaration of fundamental common-law rights and as such a proper
source of principles limiting states.[39]

Thus the fabric of the original Bill of Rights,
interweaving freedom and federalism, was unrav-
eling under the strain of slavery. And once the
Civil War came, *Barron* seemed plainly anachro-
nistic. For if the years prior to the Revolutionary
War had dramatized the special danger of *central*
tyranny, the Civil War era demonstrated that
states too could be tyrannical and needed to be
constitutionally restrained. The abolition of slavery in the Thirteenth Amendment — the first
federal constitutional amendment to restrict state

*Positive
law could
not be
relied
upon*

law — was obviously the place to start. But was it enough? When the Thirty-ninth Congress convened in December 1865, various unrepentant southern governments were in the process of resurrecting de facto slavery through the infamous Black Codes.* As with the slavery system itself, these new codes would invariably require systematic state abridgments of the core rights and freedoms in the Bill of Rights. These abridgments would hit blacks the hardest, but the resurrection of a caste system would also require repression of any whites who might question the codes or harbor sympathy for blacks.[40] In response, the Thirty-ninth Congress drafted the Civil Rights Act of 1866 and the Fourteenth Amendment.

*Laws enacted in ex-Confederate states shortly after the Civil War to restrict the freedoms of the newly freed slaves so as to ensure a supply of inexpensive agricultural labor and maintain white supremacy.

IX

THE FOURTEENTH AMENDMENT

How the Fourteenth Amendment was debated and framed by the Thirty-ninth Congress . . . The meaning of the words in its section 1 . . . How its drafters rejected the Supreme Court's holding in the Barron decision that the mandates of the Bill of Rights were not applicable to the states . . . How these legislative arguments laid the groundwork for the judicial doctrine and process of incorporation.

THE FOURTEENTH AMENDMENT
SECTION 1

" . . . No State shall make or enforce any law which shall abridge the privileges or immunities of citizens of the United States; nor shall any State deprive any person of life, liberty, or property, without due process of law; nor deny to any person within its jurisdiction the equal protection of the laws . . . ."[*]

Under the leadership of Representatives John Bingham, James Wilson, and Thaddeus Stevens, as well as Senator Jacob Howard, the Fourteenth Amendment was proposed by the Thirty-ninth Congress in 1866 and ratified by the states in 1868. A close examination of the key sentence of this Amendment and of the legislative history surrounding this sentence will show that it was designed to make the various fundamental rights in the federal Bill of Rights applicable **Barron is** against state governments, and thus to repudiate **repudiated** the Supreme Court's 1833 *Barron* decision. With this Amendment, the Reconstruction Congress laid the groundwork for the Supreme Court's eventual process of "incorporation" of the Bill of Rights against the states.

AN ANALYSIS OF THE WORDS IN THE SECOND SENTENCE OF SECTION 1

Drafted by John Bingham of Ohio, the key words of section 1 are critically important to a modern

*Many of the other provisions of the Fourteenth Amendment, while actually more important to Civil War era politicians than this key sentence of section 1, are today largely ignored. The entire amendment is set forth in the Appendix.

understanding of our Bill of Rights. It is therefore worth weighing each word with care.

"No State shall . . ."

This same phrase is found in Article I, section 10 of the U.S. Constitution, imposing various limitations on states, including several important rights designed principally for the benefit of in-state residents: *"No State shall . . . pass any Bill of Attainder, ex post facto Law, or Law impairing the Obligation of Contracts,* * or grant any Title of Nobility."* In 1810, Chief Justice Marshall's opinion for the Court in *Fletcher v. Peck* declared that the language of Article I, section 10 "may be deemed a bill of rights for the people of each state,"[1] a phrase repeated by the Supreme Court in 1853 and again in 1866, the same year in which the Fourteenth Amendment was drafted.[2] Of course, the Court did not mean to suggest that the catalogue of section 10 rights was identical to the list laid out in the first ten amendments — otherwise the entire debate over the *Barron* decision and incorporation would be meaningless. In *Barron*, a unanimous Supreme Court stated instead that, had the framers of the original Bill of Rights meant to impose its rules on states, they

The Constitution's Article I, section 10 rights were not identical to those of the Bill of Rights

*That is, laws singling out named persons for special disadvantage, laws retroactively criminalizing actions that were innocent when done, and special interest laws frustrating vested creditor rights.

The Jus-
tices
were ask-
ing for
"Simon
says" lan-
guage
would have used the Article I, section 10 phrase
"No State shall" or some reasonable facsimile.
The Justices were apparently asking for "Simon
says" language — and that's exactly what John
Bingham's Fourteenth Amendment gave them.

> " . . . *make or enforce any law*
> *which shall abridge . . .*"

The critical words of the next phrase — make,
any, law, and abridge — call to mind the First
Amendment's precisely parallel language in parallel sequence — *make, no, law,* and *abridging*.[3]
(The word *abridge* in the Fourteenth Amendment is especially revealing, for nowhere outside
the First Amendment had this word appeared in
the Constitution before 1866.) However, there
are three significant differences.

First, in keeping with the basic idea of incorporation, the Fourteenth Amendment imposes
an express prohibition on states, whereas the
First Amendment explicitly limits only Congress.

Second, the Fourteenth Amendment uses the
word *any* where the First uses *no*. The reason
here is obvious. Following the "Simon Says"
rules of *Barron* to the letter, the Fourteenth uses
negative phrasing ("No State shall . . .") where
the First used affirmative ("Congress shall . . .").
The substitution of *any* for *no* works simply to
balance out this earlier difference in phrasing.

Finally, the Fourteenth Amendment speaks of

law "enforce[ment]" as well as lawmaking. Once again, this makes perfect sense if its purpose was to incorporate the rights and freedoms of the original Bill of Rights. Many of the Bill's provisions, especially those in Amendments V–VIII, dealt centrally with the enforcement of laws by executive and judicial officers.

" . . . the privileges or immunities . . ."

These exact words do not appear in the Bill of Rights, but the words *right* and *freedom* speckle the Bill.[4] The plain meanings of these four words are roughly synonymous; indeed, the *Oxford English Dictionary* definition of *privilege* includes the word *right*; and of *immunity, freedom*.[5] What could be more common today than to speak of the "privilege" against compelled self-incrimination, or "immunity" from double prosecution? Nor is modern usage here any different from that of the eighteenth and nineteenth centuries. To pick only one pre-Revolutionary example, the entitlements to civil and criminal juries, labeled in the Sixth and Seventh Amendments as "right[s]," were described by the 1775 Declaration of the Causes and Necessity of Taking Up Arms as the "inestimable *privilege* of trial by jury"; and in *The Federalist*'s most extended discussion of a possible bill of rights, Alexander Hamilton explained that "bills of rights are, in their origin, stipulations between kings and their

The words *right* and *freedom* speckle the Bill

subjects, abridgments of prerogative in favor of *privilege*, reservations of rights not surrendered to the prince."[6]

A couple of generations later, Circuit Justice William Johnson was to characterize a congressional bill of 1822 as "in nature of a bill of rights, and of *privileges,* and immunities" of inhabitants of the Florida territory.[7] Among the rights listed in this bill were "freedom of religious opinions," "the benefit of the writ of habeas corpus," and protections against "excessive bail," "cruel and unusual punishments," and confiscation without "just compensation" — protections phrased almost identically with their federal Bill of Rights counterparts.[8]

Justice Johnson's phrasing was common: throughout the nineteenth century, Congress entered into various treaties of territorial accession guaranteeing to territorial inhabitants the privileges, rights, and immunities of the citizens **Territorial** of the United States. Such treaties were widely **treaties** **guaranteed** understood as encompassing (among other **privileges,** things) all the rights and freedoms listed in the **rights, and** original Constitution and its Bill of Rights. In **immunities** 1862 and 1867, for example, Congress extended the Bill of Rights to the Ottawa Indians and Alaskans, respectively, using the language of "rights" and "immunities" of "citizens of the United States"; and in 1868 Congress guaranteed the Sioux "all the privileges and immunities of such citizens."[9]

Even earlier than the examples we have cited thus far, when we turn to Blackstone we find the words *privileges* and *immunities* used to describe various entitlements embodied in the landmark English charters of liberty — Magna Carta, the Petition of Right, and the English Bill of Rights of 1689.[10] These English documents were the fountainhead of the common law and the acknowledged forebears of many particular rights that later appeared in the American Bill of Rights, sometimes in identical language.[11]

The words *privileges* and *immunities* are also to be found in the English charters of liberty

" . . . of citizens of the United States . . ."

Once we recognize that various "rights" and "freedoms" in the Bill are in every respect and for every purpose "privileges" and "immunities," there remains one final textual stumbling block. Can we really say that the Bill's "rights" and "freedoms" are "privileges and immunities" of "*citizens* of the United States"?

Of course we can. In ordinary, everyday language we often speak of the United States Constitution and Bill of Rights as declaring and defining rights of Americans as Americans. This ordinary, everyday understanding of the Constitution is emblazoned in its Preamble in words familiar to every generation of Americans: "*We the People of the United States,* in Order to . . . secure the Blessings of Liberty to *ourselves and our Pos-*

terity, do ordain and establish this Constitution *for* the United States."

At the time of the Fourteenth Amendment, the best-known case on the scope of the Bill of Rights was *Dred Scott v Sandford*, which involved, among other issues, questions arising under the due-process clause of the Fifth Amendment. The Supreme Court's ruling in *Dred Scott* declared that the rights in the Bill were not simply privileges, but "privileges of the citizen."[12] This passage must be read in combination with the rest of the Court's opinion that since Dred Scott was a black man, he was not a citizen of the United States and could not enjoy any of the "rights, and privileges, and immunities, guarantied by [the Constitution] to the citizen."[13] The central meaning and logic of the Court's opinion, which took pains to stress the words of the Preamble to the Constitution,[14] was that the Constitution and the Bill of Rights were ordained and established by citizens of the United States, and for their benefit only.

It is clear that the framers of the Fourteenth Amendment relied on the words used by the Supreme Court in *Dred Scott* no less than the Court's language in *Barron,* even as they were seeking to overrule both of these decisions by using the "Simon Says" language suggested by the Court itself. John Bingham not only cited *Dred Scott* in a speech before the House in early 1866 but quoted the following key language:

The *Dred Scott* decision

"The words 'people of the United States' and 'citizens' are synonymous terms."[15] Though many aspects of *Dred Scott* were highly offensive to members of the Thirty-ninth Congress, there was widespread support for the idea that the Bill of Rights was a catalogue of privileges and immunities of "citizens."[16]

> ". . . *nor shall any State deprive any person of life, liberty, or property without due process of law . . .*"

"During the drafting of section 1, one of the goals of Bingham, Senator Jacob Howard, and their colleagues was to extend the benefits of state due process to aliens. But for this, a special clause — speaking not of *"citizens"* but of *"persons"* — was needed. As Bingham explained this aspect of the amendment on the floor of the House: "Is it not essential to the unity of the people that the citizens of each State shall be entitled to all the privileges and immunities of citizens [of the United States]? Is it not essential . . . that all persons, *whether citizens or strangers,* within this land, shall have equal protection in every State in this Union in the rights of life and liberty and property?"[17]

"All persons, whether citizens or strangers, shall have equal protection"

Senator Howard's explanation to the Senate was identical. After emphasizing that the privileges and immunities of citizens of the United States included "the personal rights guarantied and secured by the first eight amendments of the Constitution," he elaborated that the subsequent clauses of section 1 were needed to "disable a State from depriving not merely a citizen of the United States, but any person, whoever he may be, of life, liberty, or property without due process of law, or from denying to him the equal protection of the laws of the State."[18] The views of Bingham and Howard were widely shared by their Reconstruction colleagues.[19]

DEBATE AND RATIFICATION

As Republican delegates to the Thirty-ninth Congress began debate on the Fourteenth Amendment, the Civil War hovered over their thoughts. The experience of the war provided powerful ideological, almost religious, reinforcement of the freedoms declared in the Bill of Rights. The war had taken a terrible toll in lives and limbs, and even victory tasted bittersweet. Republicans in 1866 needed to convince their constituents that all had not been in vain, that the noble goals of the Union — preservation of nation and (later) freedom — had been worth the fight

A perfect symbol of the noble goals of the Union and had been won.[20] The Bill of Rights was a perfect symbol of both goals, proven by the Civil War experience to be even better in some ways than the Declaration of Independence and the original Constitution. The Declaration's language of "free and independent states" had been repeatedly invoked by southern legislators on behalf of secession.[21] And the original Constitution had been tainted by its open compromises with slavery, and could also be seen as the product of independent state conventions, none of which could bind any other (points likewise emphasized by secessionists).[22] The Bill of Rights, by contrast, clearly derived from America as a nation. It proclaimed freedom, not slavery.

Unlike the Declaration of Independence and the Constitution, the Bill of Rights derived from America as a nation

The vast majority of Republican leaders in 1866 disagreed with the Supreme Court's holding in *Barron* that the mandates of the Bill of Rights should not apply to the states.[23] Some, like Bingham, were highly conscious of *Barron*, while others had apparently never heard of the case. Yet all could agree that Bingham's section 1 was simply declaratory of preexisting rights and freedoms of citizens, many of which had already been declared by the Founding Fathers.[24]

Nor did Democratic critics of the amendment directly challenge this understanding. After all, who wants to campaign against a Bill of Rights? With only a few exceptions the substance of the rights and freedoms in the federal Bill of Rights did not greatly diverge from rights already formally protected under state laws and state constitutions. True, the slavery experience led many states to betray their own constitutional safeguards of speech, press, personal security, and the like; but the principles themselves were deeply etched in both the popular and the legal mind. Given this, one would expect that the main Democratic opposition to section 1 would find expression in the basic language of federalism: although the rights of citizens should be preserved, responsibility for securing citizens' rights, freedoms, privileges, and immunities should not be handed over to Congress and federal courts but should remain with the states. And this is exactly the kind of rhetoric that one does find during debate and ratification.[25]

In 1859, seven years prior to the Thirty-ninth Congress' debate over the Fourteenth Amendment, John Bingham had argued before the House that "whenever the Constitution guaranties to its citizens a right, either natural or conventional, such guarantee is in itself a limitation upon the States."[26] At that time, he made clear that such "guarantees" that "no State may rightfully . . . impair" included the due-process and just-compensation mandates of the "fifth article of amendments," the trial by jury," and the "right to know; to argue and to utter, according to conscience" — guarantees he described as "privileges and immunities of citizens of the United States."[27] *Citizens* here meant just that, as Bingham illustrated by quoting *Dred Scott* and other commentary.[28] In a nutshell, Bingham's position was that no state could violate the Constitution's "wise and beneficent guarantees of political rights to the citizens of the United States, as such, and of natural rights to all persons, whether citizens or

No state could violate the political rights of citizens or the natural rights of persons

strangers."[29] These views, expressed in 1859, track almost perfectly the natural meaning of the words Bingham was later to draft as section 1 of the Fourteenth Amendment.

Thus we find Bingham in 1866 repeating in speeches before the House the arguments he had made seven years earlier. He once again quoted from *Dred Scott* on constitutional rights of "citizens" as "citizens," yet repeated his claim that *Dred Scott* was too stingy in refusing certain due-process protections to "persons, whether citizens or strangers."[30] In another nutshell, Bingham's argument was that no state should be allowed to violate "the privileges and immunities of all the citizens of the Republic and the inborn rights of every person within its jurisdiction."[31]

But what, precisely, were the "privileges or immunities of citizens of the Republic"? In 1859, Bingham had offered no comprehensive summary, but strongly implied that all rights and freedoms guaranteed by the Constitution were included. Though he did not use the magic words *Bill of Rights,* he either quoted or paraphrased the rights to speech, press, religion, due process, just compensation, and jury trial. In key congressional debates in 1866, he spoke to the issue at much greater length and made himself abundantly clear. Over and over he described the privileges-or-immunities clause as encompassing "the bill of rights" — *a phrase he used more than a dozen times in a key speech on February 28.*[32] In

> What were the "privileges or immunities of citzens?"

that speech he also explained why a constitutional amendment was necessary, citing by name and quoting from the Supreme Court's opinions in *Barron* and a later case that adhered to *Barron's* holding, *Livingston v. Moore*.[33] Six weeks later he again held forth on the need for his amendment, reminding his colleagues that it "has been solemnly ruled by the Supreme Court of the United States" that "the bill of rights . . . does not limit the powers of States."[34]

Bingham again reminds his colleagues that the amendment would overrule *Barron*

Then, in a speech in January 1867, while the amendment was pending ratification in the states, Bingham again reminded his audience that his amendment would overrule *Barron*.[35]

Finally, in 1871, several years after the Fourteenth Amendment was ratified, Bingham was once more called upon to explain its words. He yet again cited by name and quoted from *Barron*,[36] and here, too, he immediately linked "the privileges and immunities of citizens of the United States" with the Bill of Rights:

> [T]he privileges and immunities of citizens of the United States, as contradistinguished from citizens of a State, are chiefly defined in the first eight amendments to the Constitution of the United States. Those eight amendments are as follows. [Bingham then proceeded to read the first eight amendments word for word.] These eight articles I have shown never were limitations upon the power of the States, until made so by the fourteenth amendment.[37]

Two years before Bingham introduced his amendment, Representative James Wilson had made clear that he too understood the "privileges and immunities of citizens of the United States" to include the guarantees of the amendments. His words also show that he deemed all rights and freedoms in the Bill to be binding on state governments:

> Freedom of religious opinion, freedom of speech and press, and the right of assemblage for the purpose of petition belong to every American citizen . . . . With these rights no State may interfere. . . .
>
> Sir, I might enumerate many other constitutional rights of the citizen which slavery has disregarded and practically destroyed, but I have [said] enough to illustrate my proposition: that slavery . . . denies to the citizens of each State the privileges and immunities of citizens. . . .
>
> The people of the free States should insist on ample protection to their rights, privileges and immunities, which are none other than those which the Constitution was designed to secure to all citizens alike. . . .[38]

All rights and freedoms in the Bill would be binding on states

Shortly before the Fourteenth Amendment came before the House for final approval, the political leader Thaddeus Stevens delivered a speech describing its provisions. Here are his opening words on section 1: "I can hardly believe that any person can be found who will not admit that every one of these provisions is just. They are all asserted, in some form or other, in our

DECLARATION or [of?] organic law. But the Constitution limits only the action of Congress, and is not a limitation on the States. This amendment supplies that defect. . . ."[39]

In the Senate, Jacob Howard offered a comprehensive analysis of section 1, defining the "privileges and immunities of citizens" to include:

Senator Howard's analysis of section 1

> the personal rights guaranteed and secured by the first eight amendments of the Constitution; such as freedom of speech and of the press; the right of the people peaceably to assemble and petition the Government for a redress of grievances, a right appertaining to each and all of the people; the right to keep and bear arms; the right to be exempted from the quartering of soldiers in a house without the consent of the owner; the right to be exempt from unreasonable searches and seizures, and from any search or seizure except by virtue of a warrant issued upon a formal oath or affidavit; the right of an accused person to be informed of the nature of the accusation against him, and his right to be tried by an impartial jury of the vicinage; and also the right to be secure against excessive bail and against cruel and unusual punishments.
>
> . . . [T]he course of decision of our courts and the present settled doctrine is, that all these immunities, privileges, rights, thus guaranteed by the Constitution or recognized by it . . . do not operate in the slightest degree as a restraint or prohibition upon State legislation.
>
> . . . [T]hese guarantees . . . stand simply as a bill of rights in the Constitution . . . [and] States are not restrained from violating the principles embraced in them. . . . The great

object of the first section of this amendment is,
therefore, to restrain the power of the States
and compel them at all times to respect these
great fundamental guarantees.[40]

To evaluate the impact of these statements upon the members of the Thirty-ninth Congress, consider the sources. John Bingham was the author of section 1. Thaddeus Stevens was not only the political leader of the House but also head of the all-important Committee on Reconstruction that first drafted the Amendment. Jacob Howard was Stevens's acting Joint Committee counterpart in the Senate. James Wilson was chairman of the House Judiciary Committee and sponsor of the Civil Rights Act of 1866, whose provisions section 1 was consciously designed and widely understood to embrace.

The substantial impact of these statements upon members of the Thirty-ninth Congress

Consider next the context. Bingham's audience knew he was the author of section 1 and thus paid particular attention to his speeches.[41] *The New York Times* covered his major speeches, summarizing one as "a proposition to arm the Congress . . . with power to enforce the Bill of Rights as it stood"; and Bingham published his speech as a popular pamphlet subtitled "in support of the proposed amendment to enforce the bill of rights."[42] Stevens delivered a written speech (a rarity for him, as the *New York Herald* noted the next day)[43] in his formal capacity as House chairman of the Joint Committee. Howard, too, purported to speak on behalf of the committee, addressing a packed gallery in a speech whose passage on the Bill of Rights was reprinted in full on the front page of both the *New York Times* and the *Herald*.[44] (The latter ranked as the nation's best-selling newspaper at the time.)[45] And not a single person in either house spoke up to deny these interpretations of section 1. Most certainly, if the words of section 1 meant something different, this was the time to stand up and say so.

Consider, finally, that all these men offered arguments that mesh perfectly with each other and, most importantly, with the plain meaning of the words of section 1.

Bingham's imagery
Bingham's imagery in the Fourteenth Amendment debate also bears notice. For him the Bill of Rights was not simply "immortal,"[46] as he preached in his maiden sermon in support of his amendment, but "sacred," a word that punctuates his most extended meditation on the Bill:

> As a further security for the enforcement of the Constitution, and especially of this sacred bill of rights, to all the citizens and all the people of the United States, it is further provided that the members of the several State Legislatures and all executive and judicial officers, both of the United States and of the several States, shall be bound by oath or affirmation to support this Constitution. The oath, the most solemn compact which man can make with his Maker, was to bind the State Legislatures, executive officers,

and judges to sacredly respect the Constitution and all the rights secured by it. . . .

[The Bill of Rights encompasses] all the sacred rights of person — those rights dear to freemen and formidable only to tyrants — and of which the fathers of the Republic spoke, after God had given them the victory. . . .[47]

Not all of Bingham's colleagues shared his faith, but they, too, had reasons to value virtually every privilege and immunity in the Bill. Even if not sacred because given from above (from the Fathers, the People, or the Almighty), the Bill had proved its secular value — *if only by its unavailability* — in the trenches of the antebellum crusade against slavery. Slavery led to state repudiation of virtually every one of the Bill's rights and freedoms. As it had for Antifederalists in the 1780s, the Bill provided to Reconstruction Republicans in the 1860s an armory of indispensable weapons against a tyranny that people had seen with their own eyes. The difference, of course, was that unlike the tyranny of George III, the tyranny of slavery could not be blamed on a distant and dictatorial center, but instead had been perpetrated by local democracies. Just as the price of peace and union in 1789 was a bill of rights against the center, so the price of peace and (re)union in 1866 was a bill of rights against the periphery.

The Bill of Rights thus stood as a handy

The Bill had proven its value in the antebellum crusade against slavery

Congress
could
refuse
readmis-
sion to
the Union
of states
that vio-
lated the
Bill

pledge of the good faith of the South, enforceable by congressional refusal to readmit states that continued to violate its provisions. Senator James Nye proclaimed that Congress had "no power to invade" such privileges of the Bill as "freedom of speech," "freedom of the press," "freedom in the exercise of religion," and the "security of person," but that Congress did have power to "restrain the respective States from infracting them" by continuing to exclude as unrepublican any state violating these "personal rights."[48] Representative Roswell Hart defined a "republican" government as one where: "citizens shall be entitled to all privileges and immunities of other citizens"; where "no law shall be made prohibiting the free exercise of religion"; where "the right of the people to keep and bear arms shall not be infringed"; where "the right of the people to be secure in their persons, houses, papers and effects, against unreasonable searches and seizures, shall not be violated"; and where "no person shall be deprived of life, liberty, or property without due process of law."[49] Congressman Samuel Moulton argued against readmittance of various southern states because "there is neither freedom of speech, of the press, or protection to life, liberty, or property"; Representative Sidney Clarke opposed restoration of Mississippi to Congress because the state's policies disarming blacks violated the Second Amendment command that "the right of the people to keep and bear arms shall not be infringed"; and Representative Leonard Myers sought to exclude Alabama because of its "anti-republican laws" that banned firearms.[50]

In its various roles — as a beacon for judges trying to find higher law, as a sacred gift from above, as a time-tested arsenal against tyranny, as a ready-made pledge of states' good faith, as a definition of republican government, and as a prudent bar against hasty readmission of the South — the Bill of Rights was central to the Reconstruction vision. In both the Fourteenth Amendment's text and in their explanations of that text, members of the Thirty-Ninth Congress made it clear that the rights and freedoms of this Bill should in the future apply against states.

The Bill of Rights was central to the Reconstruction vision

POST-RATIFICATION COMMENTARY FORETELLING THE JUDICIAL DOCTRINE AND PROCESS OF INCORPORATION

After the Fourteenth Amendment's ratification in 1868, when we turn to what important decision makers said when they focused on the relation between the Fourteenth Amendment and the Bill, we find powerful statements foreshadowing the eventual development of the doctrine and process of incorporation. In the years between 1868 and 1873, various members of Congress, both Democrats and Republicans, sug-

Statements foreshadowing development of the incorporation doctrine

gested that the Bill of Rights defined privileges and immunities of Americans that no state could abridge.[51]

In 1872 Republican Senator John Sherman declared that the "privileges, immunities, and rights, (because I do not distinguish between them, and cannot do it,) of citizens of the United States" may be found in "the common law," "the great charters of England," "the Constitution of the United States," "the constitutions of the different States," the "Declaration of Independence," and other authoritative declarations.[52]

In the 1871 circuit court case *United States v. Hall*, Judge (later Justice) William Woods' opinion plainly supported incorporation: "We think, therefore, that the . . . rights enumerated in the first eight articles of amendment to the constitution of the United States are the privileges and immunities of citizens of the United States."[53]

A leading judicial figure of the time, Justice Joseph Bradley, endorsed Wood's approach in the *Hall* case in a letter to Woods: "The right of the people to assemble together and discuss political questions . . . is one of the most sacred rights of citizenship, and cannot be abridged by any state. . . . [This right is protected] against a state . . . as one of the privileges and immunities belonging to all citizens . . . [b]y the 14th amendment. . . ."[54]

Members of the executive branch and other

legal commentators also shared the views expressed in Bradley's letter. In another 1871 case, U.S. Attorney Daniel Corbin invoked *Barron* and then declared that "the fourteenth amendment changes all that theory, and lays the same restriction upon the States that before lay upon the Congress of the United States — that, as Congress heretofore could not interfere with the right of the citizen to keep and bear arms, now, after the adoption of the fourteenth amendment, the State cannot interfere with the right of the citizen to keep and bear arms. The right to keep and bear arms is included in the fourteenth amendment, under 'privileges and immunities.' "[55]

Justice Bradley's publicly voiced his position in 1873 in his dissenting opinion in the famous *Slaughter-House Cases*.[56] In his words:

> The people of this country brought with them to its shores the rights of Englishmen. . . . [Bradley then cited and discussed "fundamental rights" found in, among other places, Magna Charta, Blackstone's *Commentaries,* etc.] But we are not bound to resort to implication, or to the constitutional history of England, to find an authoritative declaration of some of the most important privileges and immunities of citizens of the United States. It is in the Constitution itself.[57]

"The people of this country brought with them to its shores the rights of Englishmen"

Bradley then proceeded to offer a representative sample of these privileges and immunities, including jury trial, free exercise, free speech, free press, free assembly, and security against unreasonable searches and seizures. He then concluded as follows:

> Admitting . . . that formerly the States were not prohibited from infringing any of the fundamental privileges and immunities of citizens of the United States, except in a few specified cases, that cannot be said now, since the adoption of the fourteenth amendment. In my judgment, it was the intention of the people of this country in adopting the amendment to provide National security against violation by the States of the fundamental rights of the citizen.[58]

X

THE INCORPORATION PROCESS

Although the Fourteenth Amendment's letter and spirit call for applying the Bill of Rights against states, the precise process of "incorporation" raises certain difficulties as interpreters seek to fit Creation-era pegs into Reconstruction-era holes.

As we have previously discussed, incorporation is a doctrine and a process by which courts apply the provisions of the Bill of Rights to the states by interpreting the Fourteenth Amendment's section 1 as encompassing (or "incorporating") those provisions. The process began in the late nineteenth century, moved forward in the early twentieth century, and culminated in a series of cases in the 1960s during the Warren Court era.

Incorporation presents a number of complex questions that have occupied the thinking of

American legislators, judges, constitutional lawyers, and legal scholars ever since the Fourteenth
Amendment was ratified in 1868. These questions have framed a debate that, in the words of
Judge Henry Friendly, "go[es] to the very nature
of our Constitution" with "profound effects for all
of us."[1] Professor William Van Alstyne has written that "it is difficult to imagine a more conse-
quential subject,"[2] an assessment confirmed by
the extraordinary number of twentieth-century
legal giants who locked horns in the debate —
Justices Hugo Black, Felix Frankfurter, and William Brennan, to name only a few.

When we examine decisions of the Supreme
Court over the last century, we also find com-

**The cen-
trality of
the incor-
poration
debate**

pelling evidence of the centrality of the incorporation debate. A list of cases applying various
parts of the Bill of Rights against states reads like
the "greatest hits"[3] of the modern era: *New York
Times v. Sullivan,*[4] *Abington School District v.
Schempp,*[5] *Mapp v. Ohio,*[6] *Miranda v. Arizona,*[7]
Gideon v. Wainwright,[8] *Duncan v. Louisiana,*[9]
and on and on.

And yet, despite the importance of the topic of
incorporation and all the attention devoted to it,
there is still a good deal of confusion regarding
the precise relation between the first ten amendments and the Fourteenth. One of the reasons is
the differing architectures of the Bill of Rights
and the Fourteenth Amendment. As we saw in
earlier chapters, at its Creation the original Bill of

Rights tightly knit together *citizens' rights and states' rights;* but during its Reconstruction in the Fourteenth Amendment unraveled this fabric, *vesting citizens with rights against states.* The original Bill focused centrally on empowering the people collectively against government agents following their own agenda. The Fourteenth Amendment, by contrast, focused on protecting minorities against even responsive, representative, majorities. Over and over, the 1789 Bill proclaimed 'the right[s]" and "the powers" of "the people" — phrases conjuring up civic republicanism, collective political action, public rights, and positive liberty. The complementary phrase in the Fourteenth Amendment —"privileges or immunities of citizens" — indicates a subtle but real shift of emphasis, reflecting a vision more liberal than republican, more individualistic than collectivist, more private than public, more negative than positive.

It should come as no surprise that attempting to incorporate the Founders' Bill of Rights into the Reconstructionists' Fourteenth Amendment should present major difficulties. After all, the two texts are separated by nearly one hundred years of history, addressed to different constituencies, and aimed at solving different political problems. You might say incorporation requires nothing less than fitting Creation pegs into Reconstruction holes.

A single example — the Second Amendment

Attempting to incorporate the Bill of Rights into the Fourteenth Amendment presents major difficulties

— should suffice to illustrate this point. In 1789 the amendment was intimately connected with the Founding Fathers' concerns about a federally controlled standing army that might seek to over-awe state-organized militias. But fourscore years later, Reconstruction Republicans like John Bingham, Jacob Howard, and Thaddeus Stevens were hardly in the mood to rail against a federal standing army. These men wanted to use precisely such an army to reconstruct defiant southern states. How, then, to square their understanding of "the right . . . to keep and bear arms" with the rather different vision of the Second Amendment's Antifederalist architects?

Originally the Second Amendment focused on arms-bearing as a political right

Another problem: the Second Amendment focused on arms-bearing as a political right akin to voting. Thus, a strong argument could be made that the original amendment protected only adult male citizens. These men, of course, constituted the "militia" of the amendment's preamble, and we can sensibly read the phrase *the people* in the amendment's main clause as synonymous with *the militia*.[10] Such a reading also draws support from the original Constitution's use of the phrase *the people* to connote voters — the same adult male citizens who, roughly speaking, constituted the militia.[11] By contrast, the privileges-or-immunities clause of the Fourteenth Amendment spoke not of *the people*, but of *all citizens*, pointedly including women and children, as made clear by the words immediately preceding Bingham's key sentence defining citizens to include "[a]ll persons born or naturalized in the United States." Moreover, time and again members of the Thirty-ninth Congress in 1866 declared that section 1 of the Fourteenth Amendment focused on "*civil rights*," not "*political rights*" like voting and militia service. But how to fit that vision together with the original Second Amendment?

But the Fourteenth Amendment focused on civil rights

Thus far, the Supreme Court has avoided these puzzles by refusing to review cases involving the possible incorporation of the Second Amendment.[12] Perhaps the Supreme Court has assumed that the Second is concerned with a purely federalism-based right of organized state militias and is thus inappropriate for incorporation against states. If so, the Court's assumption rests on a dubious reading of the word *militia* as well as inattention to the grammar and syntax of the Amendment, which speaks of a right of "*the people*," not "*the states*."[13]

Similar questions can be raised about other provisions of the original Bill of Rights. In addition to the right to keep and bear arms, three other rights in Amendments I-VIII have yet to be incorporated: the Third Amendment's right against quartering soldiers, the Fifth Amendment's right to a grand jury, and the Seventh Amendment's right to a civil jury. Also, the Ninth and Tenth Amendments have yet to be incorporated, in keeping with the generally accepted wisdom that since these amendments affirm principles of federalism and enumerated federal power, it would make little sense to apply them against the states.

The best way to confront the problem of fitting Creation pegs into Reconstruction holes is to take another look, one by one, at the provisions of the Bill of the Rights, and to see how these provisions were often reconceptualized — reconstructed, if you will — in the aftermath of the Civil War. In our next chapter we shall do just that for a series of illustrative rights.

XI

RECONSTRUCTING RIGHTS

Reacting to the Civil War and the events of the antebellum and Reconstruction eras, the Thirty-ninth Congress in effect redefined various provisions of the Founders' Bill of Rights.

In the process of debating and enacting the Fourteenth Amendment, the Thirty-ninth Congress also redefined (or as you might say, in reference to the political climate of 1866, reconstructed) most of the rights in the Founders' Bill, including the First Amendment's rights to freedom of expression, assembly, and religion; the Second Amendment's right to keep and bear arms; and the Fifth, Sixth, and Seventh Amendments' rights to grand, petit, and civil juries. In the course of explaining why these rights (and others) should apply against states, Reconstruction congressmen offered up images of these rights that differed in key ways from the corresponding images of the Founding Fathers.

FREEDOM OF SPEECH

"Congress shall make no law . . . abridging the
freedom of speech, or of the press;"

The Thirty-ninth Congress redefined and changed
the focus of the First Amendment's freedom of
speech clause, making the rights associated with
religious speech, artistic speech, and most especially, minority speech, more important than
they had been in the original First Amendment.

In the eighteenth century, freedom of expression issues were primarily focused on individuals
like John Peter Zenger and James Callender,[1]
relatively popular publishers saying relatively
popular things that were critical of less popular
government officials. In the mid-nineteenth century the focus shifted to the Unionist, the abolitionist, and the freedman, to speakers like Samuel Hoar, Harriet Beecher Stowe, and Frederick
Douglass. Hoar was a Massachusetts lawyer who
in 1844 went to South Carolina with his daughter
to defend the rights of free blacks, only to be rid-
den out of town on a rail by an enraged populace
after the South Carolina legislature passed an act
of attainder and banishment.[2]* A generation
later, Hoar's case still burned bright in the mem-
ories of members of Congress, who repeatedly

*Broadly speaking, attainers imposed penalties on spe-
cial named individuals, and were frequently accompanied by banishment (exile) from the jurisdiction..

cited the incident.[3]   Harriet Beecher Stowe penned the "incendiary" best-seller *Uncle Tom's Cabin* — a novel that outraged the proslavery South and inspired the antislavery North in the 1850s, leading Lincoln to describe her as "the little woman who wrote the book that made this great war."[4] Frederick Douglass escaped from slavery in Maryland in 1838, published a daring autobiography in 1845, founded a leading abolitionist newspaper, and became a preeminent orator on behalf of civil rights and suffrage (voting rights) for both women and freedmen.

The shift of focus from Zenger and Callender to Hoar, Stowe, and Douglass was subtle but significant. All of these individuals can be seen as outsiders, but with an important difference. As representatives of the Fourth Estate, Zenger and Callender were outside the government that sought to censor them, but Hoar, Stowe, and Douglass were outsiders in a much deeper sense. Vis-a-vis the southern society that tried to suppress their speech, Hoar, Stowe, and Douglass were geographic, cultural, and ethnic outsiders who were critical of the South's dominant social institutions and opinions.[5] Their experiences dramatized why even those in the majority should logically support strong First Amendment protections for offensive and provocative speech of minority fringe groups. For if allowed to preach its gospel freely, a zealous fringe group in one

A significant shift of focus

era (like proponents of abolition, equality, and black suffrage in 1830) could conceivably convert enough souls to the crusade to become a respectable or even dominant political force over the next generation (like the Republican Party of the 1860s).

Republicans understood the religious roots of abolitionism   Republicans understood the religious roots of abolitionism and often stressed the need to protect religious speech. On the campaign trail in 1866, John Bingham reminded his audience that men had been imprisoned in Georgia for teaching the Bible, and made clear that the Fourteenth Amendment would put an end to such state action, a theme to which he returned in a key speech on the amendment before the House in 1871.[6] In a speech before the Senate in early 1866, Lyman Trumbull stressed the need to protect the freedom "to teach" and "to preach," citing a Mississippi Black Code punishing any "free negroes and mulattoes" who dared to "exercis[e] the functions of a minister of the Gospel."[7] A few weeks later, Senator Henry Wilson painted in more vivid colors, accusing the Slave Power of "murder[ing] editors" and hanging "ministers of the living God for questioning the divinity of slavery."[8] Similarly, in 1865 Representative James M. Ashley linked religion to freedom of speech — "[the Slave Power] has silenced every free pulpit within its control . . . and made free speech and a free press impossible within its domain" — and in 1864 Representative Ebon Ingersoll stressed the role of antislavery speech of "minister[s] of the gospel."[9] On this point, the voices of northern white Republicans harmonized with those of southern black freedmen. Thus we find an 1865 convention of South Carolina blacks linking "the school, the pulpit, [and] the press."[10]

These sentiments had been maturing for forty years as the American antislavery movement wandered in the political wilderness in search of the promised land of freedom. As early as 1819, Maryland had arrested and prosecuted a Methodist minister, the Reverend Jacob Gruber, for preaching a sermon that the authorities feared might incite slaves to revolt.[11] And Maryland was hardly unique. An antebellum Louisiana law made it a capital offense to use "language in any public discourse, from the bar, the bench, the stage, *the pulpit*, or in any place whatsoever" that might incite "insubordination among the slaves."[12] In 1849 Virginia convicted a minister, Jarvis Bacon, for an ambiguous antislavery allusion in a sermon.[13] Jesse McBride, an antislavery preacher visiting North Carolina from Ohio, was sentenced to imprisonment for a year, to an hour in a pillory, and to twenty lashes.[14] In 1859 North Carolina sentenced the elderly Reverend Daniel Worth to a year in prison for circulating an antislavery tract. Then the state rewrote its laws to make "incendiary" antislavery expression punishable by death for the first offense.[15]

In response, the forces of freedom increasingly

Voices of white Republicans harmonized with those of black freedmen stressed the linkage between expressive freedom and religious freedom.[16] On the campaign trail in 1860, Abraham Lincoln condemned sedition laws "suppressing all declarations that slavery is wrong, whether made in politics, in presses, in pulpits, or in private."[17] The religion-speech linkage was also prominent in congressional debates on the eve of the Civil War. Ohio Representative Cydnor Tomkins, for example, attacked southern laws that tried "to seal every man's lips, and stop every man's mouth," laws that made a felon of "the man who dares proclaim the precepts of our holy religion."[18] Similarly, Congressman Owen Lovejoy railed against southern laws that "imprison or exile preachers of the Gospel," and proclaimed the right of discussing slavery as one of "the privileges and immunities of the Constitution . . . which guaranties to me free speech."[19]

The recognition of the importance of religious speech in the 1860s proved especially significant for women. Though excluded from exercising the formal political rights of voting, holding public office, and serving on juries or militias, women played leading roles in religious organizations.[20] These organizations engaged in moral crusades with obvious political overtones — antigambling, antiprostitution, temperance, abolition, and (eventually) suffrage. As a result, the voices of women were much harder to ignore in the 1860s than they had been in the 1790s.[21] At that time, in the debates over the Constitution and

Lincoln condemned sedition laws suppressing religious speech

The importance of religious speech was especially significant to women

Bill of Rights, only one woman, Mercy Otis Warren, participated prominently, and even then under a pseudonym. But in 1866, in a campaign orchestrated by Susan B. Anthony and Elizabeth Cady Stanton, thousands and thousands of women flooded the Thirty-ninth Congress with petitions for women's suffrage (which had been a nonissue for the Founding Fathers).[22] At least five petitions from women on the suffrage issue were presented on the floor of Congress in the first two months of 1866 alone.[23] Two years earlier, on February 9, 1864, the Women's National Loyal League had presented Congress with a mammoth emancipation petition bearing exactly one hundred thousand signatures, nearly two-thirds of them women's signatures; eventually, the league gathered about four hundred thousand names.[24] It is obvious that women were central exercisers of First Amendment freedoms in the 1860s in a way they had not been in the 1790s — yet another example of the rising importance of outsider speech.

Northern states had also sinned in the antebellum era, at times abridging expression and association, and violating the Constitution's Article IV privileges and immunities of out-of-state citizens. Here, too, one of the most famous antebellum cases involved women and religion. Prudence Crandall was a Quaker who ran a school for girls in Canterbury, Connecticut. When she began admitting black girls in the early 1830s,

Northern states also abridged expression and association

the state passed a law restricting the right of various "school[s]," "academ[ies]" and "literary institution[s]" to teach nonresident blacks.[25] In 1833 the state prosecuted Crandall for teaching students like Ann Eliza Hammond, a black seventeen-year-old from Rhode Island.[26] Crandall's case grabbed nationwide attention and galvanized the early abolitionist movement.

The new emphasis on religious speech also helped blacks

This new emphasis on religious speech also helped blacks. The exclusion of blacks from formal political rights like voting underscored the importance of their participation in other organizations, like churches, that could help gather the voice of the community.[27] Southern governments, of course, were all too aware of the "incendiary" dangers posed by any assembly of blacks, even (or perhaps especially) an assembly of God. After all, Nat Turner, who led a famous slave revolt in the 1830s, had been a black preacher — hence the adoption of the Mississippi Black Code prescribing thirty-nine lashes for any black exercising the functions of a minister.[28] But Republicans strongly affirmed the "civil" rights of blacks to assemble and preach, even as these same Republicans disclaimed any intent to confer upon blacks "political" rights like the right to vote.[29] Senator Charles Sumner provided the Joint Committee on Reconstruction an especially dramatic example of black speech, laying before the committee a petition "from the colored citizens of South Carolina," claiming to represent "four hundred and two thousand citizens of that State, being a very large majority of the population." Unsurprisingly, the petition prayed for "constitutional protection in keeping arms, in holding public assemblies, and in complete liberty of speech and of the press."[30] As W. E. B. Du Bois later explained, "For the first time in history the people of the United States listened not only to the voices of the Negroes' friends, but to the Negro himself."[31]

FREEDOM OF ASSEMBLY

"Congress shall make no law . . . abridging . . . the right of the people peaceably to assemble, and to petition the Government for a re-dress of grievances."

We can chart a similar expansion of the First Amendment's "right of the people peaceably to assemble, and to petition." In the view of the Founding Fathers, the right to assemble and petition was in its strictest sense a *political*, not a *civil* right. The words, "the people" encompassed voters — the same adult male citizens who constituted "the militia."

The right to assemble and petition was also expanded

But by 1866 all this had subtly changed. The phrase *the people* now clearly encompassed those who were not political rights holders. For example, the 1866 Congress was deluged by petitions from women precisely because they were *not* voters. Sumner's petition from the South

Carolina "convention" of "colored citizens" came from blacks who were excluded from the vote, the militia, and the jury.[32]

For these blacks, the core right of assembly at issue was "to assemble peaceably on the Sabbath for the worship of [the] Creator."[33] This was, of course, a right that southern states had continued to violate. The framers of the Fourteenth Amendment thus took direct aim at exclusionary laws like the one Virginia had passed in 1833 proclaiming that "[e]very *assemblage* of negroes for the purpose of religious worship, when such worship is conducted by a negro, . . . shall be an unlawful *assembly*."[34]

By 1866 the rights of assembly and petition were being characterized as *civil*, not *political*

In short, by 1866 the hybrid rights of assembly and petition were increasingly being characterized as *civil*, not *political* rights — a shift reflected in and perhaps caused by the exercise of these rights by women and blacks.

THE PROHIBITION AGAINST THE ESTABLISHMENT OF RELIGION

"Congress shall make no law respecting an establishment of religion, or prohibiting the free exercise thereof;"

We have seen how, in the cases of speech, press, assembly, and petition, the same words meant slightly different things when first inscribed in the

1790s and when later restated in the 1860s. Could the same thing be true of the First Amendment's establishment clause prohibiting Congress from making any law "respecting an establishment of religion?" Earlier in the book we discussed these words, as originally written, focused on federalism and states' rights. Congress could make "no law respecting [state] establishment [policy]" — that is, no law either establishing a national church or *dis*-establishing a state church. In this sense, the original clause was completely neutral on the issue of whether establishment was or was not a good thing. It simply mandated that the issue be decided state by state and that Congress keep its hands off: that Congress make no law "respecting" the vexed question. In short, the original establishment clause was a home rule-local option provision mandating federal neutrality.

In 1789 the First Amendment's establishment clause was neutral

Federal neutrality and home rule made a good deal of political sense in 1789, when half the states gave specified sects privileged status and the other half didn't. Proestablishment New Hampshiremen and antiestablishment Virginians might sharply disagree on the substantive issue of church-state relations but could agree on the jurisdictional idea that Congress should keep out: this was the lowest common denominator.

The precise wording of the clause, though, gave rise to a critical ambiguity: what about federal territories? The ratification debates in each state in the 1780s and 1790s paid remarkably little heed to the territories. Ratification took place only within existing states, and Americans living outside a state had no formal role.

Given that Article I of the Constitution had provided Congress no enumerated power to intermeddle with religion in the states, perhaps the words of the First Amendment prohibited only congressional laws that interfered with laws "respecting" *state* "establishment" policy. On this view, because Article IV of the Constitution had given Congress absolute power over federal territories, perhaps the establishment clause was not meant to modify this granted power.

Congress initially permitted the territories to aid and sponsor religion

For example, on the very day it debated an early version of the establishment clause, the First Congress pushed forward an ordinance governing the western territory by extending the Confederation Congress's Northwest Ordinance of 1787, a legislative enactment that one leading scholar has described as "suffused with aid, encouragement, and support for religion."[35] And over the next two decades, Congress applied this pattern to other territories, and allowed these territorial governments to aid and sponsor religion in a variety of ways.[36]

On a narrow states'-rights reading of the original establishment clause, when exercising its absolute power over a *territory*, perhaps Congress could legislate just like a state legislature could, and like a state, was free to adopt any kind of proreligion legislation it desired.[37]

But as the nineteenth century wore on, a different, anti-establishment reading took root; and as various territorial legislatures matured into state legislatures, it seemed natural to bind them to the same nonestablishment rule to which Congress was bound, using language borrowed from the First Amendment. For example, when Iowa gained statehood in 1846, its first state constitution proclaimed in its Bill of Rights that "[t]he general assembly shall make no law respecting an establishment of religion or prohibiting the free exercise thereof," words repeated verbatim in its Constitution of 1857.[38] Virtually identical phrases appeared in the territorial Constitution of Deseret in 1849, and its successor Utah Territory draft constitution of 1860.[39] Similarly, in the 1859 Constitution of the Jefferson Territory (today known as Colorado), we find the following clause: "The General Assembly shall make no laws respecting an establishment of religion, nor shall any religious test be required of any citizen."[40] And in his influential constitutional treatise of 1868, the respected Michigan jurist Thomas Cooley likewise wrote that, under prevailing state constitutions, state legislatures were barred from creating "[a]ny law respecting an establishment of religion."[41]

Whereas in the 1780s half the states operated

But as territories matured into states, they became bound to a non-establishment rule

under laws that featured specific sects, by the 1860s none did. Of course, virtually all states in the mid-nineteenth century favored religion generally, and some granted advantages to Christianity or Protestantism above other religions; but none singled out one Christian sect for special favor. The common denominator among states had thus shifted dramatically, and popular understandings of the establishment clause may have reflected this shift. What began as a neutral but strict federal rule — *no law* intermeddling with state religious policy — was gradually mutating into a less restrictive but substantively anti-establishment rule: religion in general could be promoted, but not one sect at the expense of others. Whereas one of the key concerns of the Founding Fathers in the 1780s was congressional power in the *states*, by the 1850s Americans were fighting out many of the most intense constitutional issues of the day in and over the *territories*. Whereas the original Bill of Rights had in many cases borrowed language from older state constitutions, newer states were now returning the compliment by borrowing from (and in the process redefining) the words of the federal Bill of Rights. By 1866 half the states had begun as federal territories; the typical state was no longer Madison's Virginia, but Bingham's Ohio.

But even if by 1866 the establishment clause was no longer a state right, pure and simple, can

The original strict federal rule had mutated into one less restricted

we really say that it was a private right of certain individuals, as opposed to a right of the public at large? To the extent that a state created a coercive or compulsory religious establishment, decreeing that individuals profess a state creed or attend a state service or pay money directly to a state church, such coercion would threaten the bodily liberty and property of individuals and would thus obviously intrude upon the privileges and immunities of citizens. But what of a noncoercive establishment — say, a simple state declaration on a state seal proclaiming Utah "the Mormon State"?

If we look to Blackstone, we will not find this kind of nonestablishment right classified as a common-law "privilege" or "immunity." And the historical evidence from the 1860s and early 1870s is somewhat sparse and rather mixed. However, strong support for the argument that there is a nonestablishment right even against the noncoercive establishment of religion by a state came from Thomas Cooley's 1868 treatise. Under prevailing state constitutions, wrote Cooley, states generally could not enact "[a]ny law respecting an establishment of religion. . . . There is not religious *liberty* where any one sect is favored by the State . . . . It is not toleration which is established in our system, but religious *equality*."[42] Even a noncoercive establishment, Cooley suggested, violated principles of religious liberty and religious equality — violated norms of equal rights and privileges.

THE RIGHT TO THE FREE EXERCISE OF RELIGION

"Congress shall make no law . . . prohibiting the free exercise [of religion];"

Let us now turn to the First Amendment's free-exercise principle and trace how it, too, was reconstructed by the Fourteenth Amendment.

Outraged by decades of religious persecution in the antebellum South, prominent Republicans in the Thirty-eighth and Thirty-ninth Congresses repeatedly stressed the need to protect "freedom of religious opinion," "a free exercise of religion," "freedom of conscience," "freedom in the exercise of religion," and "the free exercise of religion."[43] In some form or other, they insisted that henceforth this basic First Amendment freedom apply against states.

The right of free exercise of religion was also reconstructed

But in what form, exactly? The original free-exercise clause of the First Amendment merely barred those laws which targeted religious exercise as such; its letter and spirit allowed Congress to make genuinely secular laws, even though those laws might obstruct particular religious practices. Perhaps the Fourteenth Amendment sweeps more broadly in its language of *privileges*: for example where only believers in a specific

religion are involved in a religious practice —
with no direct invasions of the lives, limbs, or
property of nonbelievers — such a religious practice could be deemed suitably "priv[ate]" and
hence "privilege[d]" from intruding legislation.[44]
Under this definition, a secular law like, say,
murder, would take precedence over the religious
claims of a cult that demanded human sacrifice of
nonbelievers; but the Catholic Church would be
"privileged" to employ only male priests regardless of general laws outlawing sex discrimination
in employment.[45]

Professor Kurt Lash has argued that this textually possible reconstruction of free exercise is
also historically plausible.[46] Reconstruction Republicans, Lash argues, at times sought to shield
religion even from secular laws. Southern laws
making it a crime to teach blacks to read were
secular enough, but these laws outraged Republicans because of their devastating effect on
(Protestant) religion; they outlawed teaching
blacks to read the Holy Bible, the word of God.[47]

If, then, as Lash claims, "freedom of religion"
in the 1860s meant autonomy from governmental intrusion in ways that it did not in the 1790s,
this shift fits snugly into our overall story of rights
reconstruction. Under the Founding Fathers'
vision of free exercise in 1791, Congress might,
but need not, choose to exempt a given religious
practice from a general secular law. At that time,
large, politically powerful religions consisting of a

majority of voters could win exemptions more easily than could fringe minority sects. But the Fourteenth Amendment accentuated minority liberty, and this accent perhaps invites special judicial accommodation of minority sects.

THE RIGHT TO KEEP AND BEAR ARMS

"A well regulated Militia, being necessary to the security of a free State, the right of the people to keep and bear Arms, shall not be infringed."

The right to keep and bear arms meant different things in 1789 than it did in 1866

The right to keep and bear arms was, at its core, a "privilege" of "citizens of the United States." But the right in 1789 and the right in 1866 meant different things.

The Founding Fathers, among them republicans like Patrick Henry, George Mason, and Elbridge Gerry, proclaimed that freedom ultimately rested on the bedrock of an arms-bearing citizenry. Some fourscore years later, Republicans of the Reconstruction period, most prominently Lyman Trumbull, Jacob Howard, Charles Sumner, James Nye, Samuel Pomeroy, Sidney Clarke, Josiah Grinnell, Roswell Hart, Henry Raymond, Nathaniel Banks, Thomas Eliot, George Julian, and Leonard Myers, echoed their forebears' odes to arms in speeches in the Thirty-ninth Congress.[48]

But sometimes the same sounds mean different things.[49] We should not confuse the small-r republicans of the 1780s with the capital-R Republicans of the 1860s; when these two sets of men spoke of the need to protect the right to arms, they had decidely different pictures in mind.[50]

For the Founding Fathers, the Second Amendment was a cornerstone of federalism; state-organized militias were to keep central tyranny at bay and discourage easy resort to that bane of classical republicanism, a central standing army. But after the Civil War, the world looked different to Reconstruction Republicans. Massachusetts militiamen may have fought for freedom at Lexington and Concord in 1775, but Mississippi militiamen had killed for slavery at Vicksburg in 1863. In 1866 various southern white militias, often "composed of Confederate veterans still wearing their gray uniforms, . . . frequently terrorized the black population, ransacking their homes to seize shotguns and other property and abusing those who refused to sign plantation labor contracts."[51] A federal standing army was less a republican (small r) bane than a Republican (capital R) boon, because in the uneasy years that lay ahead a freedom-loving Union government might need to use a central army to reconstruct the South, making it safe for all true republicans and especially for all true Republicans.[52]

For the Founding Fathers, the right of the

For the Founders, the right to keep and bear arms was the cornerstone of federalism people to keep and bear arms stood shoulder to shoulder with the right to vote; arms-bearing in militias embodied an important *political* right flanking the other main political rights of voting, office holding, and jury service. Therefore "the people" and the "militia" at the heart of the Second Amendment were voters and jurymen personified: the same "people" that appeared in the Constitution's Preamble and in its Article I, section 2, as well as in the First, Fourth, Ninth, and Tenth Amendments. But Reconstruction Republicans recast arms-bearing as a core *civil* right, utterly divorced from the militia and other political rights and responsibilities. Arms were needed not only as part of political and politicized militia service but also to protect one's individual homestead. Everyone — even nonvoting, nonmilitia-serving women — had a right to own a gun for self-protection.

According to Reconstruction Republicans, everyone had a right to own a gun

In the era when the original Bill of Rights was drafted, arms-bearing was collective, exercised in a well-regulated militia embodying a republican right of the people, collectively understood. In the Reconstruction era, gun-toting was individualistic, accentuating not group rights of the citizenry but self-regarding "privileges" of individual "citizens" to self-protection. The first vision was public, with the militia muster on the town square; the latter was private, with individual freedmen keeping guns at home to ward off Klansmen and other ruffians.

Time and again republicans in 1789 spoke of "the militia"; Republicans in 1866 almost never did. For them, allowing blacks to serve in the militia presented a major problem: If blacks had a right to be in militias, why not in juries, or voting booths, or legislative assemblies? The basic analytic framework holding together the Fourteenth Amendment — the distinction between civil rights like worship, speech, property, and guns on the one hand and political rights like voting and jury service on the other — would have come unglued.[53]

So how, exactly, did Reconstruction Republicans accomplish their remarkable rereading of the arms right? And where, precisely, does the Fourteenth Amendment work its noteworthy rewriting of the arms right, now organized around the distinction between civil and political rights? Finally, what, ultimately, was the new vision of arms offered by the Reconstruction Republicans, and why did they deem it so fundamental?

Just how did Reconstruction Republicans redefine the right to keep and bear arms?

Once we remember that 1860s Reconstruction Republicans sought to hold states to various principles of the Bill of Rights *as these Republicans themselves understood these rights through the prism of their own lived experience*, it is hardly surprising that they invoked only the operative rights clause of the Second Amendment ("to keep and bear arms") while utterly ignoring the ode to the militia in its first clause.[54] (As noted above, these Reconstructors obviously had good functional and ideological reasons for downplaying militias.) Moreover, when they paraphrased or quoted the Second Amendment's second clause, they often subtly recast it. For them, it was now less a right of the people, and more an individualistic privilege of persons. Many examples could be given, but perhaps the most vivid came from Congress's 1866 Freedman's Bureau Act: "laws . . . concerning *personal* liberty, *personal* security, and the acquisition, enjoyment, and disposition of estate, real and *personal, including the constitutional right to bear arms,* shall be secured to and enjoyed by all the citizens."[55]

The three-part phraseology of the 1866 Freedman's Bureau Act — affirming rights of "personal liberty," "personal security," and property — derived directly from Blackstone's influential chapter on the "Absolute Rights of Individuals."[56] Blackstone affirmed an individual right of the subject to "hav[e] arms" to protect his "three great and primary rights, of personal security, personal liberty, and private property" and his ultimate individual right of "self-preservation."[57] The accent here is distinctly individualistic, private, and nonmilitary. Note that Blackstone uses the phrase *having arms* rather than the more military sounding phrase, *bearing arms*. Clearly, the Founding Fathers' conception of arms' use in the original Second Amendment, as we have noted before, was military. The musketed Min-

A reaffirmation of Blackstone

utemen stood at center stage, pushing Blackstone
to the wings.

But events over the next eighty years in
America conspired to move Blackstone to the
center. Southern states, ever fearful of slave
insurrections, enacted sweeping antebellum laws
prohibiting not just slaves but free blacks from
owning guns.[58] In response, antislavery theorists
emphasized the personal right of all free citizens
— white and black, male and female, northern
and southern, visitor and resident — to own guns
for self-protection. In his highly influential antislavery treatise, here is what Joel Tiffany had to
say about the Second Amendment in 1849:

**In the
antebellum
period, an-
ti-slavery
theorists
champi-
oned the
right of all
free citi-
zens to
own guns**

> Here is another of the immunities of a citizen
> of the United States, which is guaranteed by the
> supreme, organic law of the land. This is one of
> the subordinate rights, mentioned by Black-
> stone, as belonging to every Englishman. It . . .
> is accorded to every subject for the purpose of
> protecting and defending himself, if need be, in
> the enjoyment of his absolute rights of life, lib-
> erty and property. . . . The colored citizen, under
> our [federal] constitution, has now as full and
> perfect a right to keep and bear arms as any
> other; and no State law, or State regulation has
> authority to deprivehim of that right.[59]

Tiffany's treatise became a basic handbook for
many Republicans who later served in the Thirty-ninth Congress.[60]

To be sure, arms-bearing for blacks also had

huge symbolic significance. The gun was an emblem of freedom. In an appendix to his edition of Blackstone's *Commentaries*, St. George Tucker reminded his readers of the ancient law of William the Conqueror, under which English villeins* were emancipated as follows: "If any person is willing to enfranchise [that is, free] his slave, let him . . . deliver him free arms, to wit, a lance and a sword; thereupon he is a free man."[61]

But a gun was far more than a symbol. Even free blacks (to say nothing of slaves) had suffered unspeakable violence at the hands of white governments, white mobs, and white thugs; and in the wake of Emancipation, many southern governments passed legislation (the notorious Black Codes) forbidding, among other things, gun ownership among blacks but not whites.[62] Blacks immediately sensed the grave threat posed by this aspect of the Black Codes and took quick action. In November 1865 South Carolina blacks assembled in convention and petitioned Congress in bold words: "We, the colored people of the State of South Carolina, in Convention assembled, . . . ask that, inasmuch as the Constitution of the United States explicitly declares that the right to keep and bear arms shall not be infringed

Blacks petitioned against Black Codes that prohibited their ownership of guns

*One of a class of feudal serfs who held the legal status of freemen in their dealings with all persons except their lord.

. . . that the late efforts of the Legislature of this State to pass an act to deprive us [of] arms be forbidden, as a plain violation of the Constitution."[63]

Congress then passed laws redressing the blacks' grievances

In response, Congress passed the Civil Rights Act of 1866, the Freedman Bureau Act of 1866, and the Fourteenth Amendment. These related laws were designed to redress the grievances of such petitions as that of the South Carolina blacks, outlaw the infamous Black Codes, and affirm the full and equal right of every citizen to self-defense and other basic freedoms. Thus in introducing the Civil Rights Bill, whose first draft proclaimed blacks "citizens of the United States" and affirmed their "civil rights," Senator Lyman Trumbull explicitly took aim at a Mississippi law that prohibited "any negro or mulatto from having fire-arms."[64] Moments later, he read to his colleagues excerpts from Blackstone's famous chapter on the "Absolute Rights of Individuals."[65]

As the congressional debate continued, many other voices spoke out in favor of gun possession for blacks. Representative Josiah Grinnell attacked a Kentucky Black Code that forbade blacks to "keep" or "buy[]" a "gun" — even "a musket which he has carried through the war."[66] Senator James Nye was more explicit, noting the role of black men in the Union army, and then immediately accenting private gun ownership: "As citizens of the United States they have equal right to protection, and to keep and bear arms *for self-defense*."[67] Senator Samuel Pomeroy likewise linked guns with the private rather than the political: "Every man should have a homestead, that is, the right to acquire and hold one, and the right to be safe and protected in that citadel of his love. . . . He should [also] have the right to bear arms for the defense of himself and family and his homestead. And if the cabin door of the freedman is broken open and the intruder enters for purposes as vile as were known to slavery, then should a well-loaded musket be in the hand of the occupant . . ."[68] Representative Henry Raymond opined on the nature of civil rights owing to all citizens and conjured up a similar home-centered vision, affirming that the freedman "has a country and a home; a right to defend himself and his wife and children; a right to bear arms; a right to testify in the Federal courts."[69] Raymond was editor of the *New York Times*, but even the rival *New York Evening Post* shared his views on the meaning of the Civil Rights Bill. The *Post* advised its readers that though the Bill did not enfranchise blacks or grant them other political rights, it did affirm their civil rights to own firearms.[70]

A home-centered vision of gun possession

Southern blacks sang in the same key as did these northern whites. Consider, for example, an editorial that appeared in the *Loyal Georgian*, a prominent black newspaper, one month before the congressional speeches of Nye, Pomeroy, and Raymond:

> Have colored persons a right to own and carry fire arms? . . . [Blacks] are not only free

but citizens of the United States and as such
entitled to the same privileges granted to other
citizens by the Constitution. . . .

Article II, of the amendments to the Constitution of the United States, gives the people the
right to bear arms and states that this right shall
not be infringed. Any person, white or black,
may be disarmed if convicted of making an
improper or dangerous use of weapons, but no
military or civil officer has the right or authority
to disarm a class of people, thereby placing them
at the mercy of others. All men, without distinction of color, have the right to keep arms to
defend their homes, families or themselves.[71]

In these words, we hear the Second Amendment being invoked to limit state government
with heavy stress placed on the "privileges" of
national "citizens." And if we listen closely, we **A subtle**
can also hear in these words the subtle privatiza- **privatiza-**
tion of the Second Amendment — the shift from **tion of the**
"keep" to "own," from "bear" to "carry," from **Second**
"arms" to "fire arms," from "militia" to "per- **Amendment**
sons," and from collective self-defense ("the security of a free state") to individualized self-defense
(of persons' "homes, families or []selves").

In short, between 1775 and 1866 the poster
boy of arms shifted from the Concord minuteman
to the Carolina freedman. The motto of the original Second Amendment, in effect, was that if
arms were outlawed, only the central government
would have arms. In the Reconstruction era a
new vision was aborning: when guns were out-

lawed, only the Klan would have guns. This idea, focusing on private violence and the lapses of local government rather than on the public violence orchestrated by central soldiers, is far closer to the unofficial motto of today's National Rifle Association: "When guns are outlawed, only outlaws will have guns." Curiously, today's NRA — an organization founded shortly after the Civil War by ex-Union army officers — devotes less attention to the Reconstruction than to the Founding, even though it is the Reconstruction that best supports the NRA's vision.

The Reconstruction best supports the NRA's vision of the Second Amendment

JURY RIGHTS

(From the Fifth Amendment)

"No person shall be held to answer for a capital, or otherwise infamous crime, unless on a presentment or indictment of a Grand Jury . . ."

(From the Sixth Amendment)

"In all criminal prosecutions, the accused shall enjoy the right to a speedy and public trial, by an impartial jury . . ."

(From the Seventh Amendment)

"In Suits at common law . . . the right of trial by jury shall be preserved . . ."

In 1866 juries — grand, petit, and civil — had long been recognized as "inestimable privilege[s]" of Americans[72] and as basic components of due process of law, with roots in a mythic ancient constitution and Magna Carta. According to Blackstone's influential *Commentaries*, "The trial by jury, . . . as the grand bulwark of [every Englishman's] liberties, is secured to him by the great charter [in its 'law of the land' precursor of 'due process']."[73] The Thirty-ninth Congress therefore intended that the Fourteenth Amendment should provide for some sort of incorporation of jury rights against states, drawing upon both the privileges-or-immunities clause and the due-process clause of the amendment's section 1. But while the Reconstructors' definition of jury rights invoked the Founding Fathers' model, at the same time (at least initially) they inverted it. Whereas the Founding Fathers emphasized Americans' rights to participate in government by *serving in juries*, the Reconstruction Congress at first emphasized *the right to be tried by juries*.[74] Yet again, we see an original 1790s "political" right mutating (at least initially) into a Reconstruction "civil" right. (But as we shall see later in this chapter, with passage of the Fifteenth Amendment in 1870, the Reconstructors reversed themselves and reverted back to the Founding Fathers' model.)

Initially the Reconstructors inverted the jury right

In the forty years that led up to the drafting of section 1, abolitionists had repeatedly stressed the fundamentality of jury trials. They attacked slavery as a legal system that deprived human beings of their lives, liberty, and property with no semblance of due process, no individualized adjudication of wrongdoing in jury trials.[75]

This emphasis on jury trial was not merely high theory. It shaped the battle lines of perhaps the biggest politico-legal clash of the antebellum era: the fugitive-slave controversy. Surely a free black woman in, say, Ohio, was entitled to a jury before her liberty could be snatched away if ever some greedy white man called her his slave. So argued the abolitionist lawyer (and later chief justice) Salmon P. Chase in the famous 1837 case of Matilda Lawrence.[76] Though Chase lost the case — and Lawrence lost her freedom — various northern states responded by adopting personal-liberty laws guaranteeing alleged fugitive slaves the benefit of a jury trial.[77] However, when the Supreme Court struck down one of these state personal-liberty laws in 1842, the fugitive-slave controversy shifted from state capitals to Washington, D.C. Then in 1850 Congress adopted its infamous Fugitive Slave Act, placing an alleged fugitive's freedom entirely in the hands of a commissioner rather than a jury. In response Congressman Horace Mann complained that the act's lack of jury trial violated the Fifth Amendment due-process clause,[78] and Senator Charles Sumner thundered that

The fugitive-slave controversy

In denying the Trial by Jury [this act] is three times unconstitutional; first as the Constitution declares "the right of the people to be secure in their persons against unreasonable seizures;" secondly as it further declares, that "No person shall be deprived of life, liberty, or property, without due process of law;" and thirdly, because it expressly declares, that "in suits at common law . . . the right of jury trial shall be preserved." By this triple cord did the framers of the Constitution secure the Trial by Jury in every question of Human Freedom.[79]

Criticism of the infamous Fugitive Slave Act

In linking Seventh Amendment jury rights to Fourth Amendment rights against unreasonable seizures, Sumner carried forward the Founding Fathers' vision, but with a special twist; here the defendant (the alleged fugitive) sought the benefit of the jury rather than the plaintiff, as in the original model.

In debates over the Civil Rights Act of 1866, the leading Republican sponsors and supporters of the act took pains to deny opponents' claims that it would confer on blacks the right to serve on juries: jury service, supporters claimed, was a *political* right beyond the scope of the statute, not a *civil* right within the meaning of the act.[80]

But Republicans soon saw the practical problems of putting asunder what the Founding Fathers had joined together. Exactly how much would blacks in the South benefit if all-white grand juries refused to indict whites who terrorized blacks, or if all-white jurors acquitted these white thugs? And if a black man was indicted for a crime, how much protection would he receive from his "civil" right to be tried by a jury from which all blacks were excluded?

These questions were hardly theoretical — they arose urgently, graphically, and repeatedly in the Reconstruction era.[81] Eventually, Reconstruction Republicans came to realize that — for blacks at least — civil jury rights without political jury rights were rather empty. When the British Empire had run into American jury nullification one hundred years earlier, the Empire had little choice but to sidestep juries with vice-admiralty and other juryless tribunals. But Reconstruction Republicans facing southern jury nullification had another option at hand: they could reconstruct juries by repopulating them with blacks alongside whites.[82]

And this is exactly what they did. In 1875, towards the end of the Reconstruction era, Congress adopted a statute barring state and federal courts from excluding blacks from juries, regardless of the race of the parties.[83] The key right, proclaimed this act, was not *the defendant's civil right* but *the juror's political right*. And the source of that right was neither the Fourteenth Amendment's due-process clause, nor the Fourteenth Amendment's privileges-or-immunities clause, nor the Fourteenth Amendment's equal-protection clause. It was the Fifteenth Amendment, ratified in 1870, which provided that "The right of citizens of the United States to vote shall not be denied or abridged by the United States or by any state on account of race, color, or previous condition of servitude." The 1875 act obviously borrowed and built upon the new amendment's language: neither the federal nor the state government could deny the right of "citizens" to serve and vote on juries "on account of race, color, or previous condition of servitude."[84]

On this account, the Fifteenth Amendment, rightly read, affirms blacks' political rights — to vote, serve on juries, and hold office — just as the Fourteenth Amendment had affirmed blacks' civil rights to do virtually everything but. To put the point another way: blacks had a right to *vote*, but not just for representatives. They had a right to vote in juries, and in legislatures, too — a right to be voted for as well as to vote. *Jurors vote — that is what they do*[85] — and in America, ordinary voters had always served as jurors, as Tocqueville made clear.[86] Thus the Fifteenth Amendment helped restore much of the original political vision underlying juries that the framers of the Fourteenth Amendment had initially warped. Through the Fifteenth Amendment, black men finally won political rights — to vote, to serve on juries, and to hold office, partly in (belated) recognition of the fact that such men had nobly discharged yet another political function (military service) on the Civil War battlefields of glory.

The Fifteenth Amendment's affirmation of the political rights of blacks

XII

A NEW BIRTH
OF FREEDOM

*By reconstructing right upon
right, the Fourteenth Amendment gave Americans a dramatically new understanding
of liberty and of the Bill of
Rights as a whole — a new
birth of freedom.*

It is time to sum up. The tale we have tried to
tell in this book is, in some important ways,
textual. It takes as its subject the set of words —
the text — that we call the Bill of Rights, namely,
the first ten amendments and the interlocking
Fourteenth Amendment. The text of the Bill has
shaped both this book's basic architecture and
much of its internal analysis. Thus, after a prefa-
tory survey of the development of the concept of
political freedom in England and the American
colonies, the order of the remaining chapters
basically tracks the textual order of the amendments themselves (I-X, and then XIV), and

within each chapter, the specific words of the Bill.

This textual emphasis surely limits our tale, but it also helps empower it. The fact that the Bill of Rights is *the law* underscores the importance of textualism. Even though lawyers and judges must often go beyond the letter of the law, the text itself is an obvious starting point of legal analysis. Is it even possible to deduce the spirit of a law without looking at its letter?

A textual analysis casts light on the true spirit of the Bill of Rights

A textual analysis of the Bill of Rights also illuminates patterns and thus casts light on the true spirit of the law as a whole. Throughout our tale we have tried to show how various words in the original Constitution repeat themselves in the Bill of Rights; how various textual themes recur within the first ten amendments; and how the Fourteenth Amendment's key sentence features remarkable and revealing textual cross-references to the Constitution and the original Bill of Rights. We have also tried to show the illuminating way in which the Bill both builds on and deviates from the precise texts of such earlier landmarks of liberty as the English Bill of Rights, the Declaration of Independence, and various state constitutional declarations of rights.

Obviously a textual analysis of this type has appeal to the members of the legal community, whose profession is founded upon the use and interpretation of words. But this is a book written not for lawyers and judges but for ordinary citizens who care about their Constitution and their rights. And here, we think, lies perhaps the strongest reason for offering an account of the Bill of Rights that takes its words seriously. The American people — outside courtrooms, outside law offices — confront, and lay claim to, the Bill of Rights as a *text*. Its grand phrases —"the freedom of speech," "the right to keep and bear arms," "due process of law," etc. — define a basic vocabulary of liberty for ordinary citizens. "We the People of the United States," in whose name the Bill speaks and to whom it speaks, speak in the words of the Bill. Surely James Madison and John Bingham would be pleased by this fact of modern life; both men understood that a Bill of Rights that did not live in the hearts and minds of ordinary Americans would most probably, in the long run, fail.

The Bill of Rights defines a basic vocabulary of liberty for ordinary citizens

In the preceding pages, we have also tried to trace the deep roots of American thinking about the Bill of Rights. With these roots exposed to view, perhaps can now better understand, and in places improve upon, the conventional wisdom about the Bill of Rights described at the beginning of this book.

Early on, this book noted that "the Bill of Rights stands as the high temple of our constitutional order." But where did this view of the Bill originate? The conventional understanding focuses on those present at the Creation — on the hasty oversights and omissions in the last days of a hot summer in Philadelphia in 1789; on the centrality of the (absence of a) Bill of Rights in ratification debates; and on the quick repair worked by the First Congress, fixing in place the keystone of the arch of liberty. And we all lived happily ever after.

There is some truth in this stock story so far as it goes, but it doesn't go far enough. Most dramatically, conventional wisdom ignores all the ways in which the Reconstruction generation — not their Founding Fathers or grandfathers — took a crumbling and somewhat obscure edifice, placed it on new, high ground, and remade it so that it truly would stand as a temple of liberty and justice for all.

A separate Bill of Rights was no part of Madison's original constitutional plan We would do well to remember that a separate Bill of Rights was no part of James Madison's carefully conceived original plan at Philadelphia. To some extent, his ultimate sponsorship of the Bill must be seen as a sop — a peace offering — to Antifederalists.[1] Actually, many members of the First Congress were relatively uninterested in the Bill, finding it a "nauseous" distraction.[2] By contrast, in the Thirty-ninth Congress John Bingham placed the Bill of Rights at the center of his thinking about constitutionalism. His speeches in the Thirty-ninth Congress are far more inspired, and perhaps more inspiring, than Madison's in the First.

In the first century of our nation's existence, the Bill of Rights played a surprisingly trivial role: only once before 1866 was it used by the Supreme Court to invalidate federal action, and that one use was *Dred Scott's* highly implausible and strikingly casual claim that the Fifth Amendment due-process clause invalidated free-soil territory laws like the Northwest Ordinance and the Missouri Compromise.[3] In a review of newspapers published in 1841, Dean Robert Reinstein could find not a single fiftieth anniversary celebration of the Bill of Rights.[4]

However, since the turn of the twentieth century, in area after area, the incorporation process has enabled judges first to invalidate state and local laws — and then, with this doctrinal base thus built up, to begin to keep Congress in check.[5] Countless examples could be offered, but our First Amendment is perhaps the best. Before 1925, when the United States Supreme Court began in earnest the process of First Amendment incorporation,[6] free speech had never prevailed against a repressive state statute in that forum. Within a few years of incorporation, however, freedom of expression and religion began to win in cases involving states like Kansas (*Fiske,* 1927), California (*Stromberg,* 1931), Minnesota (*Near,* 1931), and Connecticut (*Cantwell,* 1940).[7] These and other cases began to build up a First Amendment tradition,[8] in and out of court, a tradition that could then be used against even federal officials. Not until 1965 did the Supreme Court strike down an act of Congress on First Amendment grounds, and when it did so, it

The First Amendment provides the best example of the incorporation doctrine at work

relied squarely on doctrine built up in earlier cases involving states.[9] Consider also the more recent flag-burning cases. The Supreme Court laid down the requisite doctrine in a 1989 case involving a Texas statute and then, in 1990, stood its ground on precisely that doctrine to strike down an act of Congress.[10]

The incorporation doctrine has created a swelling body of legal analysis that has spilled out of courtrooms and soaked into the vocabulary and world view of law students, journalists, activists, and ultimately the citizenry at large. Without incorporation, and the steady flow of cases created by state and local laws, the Supreme Court would have had far fewer opportunities to be part of the ongoing American conversation about liberty. Mid-twentieth-century skeptics worried that the incorporation process would ultimately weaken the Bill of Rights.[11] If the Bill were to be applied against the states, their argument went, it would need to be watered down to take account of the considerable diversity of state practice; and then in turn, the federal government would be held to only this watered-down version. In a few instances, this has proved to be true. But in general, the extension of the Bill of Rights against the states has dramatically strengthened the Bill, not weakened it. We thus see that the central role of the Bill of Rights today owes at least as much to the Reconstruction as to the Creation.

The extension of the Bill of Rights against states has strengthened it

In both legal doctrine and popular consciousness, notions of individual and minority rights
loom large today. Conventional wisdom attributes these themes to the Founding Fathers' Bill;
but as we have seen, this conventional story misreads the Creation and misses the Reconstruction. James Madison did believe in strong individual rights; in many ways, however, he was
ahead of his time, because the First Congress did
not always share his vision. Bingham and the
Thirty-ninth Congress did embrace individual-
ism, but the conventional narrative heralds Madison instead of Bingham. Madison was antiestablishment, so the original First Amendment was
too (*we tell ourselves*). Madison thought that
property rights were central, so the Fifth Amendment's takings clause was symbolic of the Founding era (*we think*). Madison stressed federal protection of minority rights in *The Federalist* No.
10, so this now-classic text must always have
been the abiding wisdom (*we suppose*). Madison
spoke of the role of judges, so the original Bill of
Rights was judge-centric (*we assume*). On all
these points, and many others, we might do we to
cast aside such suppositions and assumptions. We
might do well to study John Bingham more, and
lift some of the load from James Madison's
stooped shoulders.

A further point: modern academic discourse
about the Bill of Rights frequently confines itself
to narrow examinations of individual clauses in

*The con-
ventional
view of
the Bill of
Rights
misreads
its Crea-
tion and
misses its
Recon-
struction*

the Bill. Yet this discourse ignores the ways in which the Bill is, well, a bill — a set of interconnected provisions. There is some irony here. Madison stressed that the Bill of Rights could play an instructive role, yet his original planned amendments would have scattered various provisions throughout the original Constitution. Only late in the process — and over Madison's objections — were his proposed amendments recast into a single set to be placed together at the end of the original Constitution. Organized in this manner, each clause of the early amendments gains by its proximity to the others.[12] No one understood this better than John Bingham and his fellow legislators in 1866. Whereas others spoke of individual "articles of amendment," he and they insisted on the unity and centrality of the "Bill of Rights."

Placed together at the end of the Constitution, each clause of the first ten amendments gains by its proximity to the others

The modern notion of a self-contained federal bill of rights thus derives at least as much from Bingham as from Madison. The federal Constitution contains no explicit caption introducing a "bill of rights" — unlike many early state constitutions, which feature a self-styled "declaration of rights" preceding an explicit "frame of government." And because the first ten federal amendments ultimately came in as appendixes rather than as a preface to the Constitution, still later amendments had the effect of pushing the early amendments to the middle — ten early postscripts before later postpostscripts. It was Bingham's generation that in effect added a closing parenthesis after the first set of amendments, distinguishing these amendments from all others. As a result, Americans today can lay claim to a federal "Bill of Rights" set apart from everything else.

What, in the end, are we to make of the pervasive ways in which our stock stories have exaggerated James Madison and the Creation of the original Bill of Rights while diminishing John Bingham and its Reconstruction? If this book is right, then many of us are guilty of a kind of curiously selective ancestor worship — one that gives too much credit to Madison and not enough to Bingham, that celebrates Thomas Jefferson and Patrick Henry but slights Harriet Beecher Stowe and Frederick Douglass. As great as men like Madison and Jefferson were, they lived and died as slaveholders, and their Bill of Rights was tainted by its quiet complicity with the original sin of slavery.[13] Even as we celebrate the Founding Fathers, we must ponder the sobering words of Charles Cotesworth Pinckney in the 1788 South Carolina ratifying debates: "Another reason weighed particularly, with the members from this state, against the insertion of a bill of rights. Such bills generally begin with declaring that all men are by nature born free. Now, we should make that declaration with very bad grace, when a large part of our property consists in men who are actually born slaves."[14]

Many of us are guilty of a curiously selective ancestor worship

But the Reconstruction Amendment began with an affirmation of the freedom and citizenship of all. Those who birthed it renounced the Slave Power and all its works. These midwives were women alongside men, blacks alongside whites. After their mighty labors, more work did remain to be done — more work always remains to be done, if all are to be free and equal. But because of these men and women, our Bill of Rights was reborn.

APPENDIX

THE CONSTITUTION OF THE UNITED STATES

September 17, 1787

WE, the people of the United States, in order to form a more perfect Union, establish justice, insure domestic tranquillity, provide for the common defence, promote the general welfare, and secure the blessings of liberty to ourselves and our posterity, do ordain and establish this Constitution for the United States of America.

ARTICLE I. § 1. All legislative powers herein granted, shall be vested in a Congress of the United States, which shall consist of a Senate and House of Representatives.

§ 2. The House of Representatives shall be composed of members chosen every second year by the people of the several States; and the electors in each State shall have the qualifications requisite for electors of the most numerous branch of the State Legislature.

No person shall be a representative who shall not have attained to the age of twenty-five years, and been seven years a citizen of the United States, and who shall not, when elected, be an inhabitant of that State in which he shall be chosen.

Representatives and direct taxes shall be apportioned among the several States which may be included within this Union, according to their respective numbers, which shall be determined by adding to the whole number of free persons, including those bound to service for a term of years, and excluding Indians not taxed, three fifths of all other persons. The actual enumeration shall be made within three years after the first meeting of the Congress of the United States, and within every subsequent term of ten years, in such manner as they shall by law direct. The number of representatives shall not exceed one for every thirty thousand, but each State shall have at least one representative, and until such enumeration shall be made, the state of New Hampshire shall be entitled to choose three, Massachusetts eight, Rhode Island and Providence Plantations one, Connecticut five, New York six, New Jersey four, Pennsylvania eight, Delaware one, Maryland six, Virginia ten, North Carolina five, South Carolina five, and Georgia three.

When vacancies happen in the representation from any State, the Executive authority thereof shall issue writs of election to fill such vacancies.

The House of Representatives shall choose their speaker and other officers; and shall have the sole power of impeachment.

§ 3. The Senate of the United States shall be composed of two Senators from each State, chosen by the Legislature thereof, for six years; and each Senator shall have one vote.

Immediately after they shall be assembled, in consequence of the first election, they shall be divided as equally as may be into three classes. The seats of the Senators of the first class shall be vacated at the expiration of the second year, of the second class at the expiration of the fourth year, and of the third class at the expiration of the sixth year, so that one third may be chosen every second year; and if vacancies happen by resignation, or otherwise, during the recess of the Legislature of any State, the Executive thereof may make temporary appointments until the next meeting of the Legislature, which shall then fill such vacancies.

No person shall be a Senator who shall not have attained to the age of thirty years, and been nine years a citizen of the United States, and who shall not, when elected, be an inhabitant of that State for which he shall be chosen.

The Vice President of the United States shall be president of the Senate, but shall have no vote, unless they be equally divided.

The Senate shall choose their other officers, and also a president *pro tempore*, in the absence of the Vice President, or when he shall exercise the office of President of the United States.

The Senate shall have the sole power to try all impeachments. When sitting for that purpose, they shall be on oath or affirmation. When the President of the United States is tried, the Chief Justice shall preside; and no person shall be convicted without the concurrence of two thirds of the members present.

Judgment in cases of impeachment shall not extend further than to removal from office, and disqualification to hold and enjoy any office of honour, trust or profit, under the United States; but the party convicted shall nevertheless be liable and subject to indictment, trial, judgment, and punishment according to law.

§ 4. The times, places and manner of holding elections for Senators and Representatives, shall be prescribed in each State by the Legislature thereof; but the Congress may at any time by law make or alter such regulations, except as to the places of choosing Senators. The Congress shall assemble at least once in every year, and such meeting shall be on the first Monday in December, unless they shall by law appoint a different day.

§ 5. Each House shall be the judge of the elections, returns, and qualifications of its own members, and a majority of each shall constitute a quorum to do business; but a smaller number may adjourn from day to day, and may be authorized to compel the attendance of absent members, in such manner, and under such penalties, as each House may provide.

Each House may determine the rules of its proceedings, punish its members for disorderly behaviour, and, with the concurrence of two thirds, expel a member.

Each House shall keep a journal of its proceedings, and from time to time publish the same, excepting such parts as may, in their judgment, require secrecy; and the yeas and nays of the members of either House on any question, shall, at the desire of one fifth of those present, be entered on the journal.

Neither House, during the session of Congress, shall, without the consent of the other, adjourn for more than three days, nor to any other place than that in which the two Houses shall be sitting.

§ 6. The Senators and Representatives shall receive a compensation for their services, to be ascertained by law, and paid out of the Treasury of the United States. They shall, in all cases, except treason, felony, and breach of the peace, be privileged from arrest during their attendance at the session of their respective Houses, and in going to, and returning from, the same; and for any speech or debate in either House, they shall not be questioned in any other place.

No Senator or Representative shall, during the time for which he was elected, be appointed to any civil office under the authority of the United States, which shall have been created, or the emoluments whereof shall have been increased during such time; and no person holding any office under the United States, shall be a member of either House during his continuance in office.

§ 7. All bills for raising revenue shall originate in the House of Representatives; but the Senate may propose or concur with amendments as on other bills.

Every bill which shall have passed the House of Representatives and the Senate, shall, before it become a law, be presented to the President of the United States; if he approve he shall sign it, but if not he shall return it, with his objections, to that House in which it shall have originated, who shall enter the objections at large on their journal, and proceed to reconsider it. If after such reconsideration two thirds of that House shall agree to pass the bill, it shall be sent, together with the objections, to the other House, by which it shall likewise be reconsidered, and if approved by two thirds of that House, it shall become a law. But in all such cases the votes of both Houses shall be determined by yeas and nays, and the names of the persons voting for and against the bill shall be entered on the journal of each House respectively. If any bill shall not be returned by the President within ten days, (Sundays excepted,) after it shall have been presented to him, the same shall be a law, in like manner as if he had signed it, unless the Congress by their adjournment prevent its return, in which case it shall not be a law.

Every order, resolution, or vote, to which the concurrence of the Senate and House of Representatives may be necessary, (except on a question of adjournment,) shall be presented to the President of the United States; and before the same shall take effect, shall be approved by him, or being disapproved by him, shall be re-passed by two thirds of the Senate and House of Representatives, according to the rules and limitations prescribed in the case of a bill.

§ 8. The Congress shall have power

To lay and collect taxes, duties, imposts and excises, to pay the debts, and provide for the common defence and general welfare of the United States; but all duties, imposts, and excises shall be uniform throughout the United States:

To borrow money on the credit of the United States:

To regulate commerce with foreign nations, and among the several States, and with the Indian tribes:

To establish an uniform rule of naturalization, and uniform laws on the subject of bankruptcies throughout the United States:

To coin money, regulate the value thereof, and of foreign coin, and fix the standard of weights and measures:

To provide for the punishment of counterfeiting the securities and current coin of the United States:

To establish post-offices and post-roads:

To promote the progress of science and useful arts, by securing, for limited times, to authors and inventors, the exclusive right to their respective writings and discoveries:

To constitute tribunals inferior to the Supreme Court:

To define and punish piracies and felonies committed on the high seas, and offences against the law of nations:

To declare war, grant letters of marque and reprisal, and make rules concerning captures on land and water:

To raise and support armies: but no appropriation of money to that use shall be for a longer term than two years:

To provide and maintain a navy:

To make rules for the government and regulation of the land and naval forces:

To provide for calling forth the militia to execute the laws of the Union, suppress insurrections and repel invasions:

To provide for organizing, arming, and disciplining the militia, and for governing such part of them as may be employed in the service of the United States, reserving to the States respectively, the appointment of the officers, and the authority of training the militia according to the discipline prescribed by Congress.

To exercise exclusive legislation, in all cases whatsoever, over such district (not exceeding ten miles square) as may by cession of particular States, and the acceptance of Congress, become the seat of the government of the United States, and to exercise like authority over all places purchased by the consent of the legislature of the State in which the same shall be, for the erection of forts, magazines, arsenals, dock-yards, and other needful buildings. And,

To make all laws which shall be necessary and proper for carrying into execution the foregoing powers, and all other powers vested by this Constitution in the government of the United States, or in any department or officer thereof.

§ 9. The migration or importation of such persons as any

of the States now existing shall think proper to admit, shall not be prohibited by the Congress prior to the year one thousand eight hundred and eight; but a tax or duty may be imposed on such importation, not exceeding ten dollars for each person.

The privilege of the writ of *habeas corpus* shall not be suspended, unless when in cases of rebellion or invasion the public safety may require it.

No bill of attainder or *ex post facto* law shall be passed.

No capitation, or other direct tax, shall be laid, unless in proportion to the *census* or enumeration herein before directed to be taken.

No tax or duty shall be laid on articles exported from any State. No preference shall be given by any regulation of commerce or revenue to the ports of one State over those of another; nor shall vessels bound to, or from, one State be obliged to enter, clear, or pay duties in another.

No money shall be drawn from the treasury, but in consequence of appropriations made by law; and a regular statement and account of the receipts and expenditures of all public money shall be published from time to time.

No title of nobility shall be granted by the United States; and no person holding any office of profit or trust under them, shall, without the consent of the Congress, accept of any present, emolument, office, or title of any kind whatever, from any king, prince, or foreign state.

§ 10. No State shall enter into any treaty, alliance, or confederation; grant letters of marque and reprisal; coin money; emit bills of credit; make any thing but gold and silver coin a tender in payment of debts; pass any bill of attainder, *ex post facto* law, or law impairing the obligation of contracts, or grant any title of nobility.

No State shall, without the consent of the Congress, lay any imposts or duties on imports or exports, except what may be absolutely necessary for executing its inspection laws; and the net produce of all duties and imposts, laid by any State on imports or exports, shall be for the use of the treasury of the United States; and all such laws shall be subject to the revision and control of the Congress. No State shall, without the consent of Congress, lay any duty of tonnage, keep troops, or ships of war, in time of peace, enter into any agreement or compact with another State, or with a foreign power, or engage in war, unless actually invaded, or in such imminent danger as will not admit of delay.

ARTICLE II. § 1. The executive power shall be vested in a President of the United States of America. He shall hold his office during the term of four years, and together with the Vice President, chosen for the same term, be elected as follows:

Each State shall appoint, in such manner as the legislature thereof may direct, a number of electors equal to the whole number of Senators and Representatives to which the State may be entitled in the Congress; but no Senator or Representative, or person holding an office of trust or profit under the United States, shall be appointed an elector.

The electors shall meet in their respective States, and vote by ballot for two persons, of whom one at least shall not be an inhabitant of the same State with themselves. And they shall make a list of all the persons voted for, and of the number of votes for each; which list they shall sign and certify, and transmit sealed to the seat of the government of the United States, directed to the President of the Senate. The President of the Senate shall, in the presence of the Senate and House of Representatives, open all the certificates, and the votes shall then be counted. The person having the greatest number of votes shall be the President, if such number be a majority of the whole number of electors appointed; and if there be more than one who have such majority, and have an equal number of votes, then the House of Representatives shall immediately choose by ballot one of them for President; and if no person have a majority, then from the five highest on the list the said House shall in like manner choose the President. But in choosing the President, the votes shall be taken by States, the representation from each State having one vote; a quorum for this purpose shall consist of a member or members from two thirds of the States, and a majority of all the States shall be necessary to a choice. In every case, after the choice of the President, the person having the greatest number of votes of the electors shall be the Vice President. But if there should remain two or more who have equal votes, the Senate shall choose from them by ballot the Vice President.

The Congress may determine the time of choosing the electors, and the day on which they shall give their votes; which day shall be the same throughout the United States.

No person except a natural born citizen, or a citizen of the United States, at the time of the adoption of this Constitution, shall be eligible to the office of President; neither shall any person be eligible to that office who shall not have attained to the age of thirty-five years, and been fourteen years a resident within the United States.

In case of the removal of the President from office, or of his death, resignation, or inability to discharge the powers and duties of the said office, the same shall devolve on the Vice President, and the Congress may by law provide for the case of removal, death, resignation, or inability, both of the President and Vice President, declaring what officer shall then act as President, and such officer shall act accordingly until the disability be removed, or a President shall be elected.

The President shall at stated times, receive for his services, a compensation, which shall neither be increased nor diminished during the period for which he shall have been elected, and he shall not receive within that period any other emolument from the United States or any of them.

Before he enter on the execution of his office, he shall take the following oath or affirmation:

"I do solemnly swear, (or affirm,) that I will faithfully execute the office of President of the United States, and will, to the best of my ability, preserve, protect, and defend the Constitution of the United States."

§ 2. The President shall be commander-in-chief of the army and navy of the United States, and of the militia of the several States, when called into the actual service of the United States; he may require the opinion, in writing, of the principal officer in each of the executive departments, upon any subject relating to the duties of their respective offices, and he shall have power to grant reprieves and pardons for offences against the United States, except in cases of impeachment.

He shall have power, by and with the advice and consent of the Senate, to make treaties, provided two thirds of the

Senators present concur; and he shall nominate, and by and with the advice and consent of the Senate, shall appoint ambassadors, other public ministers and consuls, judges of the Supreme Court, and all other officers of the United States, whose appointments are not herein otherwise provided for, and which shall be established by law. But the Congress may by law vest the appointment of such inferior officers, as they think proper, in the President alone, in the courts of law, or in the heads of departments.

The President shall have power to fill up all vacancies that may happen during the recess of the Senate, by granting commissions which shall expire at the end of their session.

§ 3. He shall, from time to time, give to the Congress information of the state of the Union, and recommend to their consideration such measures as he shall judge necessary and expedient. He may on extraordinary occasions, convene both Houses, or either of them; and in case of disagreement between them, with respect to the time of adjournment, he may adjourn them to such time as he shall think proper. He shall receive ambassadors and other public ministers. He shall take care that the laws be faithfully executed; and shall commission all the officers of the United States.

§ 4. The President, Vice President, and all civil officers of the United States, shall be removed from office on impeachment for, and conviction of, treason, bribery, or other high crimes and misdemeanors.

ARTICLE III. § 1. The judicial power of the United States shall be vested in one Supreme Court, and in such inferior courts as the Congress may, from time to time, ordain and establish. The judges, both of the Supreme and inferior courts, shall hold their offices during good behaviour; and shall, at stated times, receive for their services, a compensation, which shall not be diminished during their continuance in office.

§ 2. The judicial power shall extend to all cases, in law and equity, arising under this Constitution, the laws of the United States, and treaties made, or which shall be made, under their authority; to all cases affecting ambassadors, other public ministers, and consuls; to all cases of admiralty and maritime jurisdiction; to controversies to which the United States shall be a party; to controversies between two or more States, between a State and citizens of another State, between citizens of different States, between citizens of the same State claiming lands under grants of different States, and between a State, or the citizens thereof, and foreign States, citizens or subjects.

In all cases affecting ambassadors, other public ministers and consuls, and those in which a State shall be party, the Supreme Court shall have original jurisdiction. In all the other cases before mentioned, the Supreme Court shall have appellate jurisdiction, both as to law and fact, with such exceptions, and under such regulations, as the Congress shall make.

The trial of all crimes, except in cases of impeachment, shall be by jury; and such trial shall be held in the State where the said crimes shall have been committed; but when not committed within any State, the trial shall be at such place or places as the Congress may by law have directed.

§ 3. Treason against the United States, shall consist only in levying war against them, or in adhering to their enemies, giving them aid and comfort. No person shall be convicted of treason unless on the testimony of two witnesses to the same overt act, or on confession in open court.

The Congress shall have power to declare the punishment of treason, but no attainder of treason shall work corruption of blood, or forfeiture, except during the life of the person attainted.

ARTICLE IV. § 1. Full faith and credit shall be given in each State to the public acts, records, and judicial proceedings of every other State. And the Congress may by general laws prescribe the manner in which such acts, records, and proceedings shall be proved, and the effect thereof

§ 2. The citizens of each State shall be entitled to all privileges and immunities of citizens in the several States.
A person charged in any State wit treason, felony, or other crime, who shall flee from justice, and be found in another State, shall, on demand of the executive authority of the State from which he fled, be delivered up, to be removed to the State having jurisdiction of the crime.

No person held to service or labour in one State, under the laws thereof, escaping into another, shall, in consequence of any law or regulation therein, be discharged from such service or labour, but shall be delivered up on claim of the party to whom such service or labour may be due.

§3. New States may be admitted by the Congress into this Union; but no new State shall be formed or erected within the jurisdiction of any other State; nor any State be formed by the junction of two or more States, or parts of States, without the consent of the legislatures of the States concerned, as well as of the Congress.

The Congress shall have power to dispose of and make all needful rules and regulations respecting the territory or other property belonging to the United States; and nothing in this Constitution shall be so construed as to prejudice any claims of the United States, or of any particular State.

§ 4. The United States shall guarantee to every State in this Union a republican form of government, and shall protect each of them against invasion; and on application of the legislature, or of the executive, (when the legislature cannot be convened) against domestic violence.

ARTICLE V. The Congress, whenever two thirds of both Houses shall deem it necessary, shall propose amendments to this Constitution, or, on the application of the legislatures of two thirds of the several States, shall call a convention for proposing amendments, which, in either case, shall be valid to all intents and purposes, as part of this Constitution, when ratified by the legislatures of three fourths of the several States, or by conventions in three fourths thereof, as the one or the other mode of ratification may be proposed by the Congress; provided, that no amendment, which may be made prior to the year one thousand eight hundred and eight, shall in any manner affect the first and fourth clauses in the ninth section of the first article; and that no State, without its consent, shall be deprived of its equal suffrage in the Senate.

ARTICLE VI. All debts contracted, and engagements entered into, before the adoption of this Constitution, shall be as valid against the United States, under this Constitution, as under the confederation.

This Constitution, and the laws of the United States which shall be made in pursuance thereof, and all treaties made, or which shall be made, under the authority of the United States, shall be the supreme law of the land: and the judges, in every State, shall be bound thereby, any thing in the Constitution or laws of any State to the contrary notwithstanding.

The Senators and Representatives before mentioned, and the members of the several State legislatures, and all executive and judicial officers, both of the United States and of the several States, shall be bound, by oath or affirmation, to support this Constitution; but no religious test shall ever be required as a qualification to any office or public trust under the United States.

ARTICLE VII. The ratification of the conventions of nine States, shall be sufficient for the establishment of this Constitution between the States so ratifying the same.

Done in Convention, by the unanimous consent of the States present, the seventeenth day of September, in the year of our Lord one thousand seven hundred and eighty-seven, and of the independence of the United States of America the twelfth. In witness whereof we have hereunto subscribed our names.

GEORGE WASHINGTON, PRESIDENT,
and Deputy from Virginia.

New Hampshire.—John Langdon, Nicholas Gilman.
Massachusetts.—Nathaniel Gorham, Rufus King.
Connecticut.—William Samuel Johnson, Roger Sherman.
New York.—Alexander Hamilton.
New Jersey.—William Livingston, David Brearley, William Paterson, Jonathan Dayton.

Pennsylvania.—Benjamin Franklin, Thomas Mifflin, Robert Morris, George Clymer, Thomas Fitzsimons, Jared Ingersoll, James Wilson, Gouverneur Morris.

Delaware.—George Read, Gunning Bedford, Jun., John Dickinson, Richard Bassett, Jacob Broom.

Maryland.—James M'Henry, Daniel of St. Thomas Jenifer, Daniel Carroll.

Virginia.—John Blair, James Madison, Jun.

North Carolina.—William Blount, Richard Dobbs Spaight, Hugh Williamson

South Carolina.—John Rutledge, Charles Cotesworth Pinckney, Charles Pinckney, Pierce Butler.

Georgia.—William Few, Abraham Baldwin.

Attest: WILLIAM JACKSON, *Secretary.*

AMENDMENTS I-X AND XIV

AMENDMENT I

Congress shall make no law respecting an establishment of religion, or prohibiting the free exercise thereof; or abridging the freedom of speech, or of the press, or the right of the people peaceably to assemble, and to petition the Government for a redress of grievances.

AMENDMENT II

A well regulated Militia, being necessary to the security of a free State, the right of the people to keep and bear Arms, shall not be infringed.

AMENDMENT III

No Soldier shall, in time of peace be quartered in any house, without the consent of the Owner, nor in time of war, but in a manner to be prescribed by law.

AMENDMENT IV

The right of the people to be secure in their persons, houses, papers, and effects, against unreasonable searches and seizures, shall not be violated, and no Warrants shall issue, but upon probable cause, supported by Oath or affirmation, and particularly describing the place to be searched, and the persons or things to be seized.

AMENDMENT V

No person shall be held to answer for a capital, or otherwise infamous crime, unless on a presentment or indictment of a Grand Jury, except in cases arising in the land or naval forces, or in the Militia, when in actual service in time of War or public danger; nor shall any person be subject for the same offence to be twice put in jeopardy of life or limb, nor shall be compelled in any criminal case to be a witness against himself, nor be deprived of life, liberty, or property, without due process of law; nor shall private property be taken for public use without just compensation.

AMENDMENT VI

In all criminal prosecutions, the accused shall enjoy the right to a speedy and public trial, by an impartial jury of the State and district wherein the crime shall have been committed, which district shall have been previously ascertained by law, and to be informed of the nature and cause of the accusation; to be confronted with the witnesses against him; to have compulsory process for obtaining witnesses in his favor, and to have the assistance of counsel for his defence.

AMENDMENT VII

In Suits at common law, where the value in controversy shall exceed twenty dollars, the right of trial by jury shall be preserved, and no fact tried by a jury shall be otherwise re-examined in any Court of the United States, than according to the rules of the common law.

AMENDMENT VIII

Excessive bail shall not be required, nor excessive fines imposed, nor cruel and unusual punishments inflicted.

AMENDMENT IX

The enumeration in the Constitution, of certain rights, shall not be construed to deny or disparage others retained by the people.

AMENDMENT X

The powers not delegated to the United States by the Constitution, nor prohibited by it to the States, are reserved to the States respectively, or to the people.

AMENDMENT XIV

Section 1. All persons born or naturalized in the United States and subject to the jurisdiction thereof, are citizens of the United States and of the State wherein they reside. No State shall make or enforce any law which shall abridge the privileges or immunities of citizens of the United States; nor shall any State deprive any person of life, liberty, or property, without due process of law; nor deny to any person within its jurisdiction the equal protection of the laws.

Section 2. Representatives shall be apportioned among the several States according to their respective numbers, counting the whole number of persons in each State, excluding Indians not taxed. But when the right to vote at any election for the choice of electors for President and Vice President of the United States, Representatives in Congress, the Executive and Judicial officers of a State, or the members of the Legislature thereof, is denied to any of the male inhabitants of such State, being twenty-one years of age, and citizens of the United States, or in any way abridged, except for participation in rebellion, or other crime, the basis of representation therein shall be reduced in the proportion which the number of such male citizens shall bear to the whole number of male citizens twenty-one years of age in such State.

Section 3. No person shall be a Senator or Representative in Congress, or elector of President and Vice President, or hold any office, civil or military, under the United States, or under any State, who, having previously taken an oath, as a member of Congress, or as an officer of the United States, or as a member of any State legislature, or as an executive or judicial officer of any State, to support the Constitution of the United States, shall have engaged in insurrection or rebellion against the same, or given aid or comfort to the enemies thereof. But Congress may by a vote of two-thirds of each House, remove such disability.

Section 4. The validity of the public debt of the United States, authorized by law, including debts incurred for payment of pensions and bounties for services in suppressing insurrection or rebellion, shall not be questioned. But neither the United States nor any State shall assume or pay any debt or obligation incurred in aid of insurrection or rebellion against the United States, or any claim for the loss or emancipation of any slave; but all such debts, obligations and claims shall be held illegal and void.

Section 5. The Congress shall have power to enforce, by appropriate legislation, the provisions of this article.

BIOGRAPHICAL PROFILES OF
NOTABLE FIGURES QUOTED
OR FEATURED IN
THE TEXT

Adams, John (1735–1826). First vice president and second president of the United States; delegate to the First and Second Continental Congresses; co-author with Thomas Jefferson of the Declaration of Independence.

Adams, Samuel (1722–1803). American patriot and a leading figure of the American Revolution. Adams was active and instrumental in every aspect of the pre-revolutionary struggle against Great Britain in Massachusetts. He wrote numerous political pamphlets championing rebellion, promoted the formation of the Boston chapter of the Sons of Liberty, headed the demonstrations that led to the Boston Massacre, and directed the Boston Tea Party. He became a delegate to the First and Second Continental Congresses, and was a signer of the Declaration of Independence. He ended his career as governor of Massachusetts.

Bingham, John A. (1815–1900). American lawyer and U.S. Representative from Ohio, serving from 1855 to 1863 and again from 1865 to 1873. His accomplishments include presenting the government's case in the conspiracy trial of President Abraham Lincoln's assassins, and playing a leading role in the impeachment of President Andrew Johnson.

He was also responsible for drafting the first section of the Fourteenth Amendment.

Black, Hugo (1886–1971). Justice of the U.S. Supreme Court from 1937 to 1971. He authored the landmark opinion of *Gideon v. Wainwright* in 1963, in which the Court ruled that to ensure due process of the law under the Fourteenth Amendment, local governments must provide attorneys for all poor defendants charged with serious crimes. Although his later years on the Court revealed a more conservative voting pattern, Black was nonetheless known for his dissenting opinions favoring individual freedom, racial desegregation, separation of church and state, and an absolutist view of the First Amendment wherein he opposed governmental controls over obscenity and libel.

Blackstone, Sir William (1723–1780). British jurist and legal scholar. His *Commentaries on the Laws of England* (4 vols., 1765–9) was for more than a century the foundation of legal education in Great Britain and the United States. As such, his *Commentaries* was one of the major influences upon the thinking of the Founding Fathers, most of whom were lawyers trained in the English common-law tradition.

Brennan, William Joseph, Jr. (1906–1997). Justice of the U.S. Supreme Court from 1956 to 1990 during the administrations of eight presidents. Brennan is characterized as one of the most influential justices in U.S. history.

Charles I (1600–1649). The second son of King James I, Charles ruled as the king of England, Scotland, and Ireland.

His reign included numerous attempts to secure funds needed to wage war against Spain, France, and eventually with Scotland, resulting in constant struggles with Parliament. Charles dissolved Parliament in 1629 for a period of eleven years until he needed additional funds for war with Scotland, at which time he reconvened Parliament in 1640. Tensions resumed and precipitated two civil wars between Royalists and Parliamentarians, ending with the execution of Charles in 1649 when he refused to answer charges and plead before the authority of the court.

Coke, Sir Edward (1552–1634). English jurist. Coke was one of the principal drafters of the Petition of Right, a statement of the principles of liberty that was to become an integral part of the English constitution. He was the author of the great legal classic *Institutes of the Laws of England* (4 volumes, 1628–44).

Coxe, Tench (1755–1824). American political economist, colonial legislator, and attorney general of the Province of Pennsylvania. Initially a royalist, Coxe joined the British army under General Howe in 1777. After the defeat of the British, Coxe was arrested but then paroled, at which time he became a Whig and a staunch Federalist as evidenced by one of his earliest writings, *An Examination of the Constitution of the United States*. A friend of Madison and Jefferson, he was appointed by Jefferson to the post of Purveyor of Public Supplies. Coxe's chief contribution to public service was in the area of economics, where he was influential in formulating national policy regarding agriculture, imports, exports, and free trade among states.

Cromwell, Oliver (1599–1658). Leader in the English Revolution (1640–1660) and the first commoner to rule England. During the English Civil War, Cromwell rose to distinction through his devout Calvinism and natural military genius, becoming Lord Protector from 1653 to 1658 under England's only written constitution, the Instrument of Government. Though the monarchy was restored with Charles II in 1660, during his time as Lord Protector Cromwell refused to rule without constitutional authority. His government introduced electoral reform, moderate religious toleration, and the first truly British Parliament.

Frankfurter, Felix (1882–1965). Justice of the U.S. Supreme Court from 1939 to 1962. During his time on the Court, Frankfurter's philosophy of judicial restraint — that rulings of state legislatures and Congress represent the will of the electorate and the Court should therefore not interfere — established him as the leader of the conservative members.

Gerry, Elbridge (1744–1814). Vice president of the United States in the administration of President James Madison. Gerry was a compatriot of Samuel Adams and a leader of the opposition to British rule in his home state of Massachusetts. He was a member of the Continental Congress and a signer of the Declaration of Independence.

Hamilton, Alexander (1757–1804). American statesman, aide-de-camp to George Washington as well as commander of a regiment of light infantry during the battle of Yorktown, first secretary of the treasury in George Washington's first administration, and principal co-author of *The Federalist* (1787–8).

Harlan, John Marshall (1899–1971). Justice of the U.S. Supreme Court from 1955 to 1971. Harlan was noted for his dissents from the decisions of the then-existing liberal majority of the Court, and for his technical proficiency in adjudicating complex legal matters.

Henry, Patrick (1736–1799). American statesman and orator, one of the most influential figures in the American Revolution. Henry is remembered today chiefly for two of his most famous utterances: "If this be treason, make the most of it!" and "I know not what course others may take, but as for me, give me liberty or give me death!" A prominent Virginia lawyer, Henry was a member of its House of Burgesses, its revolutionary convention, and the First and Second Continental Congresses. He also served two terms as governor of the state. He was a strong advocate of the adoption of the Bill of Rights.

Howard, Jacob Merritt (1805–1871). American lawyer, U.S. Senator from Michigan from 1862 to 1871, and prominent Republican leader who drafted the resolutions upon which the party was founded.

Jay, John (1745–1829). First chief justice of the Supreme Court of the United States, serving from 1789 to 1795. Before being appointed to the Court by President George Washington, Jay had served several terms in the Continental Congress in 1774, 1775, and again in 1778 when he was chosen as its president. Jay drafted the first Constitution of New York, and was appointed chief justice of the state in 1777. He was one of the commissioners who negotiated the Treaty of Paris with Great Britain in 1782, which brought an end to the American Revolution. He was secretary of foreign affairs from 1784 to 1789, and as a proponent of a strong national government urged ratification of the U.S. Constitution. He was a co-author of *The Federalist*. In 1794, he was sent to Paris to negotiate what has come to be known as Jay's Treaty with Great Britain. During his time in Paris, he was elected governor of New York, an office he held from 1795 to 1801.

Jefferson, Thomas (1743–1826). American political philosopher, statesman, a key leader of the American Revolution, co-author with John Adams of the Declaration of Independence, governor of Virginia, secretary of state in George Washington's first administration, and third president of the United States.

John (of England) (1167–1216). King of England from 1199–1216 and best known for signing the Magna Carta. John came to power in 1199 upon the death of his brother, Richard I, with whom he had joined forces in overthrowing their father in 1189. John's reign was tumultuous, facing a successful revolt led by his own nephew together with the forces of King Philip II of France. In attempting to regain his French holdings lost to Philip in 1214, John was presented with the Magna Carta by his barons in 1215 and forced to sign it, thereby making himself subject to the law in exchange for their support.

Lee, Richard Henry (1732–1794). A leader of the American Revolution, Lee was a member of the Virginia House of Burgesses, where he joined Thomas Jefferson and Patrick Henry in defending the rights of the Colonies against Great Britain. He was a delegate to the Continental Congress from 1774 to 1779, during which time he presented a resolution that formed the basis of the Declaration of Independence. An Antifederalist, Lee believed that the proposed Constitution infringed states' rights. He was instrumental in securing the adoption of the Tenth Amendment.

Locke, John (1632–1704). English philosopher and founder of the school of empiricism. Locke resided most of his life in continental Europe but returned to England following the Glorious Revolution of 1688 and the restoration of the Protestantism movement. Two works he published in 1689 have had a profound influence on modern philosophy: *Essay Concerning Human Understanding,* in which Locke set forth his theory that all persons are good, independent, and equal; and *Two Treatises of Government,* in which Locke argued that sovereignty did not reside in the state but in the people and that, although the state is supreme, it is bound by "natural law." Many of Locke's concepts relating to these natural rights and the duty of government to protect those rights — the value of majority rule, religious freedom, and the separation of church and state — were later embodied in the U.S. Constitution.

Madison, James (1751–1836). One of the founders of the Jeffersonian Republican Party in the 1790s, secretary of state under Thomas Jefferson (1801–9), and fourth president of the United States (1809–17). Madison's influence on the formation of the government of the United States cannot be overestimated. He is known as the "father of the Constitution" because of his draft of the Virginia Plan which became the foundation of the structure of the new federal government, the key role he played in the Constitutional Convention, and his co-authorship of *The Federalist* (1787–8). A leading advocate of the Federalist position in the constitutional debates, Madison supported a strong executive with veto power, a judiciary with the power to override state laws, and the formation of a strong central government which would be better able to defend and preserve liberty than would smaller state jurisdictions unable to form absolute national majorities. Madison played a leading role in the drafting of the Bill of Rights.

Marshall, John (1755–1835). Chief justice of the U.S. Supreme Court from 1801 to 1835. As a member of the Virginia Assembly from 1782 to 1791, Marshall became a prominent member of the Federalist Party and was elected to the U.S. House of Representatives in 1799 where he acted as the party spokesperson. Having declined an appointment by George Washington to the post of U.S. attorney general in 1795, and a later appointment of minister to France, Marshall became secretary of state in the cabinet of President John Adams in 1800. He accepted an appointment as chief justice of the U.S. Supreme Court a year later. Marshall held this position for 34 years, during which time his decisions secured the power of the Court by proclaiming its authority in constitutional matters.

Mason, George (1725–1792). American statesman. Born into the planter aristocracy of Virginia, Mason became a member of the Virginia House of Burgesses and a delegate to his state's constitutional convention in July 1775. He drafted Virginia's celebrated Declaration of Rights and a large portion of its constitution. As a delegate to the Constitutional Convention in 1789, he helped to draft the U.S. Constitution but refused to become a signer because of his opposition to the weaknesses he perceived in the document, chiefly its failure to limit slavery and to include a bill of rights. However, the Bill of Rights that was later incorporated into the Constitution was borrowed from the Virginia Declaration of Rights that Mason had drafted.

Paine, Thomas (1737–1809). Anglo-American political philosopher who enjoyed active and influential political careers in England, France, and the United States. After the publication of his *Rights of Man* (1791–2), a powerful condemnation of Edward Burke's *Reflections Upon the French Revolution*, Paine was indicted by the British government for treason. In the United States, he was an associate of major figures in the American Revolution, including Benjamin Franklin, George Washington, and Thomas Jefferson. His best known writings were: *The American Crisis* (1776–83), a series of pamphlets; and *Common Sense* (1776), in which Paine argued that common sense surely led to the conclusion that the American Colonies should become independent of Great Britain. This little pamphlet, which sold over 500,000 copies (an extraordinary figure for that time), was one of the most influential political documents in American history.

Stevens, Thaddeus (1792–1868). American lawyer and U.S. Representative from Pennsylvania from 1849 to 1853 and again from 1859 to 1868. Stevens was a leader of the Radical Republicans, a powerful group of Northern congressmen who advocated strict government protection for the rights of blacks and firm treatment of the South during Reconstruction.

Story, Joseph (1779–1845). One of the most distinguished jurists in American history. Story served as associate justice on the United States Supreme Court from 1811 until his death. He was also a professor of law at Harvard University and was instrumental in establishing the reputation of the Harvard Law School. He is best known for his *Commentaries on the Constitution of the United States* (1833).

Taney, Roger Brooke (1777–1864). Chief Justice of the U.S. Supreme Court from 1836 to 1864. Although Taney's judicial opinions were generally held in the highest esteem, he is chiefly remembered and vilified for his grossly erroneous majority opinion in the *Dred Scott* case, in which the Court held that no black — free or slave — could claim United States citizenship, and that Congress did not have the power to prohibit slavery in United States territories.

Taft, William Howard (1857–1930). Twenty-seventh president of the United States and later chief justice of the United States Supreme Court from 1921 to 1930.

Tocqueville, Alexis Charles Henri Maurice Clérel de (1805–1859). French statesman and author of the classic *Democracy in America* (1835–40). One of the most intelligent studies of American life ever published, the book is a thorough examination of our legislative, executive, and judicial systems, as well as our manners, customs, and morals during the post-Revolutionary period of early eighteenth century. For generations thereafter, it exerted a profound influence on political thought in Europe and in this country.

Washington, George (1732–1799). Commander in chief of the Continental army during the American Revolution and first president of the United State

Webster, Daniel (1782-1852). U.S. Congressman, Senator, secretary of state under four presidents, great orator, and one of the ablest lawyers and statesmen of his time. Webster was initially a Federalist leader in the House of Representatives, but became a leader of the Whig Party after its founding in 1830. He was an eloquent advocate of tariffs, and was a champion of a strong national government.

William III (of Orange) (1650–1702). Dutch Protestant noble who had married King James' daughter Mary. Following the Revolution of 1688, he and Mary became joint monarchs of Great Britain in 1689.

Zenger, John Peter (1697–1746). American journalist born in Germany who moved to America in 1710. Backed by several prominent lawyers and merchants, he began printing the *New York Weekly Journal* in 1733. The newspaper included articles attacking the administration of New York Governor William Cosby for which Zenger was tried for the crime of seditious libel. His acquittal was a landmark in the history of the freedom of the press in America.

NOTES

PREFACE
(Pages 1-49)

1, DAVID HUME, THE HISTORY OF ENGLAND, Liberty Classics, Indianapolis, 1983, I, 452.

2. *"Instructions of the Town of Braintree"*, October 14, 1765, Charles F. Adams (ed.), THE WORKS OF JOHN ADAMS, Boston, 1851, 3: 467.

3. WILLIAM HOLDSWORTH, A HISTORY OF ENGLISH LAW, Boston, 1937, 5: 449.

4. THOMAS MACAULAY, THE HISTORY OF ENGLAND, ed.. Charles H. Firth, London, 1913-1915, 3: 1311.

5. ALEXIS DE TOCQUEVILLE, DEMOCRACY IN AMERICA, London, 1835-40, 11.

6. David T. Hardy, *"Armed Citizens, Citizen Armies: Toward a Jurisprudence of the Second Amendment,"* Harvard Journal of Law and Public Policy, 587 (1986).

7. JOYCE LEE MALCOLM, TO KEEP AND BEAR ARMS; THE ORIGINS OF AN ANGLO-AMERICAN RIGHT, 1994, 142.

8. *Ex parte Grossman,* 267 U. S. 87 at 108-109.

9. William Penn (1644-1718), famous English Quaker who was granted a charter by Charles II to American territory west of the Delaware River between New York and Maryland. Promising religious liberty and inexpensive land, Penn brought a number of settlers to America and established the colony which was to become the state of Pennsylvania.

10. Bernard Schwartz, The Bill of Rights: A Documentary History, New York, 1971, 1:53.

11. Journal of the House of Burgesses of Virginia, 1761-65, 360.

Notes for pp. 19-26

12. Thomas Paine, Common Sense, Philadelphia, 1776.

13. Thomas Paine, The American Crisis, Philadelphia, 1776.

14. Charles Francis Adams (ed.), Familiar Letters of John Adams and His Wife Abigail Adams, New York, 1876, 167: David Freeman Hawke, Paine, New York, 1974, 7.

15. B. Schwartz, *supra* note 10, at 231.

16. Edmund S. Morgan and Helen M. Morgan, The Stamp Act Crisis (Chapel Hill, 1953), 290.

17. The Intolerable Acts (also known as the

Coercive Acts) were five laws passed by the British Parliament in early 1774 intended primarily to punish the people of Massachusetts for throwing tea into Boston Harbor in December 1773. While Parliament intended the laws to serve merely as local punishments, news of their enactment reverberated throughout all the American colonies, hastening the coming of the American Revolution.

18. Jefferson largely copied from three public documents: the North Carolina's Mecklenburg Resolves of May 31, 1775, using its last sentence verbatim in his declaration; the preamble to the New Hampshire Constitution of January 5, 1776; and the preamble to the South Carolina Constitution of March 26, 1776.

Notes for pp. 26–32

19. George Washington to James Warren, October 7, 1985, WRITINGS OF GEORGE WASHINGTON, Jared Sparks (ed.), (1834-7) 9: 140.

20. Text in DOCUMENTS ILLUSTRATIVE OF THE FORMATION OF THE UNION OF THE AMERICAN STATES, Charles C. Tansill, (ed.), 69th Cong., 1st Sess., 1927, House Doc. 398, 46.

21. Russell Kirk, from *Foreword* to M.E. BRADFORD, FOUNDING FATHERS: BRIEF LIVES OF THE FRAMERS OF THE UNITED STATES CONSTITUTION, 2nd ed., Lawrence, 1981, xiii.

22. THE FEDERALIST, at xx, Edward Mead Earle (ed.), New York, 1937.

23. THE COMPLETE JEFFERSON, S.K. Padover (ed.), New York, 1943, 1112.

24. *Cohens* vs. *Virginia* (1821).

25. E. Earle, *supra* note 22, at xx-xxi.

26. THE FEDERALIST NO. 84, New York, 1937, 555.

27. *Ibid*, 559.

28. B. SCHWARTZ, *supra* note 10, at 444.

29. *Ibid*, 1007.

30. *Ibid*, 983.

Notes
for pp.
32–44
31. Professor of Political Science, University of Houston.

32. Donald S. Lutz, "*The States and the U.S. Bill of Rights*," SOUTHERN ILLINOIS UNIVERSITY LAW JOURNAL, Vol. 14., 251 (1992).

33. The author has relied on the text as found in SOURCES OF OUR LIBERTIES, Richard L. Perry (ed.), American Bar Foundation, 1959, 11-22, 73-75, 245-50.

34. *Ibid* at 23-24.

35. *See* BERNARD SCHWARTZ, THE GREAT RIGHTS OF MANKIND: A HISTORY OF THE BILL

OF RIGHTS, 197 (1977); IRVING BRANT, THE BILL
OF RIGHTS: ITS ORIGIN AND MEANING (1965)
(Chapters five and six are particularly useful).

36. I Annals of Congress 436 (Joseph Gates,
Ed., 1789).

Notes
for pp.
44–49

37. The state bills of rights and their respective
constitutions can be found in THE FEDERAL AND
STATE CONSTITUTIONS, Francis N. Thorpe, (ed.),
1907.

CREATION AND RECONSTRUCTION:
AN OVERVIEW
(Pages 51-56)

1. *See, e.g.*, William J. Brennan, Jr., *Why Have a
Bill of Rights?*, 26 VAL. U. L. REV. I, 12 (1991) (Suggesting that the "salient purpose" of a bill of rights is "to
protect minorities . . . from the passions or fears of political majorities").

2. THE FEDERALIST, No. 51, at 323 (James Madison) (Clinton Rossiter ed., 1961).

Notes
for pp.
51–54

3. In 1989, Professor Levinson powerfully docu-
mented the general lack of interest in the Second
Amendment among mainstream constitutional theorists. *See* Sanford Levinson, *The Embarrassing Second
Amendment*, 99 YALE L. J. 637, 636-42 (1989). Since
then, the amendment has received more scholarly
attention but is still often ignored in constitutional law
classrooms.

4. A topic as vast as the Bill of Rights has obviously forced us to make hard choices to omit or downplay certain issues, themes, and approaches while emphasizing others. A few words about our criteria of selection are in order at the outset. This book aims to offer a general theory of the Bill of Rights — that is, an account that seeks to illuminate not simply individual clauses of the Bill but their relation to each other and to other constitutional provisions. Thus in Part I we pay special attention to questions obscured by the clausebound approach that now dominates constitutional discourse: Why are various clauses lumped together in a single amendment, and how do they interrelate? What themes connect amendments? What words, phrases, and ideas link the original Constitution and the Bill? How do structural ideas and rights fit together? In Part II we examine the intricate interplay between the Bill and the later Fourteenth Amendment.

Notes for p. 56

FIRST THINGS FIRST
(Pages 59-71)

1. *See, e.g.*, JESSE H. CHOPER, JUDICIAL REVIEW AND THE POLITICAL PROCESS 252-54 (1980). One of your authors, too, is guilty. *See, e.g.*, Akhil Reed Amar, *A Neo-Federalist View of Article III: Separating the Two Tiers of Federal Jurisdiction*, 65 B. U. L. REV. 205 1985).

Notes for pp. 59–61

2. For an elegant discussion of the differences between judicial invalidations of congressional statutes and other forms of judicial review, *see* CHARLES L.

BLACK, JR., STRUCTURE AND RELATIONSHIP IN CONSTITUTIONAL LAW 67-93 (1969).

3. OLIVER WENDELL HOLMES, COLLECTED LEGAL PAPERS 295-96 (1920).

4. *See generally* GORDON S. WOOD, THE CREATION OF THE AMERICAN REPUBLIC, 1776-1787, at 364-67 (1969) ("The Abandonment of the States").

5. *See generally* Akhil Reed Amar, *Of Sovereignty and Federalism,* 96 YALE L. J. 1500-1503 (1987).

6. *Id.* at 1451-66, 1492-1520.

7. *See id.* at 1451-66.

8 Though we shall disagree with him a great deal in Part II, we note that Dean Griswold agreed with us on at least this much. *See* Erwin N. Griswold, *Due Process Problems Today in the United States, in* THE FOURTEENTH AMENDMENT 161, 162-63, 165 (Bernard Schwartz ed., 1970).

Notes for pp. 61–67

9. U.S. CONST. art. V.

10. 2 DOCUMENTARY HISTORY OF THE CONSTITUTION OF THE UNITED STATES OF AMERICA 321-22 (Washington: Department of State, 1894) [hereinafter DOCUMENTARY HISTORY OF THE CONSTITUTION] (ellipsis in original).

11. Under this formula, each slave was counted as three-fifths of a free person. U.S. CONST. art. I, §2, cl. 3.

12. The best known exponent of this view, of course, was Montesquieu. This view resounds throughout Antifederalist speeches and writings. For a smattering, *see* CECELIA M. KENYON, THE ANTIFEDERALISTS 24, 39, 101-2, 132-33, 208, 302, 324 (1966) (reprinting work of "Centinel," "The Pennsylvania Minority," "John De Witt," "Agrippa," "The Federal Farmer," "Cato," and "Brutus").

13. For more discussion, see Akhil Reed Amar, Marbury, *Section 13, and the Original Jurisdiction of the Supreme Court*, 56 U. Chi. L. Rev. 443, 469-71 and n.128 (1989); Akhil Reed Amar, *Some New World Lessons for the Old World*, 58 U. Chi. L. Rev. 483, 485-97 (1991).

Notes for pp. 67–68

14. This was, of course, part of the Federalists' design. *See* G.WOOD, *supra* note 4, at 471-518 ("The Worthy Against the Licentious"); GARRY WILLS, EXPLAINING AMERICA 223-47 (1981).

15. *See* HERBERT J. STORING, WHAT THE ANTIFEDERALISTS WERE FOR 16-18, 41, 51-52 (1981); Carol M. Rose, *The Ancient Constitution vs. The Federalist Empire: Anti-Federalism from the Attack on "Monarchism" to Modern Localism*, 84 NW. U. L. REV. 74, 90-91 (1989), and sources cited therein; C. KENYON, *supra* note 12, at xl; *Essays of Brutus* (IV), *reprinted in* 2 THE COMPLETE ANTI-FEDERALIST 382-86 (Herbert J. Storing ed., 1981); *Letters from the Federal Farmer* (II), *reprinted in id.* at 233-34; *Letters from the Federal Farmer* (VII), *reprinted in id.* at 268-69; 2 BERNARD SCHWARTZ, THE BILL OF RIGHTS: A DOCUMENTARY HISTORY 1187 (1971) (Letter from

Richard Henry Lee and William Grayson to Virginia Speaker of the House of Representatives (Sept. 28, 1789)).

16. THE FEDERALIST NO. 10 at 83 (James Madison) (Clinton Rossiter ed., 1961); *cf.* 2 DEBATES ON THE ADOPTION OF THE FEDERAL CONSTITUTION 474 (Jonathan Elliot ed., AYER Co. reprint ed. 1987) (1836) [hereinafter ELLIOT'S DEBATES] (remarks of James Wilson at Pennsylvania ratifying convention).

17. 1 RECORDS OF THE FEDERAL CONVENTION OF 1787, at 568 (Max Farrand rev. ed., 1937).

18. *See* 2 DOCUMENTARY HISTORY OF THE CONSTI- **Notes** TUTION, *supra* note 10, at 321-90. The ratification tally **for.** in this official document corresponds with that in HER- **p. 69** MAN AMES, THE PROPOSED AMENDMENTS TO THE CONSTITUTION OF THE UNITED STATES DURING THE FIRST CENTURY OF ITS HISTORY 320 (New York: Burt Franklin, 1896), and suggests that the tallies in 2 B. SCHWARTZ, *supra* note 15, at 1203, and 1 ELLIOT'S DEBATES, *supra* note 16, at 339-40, *reprinted in* 5 THE FOUNDERS' CONSTITUTION 132 (Philip B. Kurland and Ralph Lerner, eds., 1987) at 41, are in error. Elliot omits both Vermont's ratification of all twelve amendments and Pennsylvania's eventual decision to ratify the (original) First Amendment on September 21, 1791. Elliot also erroneously states that Rhode Island ratified Congress's Second Amendment. Schwartz ignores Pennsylvania's ratification of the original First Amendment, and mistakenly implies that both Rhode Island and Pennsylvania ratified the original Second Amendment. (Apparently they did not.) *Compare* B.

SCHWARTZ at 1203, *with id.* at 1197, 1200, 1201. The Holmes Devise account of ratification is also faulty. *See* JULIUS GOEBEL, JR., 1 HISTORY OF THE SUPREME COURT OF THE UNITED STATES: ANTECEDENTS AND BEGINNINGS TO 1801, at 456 (1971).

19. 2 DOCUMENTARY HISTORY OF THE CONSTITUTION, *supra* note 10, at 322 (ellipsis in original).

Notes
for pp.
69–71

20. On the other hand, consider the argument of the Antifederalist essayist "Cornelius," who trusted state legislators to set their own pay, but distrusted congressmen. State lawmakers, he argued, were elected annually, chosen in small districts, easily monitored by constituents, and "sent but a small distance from their respective homes," to which they quickly returned to "mix with their neighbours of the lowest rank." Congressmen, by contrast, would emerge from large districts and sit for long terms, "far removed, and long detained, from the view of their constituents." Living in an imperial capital city, they would daily mix with foreign "Ambassadors," other "Ministers," and men "bred in affluence" and "luxury." *Essay by Cornelius, reprinted* in 4 THE COMPLETE ANTI-FEDERALIST 141 (Herbert J. Storing ed., 1981).

OUR FIRST AMENDMENT
(Pages 73-83)

Notes
for
p. 74

1. *See e.g.*, ALEXANDER MEIKLEJOHN, POLITICAL FREEDOM: THE CONSTITUTIONAL POWERS OF THE PEOPLE (1960); CHARLES L. BLACK JR., STRUCTURE AND RELATIONSHIP IN CONSTITUTIONAL LAW 33-50 (1969).

2. *See, e.g.*, Ronald K. L. Collins and David M. Skover, *The Future of Liberal Legal Scholarship*, 87 MICH. L. REV. 189, 214 (1988). The authors' identification of the First Amendment with minority rights is especially revealing in light of their view, to which we subscribe, that the Bill of Rights was less centrally focused on minority rights than on protecting "the entire citizenry from governmental abuses of power." *Id.; see also* William T. Mayton, *Seditious Libel and the Lost Guarantee of a Freedom of Expression*, 84 COLUM. L. REV. 91, 127 n.189 (1984) (presenting First Amendment as in large part a federalism provision; but nevertheless implying that its core concern was to prevent majority tyranny).

3. *See, e.g.*, Kingsley Pictures Corp. v. Regents, 360 U.S. 684, 688-89 (1959) (amendment's "guarantee is not confined to the expression of ideas that are conventional or shared by a majority").

Notes for pp. 74–76

4. *See supra* page 52.

5. *See* 4 WILLIAM BLACKSTONE, COMMENTARIES ON THE LAWS OF ENGLAND 150-53 (Oxford: Clarendon, 1765); 2 DEBATES ON THE ADOPTION OF THE FEDERAL CONSTITUTION 449-50 (Jonathan Elliot ed., AYER Co. reprint ed. 1987) (1836) [hereinafter ELLIOT'S DEBATES] (remarks of James Wilson at Pennsylvania ratifying convention); 3 JOSEPH STORY, COMMENTARIES ON THE CONSTITUTION OF THE UNITED STATES §1879 (Boston: Hilliard, Gray, 1833).

6. *See, e.g.*, *Letters of Centinel* (I), *reprinted in* 2 THE COMPLETE ANTI-FEDERALIST 136 (Herbert J.

Storing ed., 1981) ("[I]f I use my pen with the boldness of a freeman, it is because I know that *the liberty of the press yet remains unviolated*, and *juries yet are judges*.") (emphasis in original); *Essays by Cincinnatus* (I), *reprinted in* 6 *id.* at 9 (invoking "Peter Zenger's case" to link the "freedom of the press, the sacred palladium of public liberty" to "trial by jury"). For early state constitutions linking press freedom and jury trial, *see, e.g.*, GA. CONST. OF 1777, art. LXI; PA. CONST. OF 1790, ART. IX, §7; DEL. CONST. OF 1792, ART. I, §5; KY. CONST. OF 1792, ART. XII, §8; TENN. CONST. OF 1796, art. XI, §19.

7. Professors Monaghan and Schauer have both noted this shift, but neither points to the Fourteenth Amendment to justify or explain it — yet another illustration, perhaps, of the invisibility of the incorporation process. *See* Henry P. Monaghan, *First Amendment "Due Process,"* 83 HARV. L. REV. 518, 526-32 (1970); Frederick Schauer, *The Role of the People in First Amendment Theory*, 74 CALIF. L. REV. 761, 765 (1986). As Professor Michael Kent Curtis has noted, in many contexts, the process might be crafted so that press freedom would prevail if *either* judge *or* jury sides with the press.

8. 3 JEAN-JACQUES ROUSSEAU, DU CONTRAT SOCIAL ch. XII (1762) (emphasis added) (our translation; in original, "le Souverain ne sauroit agir que quand le peuple est assemblé").

9. 3 ELLIOT'S DEBATES, *supra* note 5, at 37 (emphasis added).

10. 2 BERNARD SCHWARTZ, THE BILL OF RIGHTS: A DOCUMENTARY HISTORY 1022 (1971) (June 8, 1789) (remarks of John Page referring to "assembling of a convention") (June 8, 1789); *see also* Akhil Reed Amar, *Philadelphia Revisited: Amending the Constitution Outside Article V*, 55 U. CHI. L. REV. 1043, 1058 (1988) and sources cited therein (linking ideas of convention and assembly); James Gray Pope, *Republican Moments: The Role of Direct Popular Power in the American Constitutional Order*, 139 U. PA. L. REV. 287, 325-26 (1990) (connecting people's right to assemble to conventions and other forms of popular sovereignty and mass mobilization).

11. GORDON S. WOOD, THE CREATION OF THE AMERICAN REPUBLIC, 1776-1787, at 312 (1969).

Notes for pp. 78–79

12. 1 WILLIAM BLACKSTONE, *supra* note 5, at 147-48.

13. *See, e.g.*, VA. CONST. OF 1776 (Declaration of Rights), pmbl.; MASS. CONST. OF 1780, pt. II, ch. VI, art. X.

14. *See, e.g.*, Kamper v. Hawkins, 3 Va. 20, 69 (1793) (opinion of Justice Tucker); McCulloch v. Maryland, 17 U.S. (4 Wheat.) 316, 403 (1819); Barron v. Baltimore, 32 U.S. (7 Pet.) 243, 249-50 (1833). *See also* JAMES M. VARNUM, THE CASE OF TREVETT V. WEEDEN 30 (1787).

15. *See* 1 RECORDS OF THE FEDERAL CONVENTION OF 1787, at 22 (Max Farrand rev. ed., 1937); 2 *id.* at 133.

16. *See* 3 ELLIOT'S DEBATES, *supra* note 5, at 37, quoted *supra* text accompanying note 9 (remarks of Edmund Pendleton at Virginia ratifying convention); *id.* at 51 (remarks of Patrick Henry at Virginia ratifying convention); Akhil Reed Amar, *The Consent of the Governed: Constitutional Amendment Outside Article V*, 94 COLUM. L. REV. 457, 494 (1994) (quoting remarks of John Smilie in Pennsylvania ratifying convention). *See also* 2 THE WORKS OF JAMES WILSON 762 (Robert Green McCloskey ed., 1967).

Notes for p. 79

17. G. WOOD, *supra* note 11, at 312; *see also* EDWARD DUMBAULD, THE DECLARATION OF INDEPENDENCE AND WHAT IT MEANS TODAY 103-5 (1950) (linking assembly, petition, conventions, and rights "of the people"); Norman B. Smith, *"Shall Make No Law Abridging . . .": An Analysis of the Neglected, But Nearly Absolute, Right of Petition*, 54 U. CIN. L. REV. 1153, 1179 (1986) (petition right "inextricably linked to the emergence of popular sovereignty").

18. *See* DECLARATION OF RIGHTS art. 8 (1774); PA. CONST. OF 1776 (Declaration of Rights), art. XVI; N.C. CONST. OF 1776 (Declaration of Rights), art. XVIII; VT. CONST. OF 1777, ch. I, §XVIII; MASS CONST. of 1780, pt. I, art. XIX; N.H. CONST. OF 1784, pt.I, art. I, §XXXII; VT. CONST. OF 1786, ch. I, §XXII; 1 ELLIOT'S DEBATES, *supra* note 5, at 328 (New York); *id* at 335 (Rhode Island); 4 *id* at 244 (North Carolina). The converse was not true: two states explicitly protected petition without mentioning assembly. *See* DEL. DECLARATION OF RIGHTS OF 1776, §9; MD. CONST. OF 1776 (Declaration of Rights), art. XI. In an otherwise superb essay on the right of petition, Professor Schnapper

appears to overlook these two counterexamples. *See* Eric Schnapper, *"Libelous" Petitions for Redress of Grievances — Bad Historiography Makes Worse Law*, 74 Iowa L. Rev. 303, 347 n.249 (1989).

19. *See* Stephen A. Higginson, *A Short History of the Right to Petition Government for the Redress of Grievances*, 96 Yale L.J. 153-55; *accord* Smith, *supra* note 17, at 1178-79.

20. For more support and elaboration, *see* E. Dumbauld, *supra* note 17, at 104 and n.5; 2 William Winslow Crosskey, Politics and the Constitution in the History of the United States 1057, 1060, 1072-74 (1953); Wilbur Katz, Religion and American Constitutions 8-10 (1964); Gerard V. Bradley, Church-State Relationships in America 76, 92-95 (1987); Stephen D. Smith, Foreordained Failure: The Quest for a Constitutional Principle of Religious Freedom 17-34 (1995); Edward S. Corwin, *The Supreme Court as National School Board*, 14 Law & Contemp. Probs. 3, 11-12 (1949); Joseph M. Snee, *Religious Disestablishment and the Fourteenth Amendment*, 1954 Wash. U. L. Q. 371; Michael A. Paulsen, *Religion, Equality, and the Constitution: An Equal Protection Approach to Establishment Clause Adjudication*, 61 Notre Dame L. Rev. 311, 321-23 (1986); William C. Porth and Robert P. George, *Trimming the Ivy: A Bicentennial Re-Examination of the Establishment Clause*, 90 W. Va. L. Rev. 109, 136-39 (1987); Daniel O. Conkle, *Toward a General Theory of the Establishment Clause*, 82 Nw. U. L. Rev. 1113, 1132-35 (1988); William K. Lietzau, *Rediscovering the Establishment Clause: Federalism*

Notes for pp. 79–80

and the Rollback of Incorporation, 39 DEPAUL L. REV. 1191 (1990); Kurt T. Lash, *The Second Adoption of the Establishment Clause: The Rise of the Nonestablishment Principle*, 27 ARIZ. ST. L. J. 1085, 1089-99 (1995); Jed Rubenfeld, *Antidisestablishmentarianism: Why RFRA Really Are Unconstitutional*, 95 MICH. L. REV. 2347 (1997).

21. *See* LEONARD W. LEVY, JEFFERSON AND CIVIL LIBERTIES: THE DARKER SIDE 5 (1963); Michael W. McConnell, *The Origins and Historical Understanding of Free Exercise of Religion*, 103 HARV. L. REV. 1409, 1437 (1990). *Cf.* G. BRADLEY, *supra* note 20, at 13 ("each of the thirteen original states generously aided and promoted religion and should therefore, according to Levy's methodology, be called establishment regimes").

22. *See* PA. CONST. OF 1776, §10; DEL. CONST. OF 1776, art. 22; N.C. CONST. OF 1776, art. XXXII; N.J. CONST. OF 1776, art. XIX. In Rhode Island, Jews and Catholics were apparently ineligible for citizenship, see G. BRADLEY, *supra* note 20, at 29.

23. THOMAS J. CURRY, THE FIRST FREEDOMS: CHURCH AND STATE IN AMERICA TO THE PASSAGE OF THE FIRST AMENDMENT 162-63, 221 (1986).

24. 3 J. STORY, *supra* note 5, at §1873.

25. *Compare* Proclamation Appointing a Day of Thanksgiving and Prayer (Nov. 11, 1779), *reprinted in* 3 THE PAPERS OF THOMAS JEFFERSON 177 (Julian P. Boyd ed., 1951) *with* Letter from Thomas Jefferson to

Attorney General Levi Lincoln (Jan. 1, 1802), *in* 8 THE WRITINGS OF THOMAS JEFFERSON 129 (Paul Leicester Ford ed., New York: G. P. Putnam's Sons, 1897); *see also* Second Inaugural Address (Mar. 4, 1805), *reprinted in id.* at 341, 344 (suggesting that states have power over religion where federal government has none).

26. Letter of Thomas Jefferson to Reverend Samuel Miller (January 23, 1808) *in* 5 THE FOUNDERS' CONSTITUTION, 98-99 (Philip B. Kurland and Ralph Lerner eds., 1987).   **Notes for pp. 81–83**

27. 1 ANNALS OF CONG. 949-50 (Joseph Gales ed., 1789) (1st ed. pagination).

28. David A. Anderson, *The Origins of the Press Clause*, 30 U.C.L.A. L. Rev. 484 (1983); *but see id.* at 488 (noting anachronism of this reading). *See also* Murray Dry, *Flag Burning and the Constitution*, 1990 SUP. CT. REV. 69, 72.

THE SECOND AND THIRD AMENDMENTS
(THE MILITARY AMENDMENTS)
(*Pages 85-103*)

1. 3 DEBATES ON THE ADOPTION OF THE FEDERAL CONSTITUTION (Jonathan Eliot ed., AYER Co. reprint ed., 1987) (1836) [hereinafter ELLLIOT'S DEBATES].   **Notes for pp. 85–87**

2. Apparently, the violent nature of revolution induced Locke to strictly limit the legitimate occasions

for the exercise of the people's right to revolt. The people, said Locke, could reclaim their sovereignty only when government action approached true and systematic tyranny. JOHN LOCKE, THE SECOND TREATISE OF GOVERNMENT §§221-43 (Thomas P. Peardon ed., 1952). Between 1776 and 1789, Americans domesticated and defused the idea of violent revolution by channeling it into the newly renovated legal instrument of the peaceful convention. Through the idea of conventions, Americans *legalized* revolution, substituting ballots for bullets. As a result, by 1789 Americans could expand the Lockean right to "revolt" — to alter or abolish government — into a right the people could invoke (by convention) at any time and for any reason. *See, e.g.*, GORDON S. WOOD, THE CREATION OF THE AMERICAN REPUBLIC, 1776-1787, at 342-43 (1969); 1 THE WORKS OF JAMES WILSON 77-79 (Robert Green McCloskey ed., 1967); 2 ELLIOT'S DEBATES, *supra* note 1, at 432-33 (remarks of James Wilson at Pennsylvania ratifying convention); Akhil Reed Amar, *The Consent of the Governed: Constitutional Amendment Outside Article V*, 94 COLUM. L. REV. 457, 458, 463-64, 475-76 (1994). Yet as the Second Amendment reminds us, even the new legal institutions ultimately rested on force — force that ideally would never need to be invoked, yet whose latent existence would nevertheless deter.

Notes for pp. 87–89

3. 3 ELLIOT'S DEBATES, *supra* note 1, at 51.

4. For arguments supporting a broad reading of the amendment as protecting arms-bearing outside of military service, *see generally* Stephen P. Halbrook, *What the Framers Intended: A Linguistic Analysis of the*

Right to Bear Arms, LAW & CONTEMP. PROBS., Winter 1986, at 151; *see, e.g., id.* at 155 (discussing essay by Tench Coxe, written days after Madison proposed his Bill of Rights, construing his proto-Second Amendment to protect the people "in their right to keep and bear their *private* arms") (emphasis added); *see also* EDWARD DUMBAULD, THE BILL OF RIGHTS AND WHAT IT MEANS TODAY 174 (1957) (quoting Pennsylvania Antifederalists linking "right to bear arms" with "killing game"). *But see, e.g.,* Aymette v. State, 21 Tenn. (2 Hum.) 154, 161 (1840) ("The phrase '*bear arms*,' . . . has a military sense, and no other. . . . A man in the pursuit of deer, elk and buffaloes, might carry his rifle every day, for forty years, and, yet, it would never be said of him, that he had *borne arms* . . . "); Don B. Kates, *Handgun Prohibition and the Original Meaning of the Second Amendment*, 82 MICH. L. REV. 204, 219-20, 267 (1983) [hereinafter *Original Meaning*] (similar). Kates has subsequently modified his position in response to Halbrook's evidence. Don B. Kates, *The Second Amendment: A Dialogue*, LAW & CONTEMP. PROBS., Winter 1986, at 143, 149. For a vigorous (if vicious) argument that Kates was more right the first time — that the phrase "keep and bear arms" is exclusively military — *see* Garry Wills, *To Keep and Bear Arms*, N.Y. REV. OF BOOKS, Sept. 21, 1995, at 62.

Notes for pp. 89–90

5. We have been importantly influenced here by the pioneering work of Elaine Scarry. *See, e.g.,* Elaine Scarry, *War and the Social Contract: Nuclear Policy, Distribution, and the Right to Bear Arms*, 139 U. PA. L. REV. 1257 (1991).

6. THE FEDERALIST NO. 28, at 180 (Alexander

Hamilton) (Clinton Rossiter ed., 1961) [hereinafter all citations are to this edition].

7. *Id.* No. 46, at 299 (James Madison).

8. *See generally* Akhil Reed Amar, *Of Sovereignty and Federalism*, 96 YALE L. J. 1425, 1494-1500 (1987).

9. *See, e.g.*, 3 ELLIOT'S DEBATES, *supra* note 1, at 48, 52, 169, 386 (remarks of Patrick Henry at Virginia ratifying convention); *id.* at 379-80 (remarks of George Mason at Virginia ratifying convention); 2 *id.* at 545-46 (Proceedings of the Meeting at Harrisburg, Pennsylvania, September 3, 1788); 3 THE RECORDS OF THE FEDERAL CONVENTION OF 1787, at 208-9 (Max Farrand rev. ed., 1937) [hereinafter M. FARRAND] (Luther Martin's *Genuine Information*); 2 DOCUMENTARY HISTORY OF THE RATIFICATION OF THE CONSTITUTION 509 (Merrill Jensen ed. 1976) (remarks of John Smilie at Pennsylvania ratifying convention) [hereinafter DOCUMENTARY HISTORY].

10. *See, e.g.*, JOHN HART ELY, DEMOCRACY AND DISTRUST 94-95, 227 n.76 (1980); LAURENCE H. TRIBE, AMERICAN CONSTITUTIONAL LAW §5-2, at 299 n.6 (2d ed. 1988). For a more detailed catalogue of Second Amendment scholarship, see Kates, *Original Meanings*, *supra* note 4, at 206-7.

11. *See* U.S. CONST. amend. X (distinguishing between "States respectively" and "the people").

12. 2 BERNARD SCHWARTZ, THE BILL OF RIGHTS: A

DOCUMENTARY HISTORY 1107 (1971) (August 17,
1789) (emphasis added).

13. *See, e.g.*, Kates, *Original Meaning*, *supra* note
4, at 214-18; David T. Hardy, *Armed Citizens, Citizen
Armies: Toward a Jurisprudence of the Second Amendment*, 9 HARV. J. L. & PUB. POL'Y 559, 623-28 (1986);
Letters from the Federal Farmer (III, XVIII),
reprinted in 2 THE COMPLETE ANTI-FEDERALIST 242,
341-42 (Herbert J. Storing, ed. 1981); *Letters of Centinel* (IX), *reprinted in* 2 *id*. at 179, 182; 2 DOCUMEN-
TARY HISTORY, *supra* note 9, at 509 (remarks of John
Smilie in Pennsylvania ratifying convention).

14. In addition to sources cited *supra* note 13, *see*
STEPHEN P. HALBROOK, THAT EVERY MAN BE **Notes**
ARMED: THE EVOLUTION OF A CONSTITUTIONAL RIGHT **for**
(1984); William E. Nelson, *The Eighteenth-Century* **p. 92**
*Background of John Marshall's Constitutional Jurispru-
dence*, 76 MICH. L. REV. 893, 920 (1978).

15. E. DUMBAULD, *supra* note 4, at 214.

16. *See, e.g.*, THE FEDERALIST NO. 25, at 166
(Alexander Hamilton); *id*. No. 29, at 184 (Alexander
Hamilton); *id*. No. 46, at 299 (James Madison).

17. *See, e.g.*, 3 ELLIOT'S DEBATES, *supra* note 1, at
425 (remarks of George Mason at Virginia ratifying
convention) ("Who are the militia? They consist now of
the whole people. . . ."); *id*. at 112 (remarks of Francis
Corbin at Virginia ratifying convention) ("Who are the
militia? Are we not militia?"); *Letters from the Federal
Farmer* (XVIII), *reprinted in* 2 THE COMPLETE ANTI-

FEDERALIST, *supra* note 13, at 341 ("A militia, when properly formed, are in fact the people themselves . . . and include . . . all men capable of bearing arms. . . .").

18. 2 DOCUMENTARY HISTORY, *supra* note 9, at 1778-80 (Microfilm supp.).

19. U.S. CONST. art. I, §8, cls. 1, 9. *See* 4 ELLIOT'S DEBATES, *supra* note 1, at 210 (remarks of Richard Spaight in North Carolina ratifying convention: "Men are to be *raised* by bounty.") (emphasis added).

20. British impressment in the 1770s was one of the major grievances triggering the American Revolution and was explicitly denounced by the Declaration of Independence. In the later impressment debate leading to the War of 1812, Secretary of State Monroe declared that impressment "is not an American practice, but is utterly repugnant to our Constitution" 28 ANNALS OF CONG. 81 (1814) (remarks of Senator Jeremiah Mason). Yet even if naval impressment were deemed permissible, army conscription power would not necessarily follow. Historically the two were distinct issues — the British government before the Revolution "did attempt to exercise in this country the supposed right of impressment for the Navy, which it never did for the Army." *Id*. As explained below, the word *army*, in contradistinction to *militia*, connoted a volunteer force. The word *navy* was more ambiguous, as illustrated by the British-American tussles over impressment. These textual and historical points can be recast into a structural argument: impressing "private" sailors who had already voluntarily agreed to abandon ordinary civilian life and submit to the harsh discipline and

command on a merchant ship involved a smaller marginal deprivation of liberty than wrenching citizen farmers from their families and land through an army draft.

21. *See, e.g.*, THE FEDERALIST NO. 24, at 161 (Alexander Hamilton) (defining *army* as "permanent corps in the pay of government"); WEBSTER'S AMERICAN DICTIONARY (1828). In addition to the sources cited *supra* notes 13-14, see JOHN REMINGTON GRAHAM, A CONSTITUTIONAL HISTORY OF THE MILITARY DRAFT (1971); Harrop A. Freeman, *The Constitutionality of Direct Federal Military Conscription*, 46 IND. L. J. 333, 337 n.14 (1971); Leon Friedman, *Conscription and the Constitution: The Original Understanding*, 67 MICH. L. REV. 1493 (1969); Alan Hirsch, *The Militia Clauses of the Constitution and the National Guard*, 56 U. CIN. L. REV. 919, 958-59 (1988); 3 JOSEPH STORY, COMMENTARIES ON THE CONSTITUTION OF THE UNITED STATES, §1179 (Boston: Hilliard, Gray, 1833).

Notes for pp. 94–95

22. *But see* Michael J. Malbin, *Conscription, the Constitution, and the Framers: An Historical Analysis*, 40 FORDHAM L. REV. 805, 824 (1972). Malbin claims that although Congress can conscript under the army clause, the militia clause is not thereby rendered trivial. According to him, had Congress not been able to rely on the militia as a backup military force, Congress would have been tempted to keep a large (and thus dangerous) standing army at all times. The militia clause removes this temptation, and thus adds something valuable, he claims. Malbin's argument fails miserably. If Congress did have army conscription power, as he claims, surely it would have the lesser power under the

army clause to draft back-up army "reserves," obviating the need for large standing armies — but · once again, this contingent draft violates the cooperative federalism safeguards imposed by the militia clause.

23. *See, e.g.,* Stephen P. Halbrook, *The Right of the People or the Power of the State: Bearing Arms, Arming Militias, and the Second Amendment*, 26 VAL. U. L. REV. 131, 195 (1991) (quoting 1791 essay contradistinguishing "a well regulated militia" and "a regular, standing army, composed of mercenaries"). The idea of a national army based on a national draft is a distinctly modern one, born in Napoleonic France in 1798 — a decade after ratification of our Constitution. *See* Harrop A. Freeman, *The Constitutionality of Peacetime Conscription*, 31 VA. L. REV. 40, 68 (1944); Friedman, *supra* note 21 at 1498-99 and n.20; Malbin, *supra* note 22, at 811. Tellingly, although many leading Antifederalists voiced loud fears about the federal government's power to mistreat conscripted militiamen, virtually nothing was said about possible mistreatment of conscripted army soldiers — the very idea bordered on oxymoron. Put another way, even the most suspicious Antifederalists generally seemed to assume that the federal government could not use the army clause to justify conscription, and no Federalists, of course, ever supported such a reading. *See* Friedman, *supra* note 21 at 1525-33; *see also Essay by Deliberator, reprinted in* 3 THE COMPLETE ANTI-FEDERALIST, *supra* note 13, at 178-79. *But see Essays of Brutus* (VIII), *reprinted in* 2 *id.* at 406 (questioning whether Congress might have impressment power under the army clause but referring to this as a draft "from the militia"). Elsewhere, Brutus took the extreme position

that the Article I enumeration of powers imposed no meaningful or sincere limits on congressional authority.

24. ROBERT A. GROSS, THE MINUTEMEN AND THEIR WORLD 71 (1976).

25. GORDON S. WOOD, THE RADICALISM OF THE AMERICAN REVOLUTION 45 (1992).

26. *See* Friedman, *supra* note 21, at 1508. States' rights advocates viewed the state appointment of officers as vital. When Madison proposed to limit states to appointments "under the rank of General," the Philadelphia convention voted overwhelmingly against him. Roger Sherman called the modification "absolutely inadmissible," and Elbridge Gerry sarcastically suggested that the convention might as well abolish state governments altogether, create a king, and be done with it. 2 M. FARRAND, *supra* note 9, at 388.

Notes for pp. 95–97

27. At least seven Revolution-era constitutions or bills of rights echoed — almost verbatim — the language of the Virginia Bill of Rights of 1776, §13: "[I]n all cases the military should be under strict subordination to, and governed by, the civil power." These provisions were invariably placed alongside paeans to "the militia" and/or guarantees of the right of "the people" to keep and bear arms. *See* PA. CONST. OF 1776 (Declaration of Rights), art. XIII; DEL. DECLARATION OF RIGHTS OF 1776, §20; MD. CONST. OF 1776 (Declaration of Rights), art. XXVII; N.C. CONST. OF 1776 (Declaration of Rights), art. XVII; VT. CONST. OF 1777, ch. 1, §XV; MASS. CONST. OF 1780, pt. I, art. XVII; N.H. CONST. OF 1784, pt. I, art. I, §XXVI. *See gener-*

ally 2 ALEXIS DE TOCQUEVILLE, DEMOCRACY IN AMER-
ICA, 279-302 (Phillips Bradley ed., Vintage, 1945).
Although not explicitly analyzing the allocation of military power under the U.S. Constitution, Tocqueville's
account of civilian versus professional armies strongly
supports our analysis.

28. United States v. Miller, 307 U.S. 174, 179
(1939) (quoting ADAM SMITH, THE WEALTH OF
NATIONS, Book V, Chapter 1).

29. I PAPERS OF DANIEL WEBSTER: SPEECHES AND
FORMAL WRITINGS 21 (Charles M. Wiltse, ed., 1986).

Notes
for pp.
97–101
30. 245 U.S. 366 (1918).

31. E. DUMBAULD, *supra* note 4, at 166.

32. THE DECLARATION OF INDEPENDENCE paras.
13-16 (U.S. 1776).

33. *See, e.g.*, DEL. DECLARATION OF RIGHTS OF
1776, §§ 18-21; MD. CONST. of 1776 (Declaration of
Rights), arts. XXV-XXVIIX; N.H. CONST. of 1784, pt.
I, arts. XXIV-XXVII; MASS. CONST. of 1780, pt. I,
arts. XXVII-XXVIII. *See also* E. DUMBAULD, *supra*
note 4, at 178, 182, 185, 190, 201; 1 ELLIOT'S DE-
BATES, *supra* note 1, at 335; M. FARRAND , *supra* note
9, at 341 (Pinckney's Report).

34. 3 ELLIOT'S DEBATES, *supra* note 1, at 410-11.
See also Morton J. Horwitz, *Is the Third Amendment
Obsolete?*, 26 VAL. U. L. REV. 209, 210 (1991) (noting
linkages between opposition to standing armies and
opposition to quartering troops).

35. *See also* SECOND CONTINENTAL CONGRESS, DECLARATION OF THE CAUSES AND NECESSITY OF TAKING UP ARMS para. 3 (1775) (condemning "quartering soldiers upon the colonists in time of profound peace"), *supra* note 33 (citing Pinckney's report).

Notes for pp. 102–103

36. Youngstown Sheet & Tube Co. v. Sawyer, 343 U.S. 579, 587-88 (1952).

37. 381 U.S. 479, 484 (1965).

THE FOURTH AMENDMENT
(SEARCHES, SEIZURES, AND FIFTH AMENDMENT TAKINGS)
(*Pages 105-121*)

1. Lawrence Delbert Cress, *An Armed Community: The Origins and Meaning of the Right to Bear Arms*, 71 J. AM. HIST. 22, 31 (1984).

2. EDWARD DUMBAULD, THE BILL OF RIGHTS AND WHAT IT MEANS TODAY 182-85 (1957) (emphasis added).

Notes for pp. 106–108

3. *Id.* at 207.

4. MASS. CONST. OF 1780, pt. I, art. XIV (emphasis added).

5. 98 Eng. Rep. 489 (C.P. 1763), 19 Howell's State Trials 1153.

6. On Wilkes *see* RAYMOND WILLIAM POSTGATE, THAT DEVIL WILKES (1929); GEORGE F. E. RUDÉ, WILKES AND LIBERTY (1962); PAULINE MAIER, FROM RESISTANCE TO REVOLUTION 162-69 (1972); Powell v. McCormack, 395 U.S. 486, 527-31 (1969). On Camden *see* TELFORD TAYLOR, TWO STUDIES IN CONSTITUTIONAL INTERPRETATION 184 n.35 (1969). (We are also grateful for helpful information furnished by Donald Grove, tour coordinator of the Baltimore Orioles, and by our resourceful research assistant Teena-Ann Sankoorikal.) On *Wood* and its companion cases *see* T. TAYLOR at 29-35 and accompanying endnotes; NELSON B. LASSON, THE HISTORY AND DEVELOPMENT OF THE FOURTH AMENDMENT TO THE UNITED STATES CONSTITUTION 43-49 (1937).

Notes for pp. 108–110

7. *See, e.g.*, Johnson v. United States, 333 U.S. 10, 14-15 (1948).

8. *See, e.g.*, WILLIAM E. NELSON, AMERICANIZATION OF THE COMMON LAW 190 n.57 (citing Massachusetts case with jury verdict that officer not guilty "If this Warrant be Lawfull in This Case," but guilty otherwise); *id*. 92 ("due issuance of a [judicial] warrant was an absolute defense to an officer who was sued for an unlawful search or arrest"). In *Wood* and *Entick*, had the warrants been lawful, each surely would have been a good defense. *See* 4 WILLIAM BLACKSTONE, COMMENTARIES ON THE LAWS OF ENGLAND 288 (Oxford: Clarendon, 1765) (general warrant "is therefore in fact no warrant at all: for it will not justify the officer who acts under it; whereas a lawful warrant will at all events indemnify the officer, who executes the

same ministerially"); Akhil Reed Amar, *Fourth Amendment First Principles*, 107 HARV. L. REV. 778-79 (1994) [hereinafter *Fourth Amendment*].

9. *See* Amar, *Fourth Amendment*, *supra* note 8, at 818 n.228; cf. Antonin Scalia, *The Rule of Law as a Law of Rules*, 56 U. CHI. L. REV. 1175, 1180-86 (1989).

10. *See* N. LASSON, *supra* note 6, at 45.

11. *Accord* T. TAYLOR, *supra* note 6, at 21-50. Professor Taylor offers a wealth of historical evidence against collapsing the Fourth Amendment's distinct requirements, but nowhere suggests the possible relevance of jury-trial issues. Although Professor Nelson suggests that arrests and searchers always required warrants in colonial Massachusetts, W. NELSON, *supra* note 6, at 17-18, he elsewhere cites two early-nineteenth-century cases holding that no arrest warrant was needed "in cases of treason and felony, and . . . to preserve the peace and to prevent outrage." *Id*. at 226 n.126. The later cases accord with Professor Taylor's extensive evidence, and with Blackstone. *See* 4 W. BLACKSTONE, *supra* note 8, at 286-92; *see generally* Amar, *Fourth Amendment*, *supra* note 8, at 764 and n.13.

Notes for pp. 110–114

12. *See supra* Chapter 2.

13. *See* STEPHEN A. SALTZBURG, AMERICAN CRIMINAL PROCEDURE 56 (4th. ed. 1992); N. LASSON, *supra* note 6, at 24-50; 3 JOSEPH STORY, COMMENTARIES ON THE CONSTITUTION OF THE UNITED STATES §1895

(Boston: Hilliard, Gray, 1833); *see also* 2 DEBATES ON THE ADOPTION OF THE FEDERAL CONSTITUTION 551 (Jonathan Elliot ed., AYER Co. reprint ed. 1987) (1836) (Maryland convention recognition that general warrants were "the great engine by which power may destroy those individuals who resist usurpation").

14. 95 Eng. Rep. 807 (C. P. 1765), 19 Howell's State Trials 1029, 1073.

15. *See* William J. Stuntz, *The Substantive Origins of Criminal Procedure*, 105 YALE L. J. 393 (1995); Eric Schnapper, *Unreasonable Searches and Seizures of Papers*, 71 VA. L. REV. 869 (1985).

Notes for pp. 114–120

16. Stuntz, *supra* note 15, at 403.

17. Zurcher v. Stanford Daily, 436 U.S. 547, 564 (1978) (citations omitted) (quoting Stanford v. Texas, 379 U.S. 476, 485 (1965) and Roaden v. Kentucky, 413 U.S. 496, 501 (1973). For criticism of *Zurcher's* failure to apply this framework properly, *see* Amar, *Fourth Amendment*, *supra* note 8, at 805-6.

18. *See* MASS. CONST. OF 1780, pt. I, art. X; *see also* VT. CONST. OF 1777, ch. I, §II; *see generally* William Michael Treanor, Note, *The Origins and Original Significance of the Just Compensation Clause of the Fifth Amendment*, 94 YALE L. J. 694 (1985).

19. Michael W. McConnell, *Contract Rights and Property Rights: A Case Study in the Relationship Between Individual Liberties and Constitutional Structure*, 76 CAL. L. REV. 267, 288-93 (1988).

20. 1 BLACKSTONE'S COMMENTARIES 305-6 app. (St. George Tucker ed., Philadelphia: Burch and Small, 1803).

21. *See* Jed Rubenfeld, *Usings*, 102 YALE L. J. 1077, 1122-23 (1993); John Jay (A Freeholder), *A Hint to the Legislature of the State of New York* (1778), *reprinted in* 5 THE FOUNDERS' CONSTITUTION 312 (Philip B. Kurland and Ralph Lerner eds., 1987) (emphasis deleted).

Notes for p. 120

THE FIFTH, SIXTH, SEVENTH, AND EIGHTH AMENDMENTS
(THE JURY AMENDMENTS)
(Pages 123-158)

1. *See* BERNARD BAILYN, THE ORIGINS OF AMERICAN POLITICS 68-70, 111 (Vintage 1970) (1967); BERNARD BAILYN, THE IDEOLOGICAL ORIGINS OF THE AMERICAN REVOLUTION 105-8 (1967) [hereinafter IDEOLOGICAL].

2. THE DECLARATION OF INDEPENDENCE para. 11 (U.S. 1776).

3. *Id.* paras. 15, 31.

Notes for pp. 125–127

4. B. BAILYN, IDEOLOGICAL, *supra* note 1, at 108.

5. *See* JACK N. RAKOVE, ORIGINAL MEANINGS 148 (1996) (describing Antifederalists' "intense suspicion" of the national judiciary, drawing "upon an older tradition that treated the judiciary itself as an agent of arbitrary power").

6. Hugo L. Black, *The Bill of Rights*, 35 N.Y. U. L. REV. 865, 870 (1960); *see also* Adamson v. California, 332 U.S. 46, 70-71 (1947) (Black, J., dissenting) (noting connection between First Amendment and limitations on "arbitrary court action" imposed by Fifth, Sixth, and Eighth Amendments); Feldman v. United States, 322 U.S. 487, 500-502 (1944) (Black, J., dissenting) (similar).

7. John H. Baker, *Criminal Courts and Procedure at Common Law* 1550-1800, *in* CRIME IN ENGLAND 1550-1800, at 15, 42 (J. S. Cockburn ed., 1977).

8. LEONARD W. LEVY, ORIGINS OF THE FIFTH AMENDMENT 332 (2d ed. 1986). *See also* William J. Stuntz, *The Substantive Origins of Criminal Procedure*, 105 YALE L. J. 393, 411-19 (1995).

Notes for pp. 128–130

9. 8 WILLIAM HOLDSWORTH, A HISTORY OF ENGLISH LAW 408 (2d ed. 1937).

10. *See* 2 THE RECORDS OF THE FEDERAL CONVENTION OF 1787, at 587-88 (Max Farrand rev. ed., 1937).

11. *See* EDWARD DUMBAULD, THE BILL OF RIGHTS AND WHAT IT MEANS TODAY 176, 181-82, 183-84, 188, 190-92, 200, 204 (1957).

12. LEONARD W. LEVY, THE EMERGENCE OF A FREE PRESS 227 (1985). For a superb overview of the central role of juries in the Founding era, *see* Alan Howard Scheiner, Note, *Judicial Assessment of Punitive Damages, The Seventh Amendment, and the Politics of Jury Power*, 91 COLUM. L. REV. 142 (1991).

13. THE DECLARATION OF INDEPENDENCE para 20 (U.S. 1776).

14. *An Old Whig* (VIII), *reprinted in* 3 THE COMPLETE ANTI-FEDERALIST 46, 49 (Herbert J. Storing ed., 1981). *See also Letters of Cato* (VII), *reprinted in* 2 *id*. at 123, 125 ("rulers in all governments will erect an interest separate from the ruled, which will have a tendency to enslave them").

15. E. DUMBAULD, *supra* note 11, at 209; *Letters from the Federal Farmer* (IV), *quoted infra* text accompanying note 28.

16. *See* Ronald F. Wright, *Why Not Administrative Grand Juries?,* 44 ADMIN. L. REV. 465, 469 (1992).

Notes for pp. 130–134

17. *See id* at 469; David A. Anderson, *The Origins of the Press Clause*, 30 U.C.L.A. L. REV. 455, 511-12 (1983).

18. MASS. CONST. OF 1780 pt. I, art. XXVI; N.H. CONST. OF 1784, pt. I, art. XXXIII (emphasis added). On the special judge-limiting nature of the Eighth Amendment, *cf.* WILLIAM RAWLE, A VIEW OF THE CONSTITUTION OF THE UNITED STATES OF AMERICA 131 (Philadelphia: Nicklin 2d. ed., 1829).

19. *See* 4 WILLIAM BLACKSTONE, COMMENTARIES ON THE LAWS OF ENGLAND 372 (Oxford: Clarendon, 1765).

20. *See id*. at 355. *See also* United States v.

Haskell, 26 F. Cas. 207, 212 (C. C. E. D. Pa. 1823) (No. 15,321) (Washington, Circuit J.) ("jeopardy" means "nothing short of the acquittal or conviction of the prisoner, and the judgment of the court thereupon"). *Compare* JOHN BOUVIER, A LAW DICTIONARY 67 (10th ed., Philadelphia: 1865) ("jeopardy" triggered by "verdict of a jury") *with id.* at 752 (11th ed., 1868) ("jeopardy" triggered when "jury has been charged with [defendant's] deliverance"). For a similar shift in Joseph Story's language, *compare* 3 JOSEPH STORY, COMMENTARIES ON THE CONSTITUTION OF THE UNITED STATES §1781 (Boston: Hillard, Gray, 1833), *with* United States v. Gibert, 25 F. Cas. 1287, 1295-96 (C. C. D. Mass. 1834) (No. 15,204) (Story, Circuit J).

Notes for pp. 134–135

21. *See, e.g.,* 3 THE PAPERS OF ALEXANDER HAMILTON 485 (Harold C. Syrett and Jacob E. Cooke eds., 1962) (1784 "Letter of Phocion" defining "due process of law" as "*indictment or presentment of good and lawful men* and trial and conviction in consequence") (quoting Coke in italicized language); 2 JAMES KENT, COMMENTARIES ON AMERICAN LAW 13 (2d ed., 1832) (parroting Coke's definition of due process of law, quoted *supra*); 3 J. STORY, *supra* note 20, at §1783 (similar). Here, as elsewhere, we do not argue that the clause cannot be applied beyond what we have called its "core" meaning. Indeed, refusal to do so here would render the provision wholly redundant, as the Supreme Court has noted. *See* Murray's Lessee v. Hoboken Land and Improvement Co., 59 U.S. (18 How.) 272, 276 (1856).

22. *See* Ralph Lerner, *The Supreme Court as Republican Schoolmaster,* 1967 SUP. CT. REV. 127.

23. *Letters from the Federal Farmer* (XV), *reprinted in* 2 THE COMPLETE ANTI-FEDERALIST, *supra* note 14, at 315, 320.

24. I ALEXIS DE TOCQUEVILLE, DEMOCRACY IN AMERICA at 295-96 (Phillips Bradley ed., Vintage 1945) (emphasis added). Francis Lieber, one of the leading constitutional commentators of the mid-nineteenth century, shared Tocqueville's assessment. *See* FRANCIS LIEBER, ON CIVIL LIBERTY AND SELF-GOVERNMENT 250 (Philadelphia: Lippincott, Grambo, 1853).

25. 1 A. DE TOCQUEVILLE, *supra* note 24, at 297.

26. *Letters from the Federal Farmer* (IV), *reprinted in* 5 THE COMPLETE ANTI-FEDERALIST, *supra* note 14 at 249; *cf. Letters of Cato* (V), *reprinted in id.* at 119 ("the opportunity you will have to participate in government [is] one of the principal securities of a free people").

Notes for pp. 136–138

27. *Letters from the Federal Farmer* (XV), *reprinted in id.* at 320.

28. *Letters from the Federal Farmer* (IV), *reprinted in* 2 THE COMPLETE ANTI-FEDERALIST, *supra* note 14, at 249-50; *see also id.* at 320 (XV).

29. Letter from Thomas Jefferson to L'Abbé Arnoux (July 19, 1789), *in* 15 THE PAPERS OF THOMAS JEFFERSON 282, 283 (Julian P. Boyd ed., 1958) [hereinafter J.

Boyd]; *see also* 2 THE WORKS OF JOHN ADAMS 253 (Charles Francis Adams ed., Boston: Little, Brown, 1850) (diary entry, Feb. 12, 1771) ("the common people, should have as complete a control" over judiciary as over legislature; the "rights of juries and of elections" stand or fall together).

30. 1 A. DE TOCQUEVILLE, *supra* note 24, at 293-94. For similar emphasis on the political nature of the jury as an institution, *see Letters from the Federal Farmer* (XV), *reprinted in* 2 THE COMPLETE ANTI-FEDERALIST, *supra* note 14, at 315, 320 ("jury trial, especially politically considered, is by far the most important feature in the judicial department in a free country"). Professor Nelson writes that jurors were typically selected "by lot from a list of freeholders, elected by the voters of a jurisdiction, or summoned by the sheriff from among the bystanders at court." William E. Nelson, *The Eighteenth-Century Background of John Marshall's Constitutional Jurisprudence*, 76 MICH. L. REV. 893, 918 n.140 (1978). Thomas Jefferson was harshly critical of this last method, which he believed vested too much discretion in permanent executive officials. *See* Petition on Election of Jurors (Oct. 1798), *reprinted in* 7 THE WRITINGS OF THOMAS JEFFERSON 284, 285 (Paul Leicester Ford ed., New York: G. P. Putnam's Sons, 1896) [hereinafter P. Ford]; First Annual Message (Dec. 8, 1801), *reprinted in* 8 *id.* at 108, 123-24 (1897); Letter from Thomas Jefferson to Sarah Mease (March 26, 1801), *in id.* at 34, 35; Letter from Thomas Jefferson to Samuel Kercheval (July 12, 1816), *in* 10 *id.* at 37, 39 (1899).

31. JOHN TAYLOR, AN INQUIRY INTO THE PRINCIPLES

Notes for p. 138

AND POLICY OF THE GOVERNMENT OF THE UNITED STATES 209 (W. Stark ed., 1950) (1814).

32. *Essays by a Farmer* (IV), *reprinted in* 5 THE COMPLETE ANTI-FEDERALIST, *supra* note 14, at 36, 38; *see also id.* at 37 (referring to jury as a "distinct branch" within the judiciary).

33. 1 A. DE TOCQUEVILLE, *supra* note 24, at 293.

34. *See supra* text at note 28; *see also Essays by a Farmer* (I), *reprinted in* 4 THE COMPLETE ANTI-FEDERALIST, *supra* note 14, at 205, 206 (proposing rotating jurors to be sent from each state to U.S. Supreme Court).

Notes for pp. 138–139

35. *See, e.g.*, GORDON S. WOOD, THE CREATION OF THE AMERICAN REPUBLIC, 1776-1787, at 521-22 (1969); *See* HERBERT J. STORING, WHAT THE ANTI-FEDERALISTS WERE FOR 17, 84 n.15 (1981); *Essays of Brutus* (XVI), *reprinted in* 2 THE COMPLETE ANTI-FEDERALIST, *supra* note 14, at 444-45; 2 DEBATES ON THE ADOPTION OF THE FEDERAL CONSTITUTION 309-11 (Jonathan Elliot ed., AYER Co. reprint ed., 1987) (1836) [hereinafter ELLIOT'S DEBATES] (remarks of Melancton Smith at New York ratifying convention). On the possible use of lotteries to achieve legislative rotation, *see* Akhil Reed Amar, Note, *Choosing Representatives by Lottery Voting*, 93 YALE L. J. 1283 (1984).

36. Letter from Thomas Jefferson to George Washington (May 2, 1788), *in* 13 J. Boyd, *supra* note 29, at 124, 128 (1956); Letter from Thomas Jefferson to

James Madison (July 31, 1788), *in id.* at 440, 442-43; Letter from Thomas Jefferson to James Madison (Dec. 20, 1787), *in* 12 *id.* at 438, 440-41 (1955); Letter from Thomas Jefferson to Francis Hopkinson (Mar. 13, 1789), *in* 14 *id.* at 649, 650.

37. 2 ELLIOT'S DEBATES, *supra* note 35, at 288.

38. Most current immunity doctrines are of a distinctly modern vintage. *See* Akhil Reed Amar, *Of Sovereignty and Federalism*, 96 YALE L. J. 1425, 1487 (1987). For a sharp criticism of both judge-created immunity doctrine and the judge-created exclusionary rule *see* Akhil Reed Amar, *Fourth Amendment First Principles*, 107 HARV. L. REV. 757 (1994).

Notes for pp. 139–141

39. *See* 2 THE WORKS OF JAMES WILSON 542 (Robert Green McCloskey, ed., 1967) (jury, in deciding legal questions, is bound by rules of legal reasoning); Henfield's Case, 11 F. Cas. 1099, 1121 (C. C. D. Pa. 1793) (No. 6,360) (Wilson, Circuit J.) (similar). For other careful distinctions between jury review and the slightly different issue of jury nullification generally, *see* United States v. Smith and Ogden, 27 F. Cas. 1186, 1242 (C. C. D. N.Y. 1806) (No. 16,342a); United States v. Wilson 28 F. Cas. 699, 700, 708-9 (C. C. D. Pa. 1830) (No. 16,730) (Baldwin, Circuit J.).

40. *See* Virginia v. Zimmerman, 28 F. Cas. 1227, 1227 (C. C. D. D. C. 1802) (No. 16,968) (opinion of Cranch, J.) (jury's right to decide law implies counsel's right to argue law to jury); United States v. Morris, 26 F. Cas. 1323, 1331-36 (C. C. D. Mass. 1851) (No. 15,815) (Curtis, Circuit J.) (preventing counsel from arguing constitutionality of statute to jury on ground that jury had no right to decide law).

41. 25 F. Cas. 239 (C. C. D. Va. 1800) (No. 14,709).

42. *See* materials in STEPHEN B. PRESSER AND JAMIL S. ZAINALDIN, LAW AND JURISPRUDENCE IN AMERICAN HISTORY 228-47 (2d ed., 1989).

43. *Proceedings in Commemoration of the 200th Anniversary of the First Session of the Supreme Court of the United States*, 493 U.S. v, x (1990) (remarks of Rex Lee).

44. 25 F. Cas. at 253.

45. *See* Marbury v. Madison, 5 U.S. (1 Cranch) 137 (1803); *see generally* Akhil Reed Amar, Marbury, *Section 13, and the Original Jurisdiction of the Supreme Court*, 56 U. CHI. L. REV. 443, 445-46 (1989).

Notes for pp. 141–145

46. *Essays by a Farmer* (IV) *reprinted in* 5 THE COMPLETE ANTI-FEDERALIST, *supra* note 14. at 36, 38; see also *id*. at 37 (referring to jury as a "distinct branch" within the judiciary).

47. *Letters from the Federal Farmer* (XV), *reprinted in* 2 THE COMPLETE ANTI-FEDERALIST, *supra* note 14, at 315, 320.

48. *Id.*

49. *See* Peter Westen and Richard Drubel, *Toward a General Theory of Double Jeopardy*, 1978 SUP.CT. REV. 81, 131-32; Peter Westen, *The Three Faces of*

Double Jeopardy: Reflections on Government Appeals of Criminal Sentences, 78 MICH. L. REV. 1001, 1012-18 (1980).

50. 1 A. DE TOCQUEVILLE, *supra* note 24, at 296.

51. Gannett Co. v. DePasquale, 443 U.S. 368, 428-29 (1979) (Blackmun, J., concurring in part and dissenting in part).

52. Patton v. United States, 281 U.S. 276, 293 (1930).

Notes for pp. 145–146

53. On the mandatory character of these other words of Article III, *see* Akhil Reed Amar, *A Neo-Federalist View of Article III: Separating the Two Tiers of Federal Jurisdiction*, 65 B.U. L. REV. 205 (1985); Akhil Reed Amar, *The Two-Tiered Structure of the Judiciary Act of 1789*, 138 U. PA. L. REV. 1499 (1990). Joseph Story, whose opinion of the Court in *Martin v. Hunter's Lessee*, 14 U.S. (1 Wheat.) 304 (1816), emphasized the plain meaning of "shall" and "all" in Article III's jurisdictional and tenure provisions, also deemed these words mandatory in the criminal jury context. *See* United States v. Gibert, 25 F. Cas. 1287, 1305 (C. C. D. Mass. 1834) (No. 15,204) (Story, Circuit J.).

54. *See, e.g.*, THE FEDERALIST No. 83, at 496 (Alexander Hamilton); 3 ELLIOT'S DEBATES, *supra* note 35, at 520-21 (remarks of Edmund Pendleton at Virginia ratifying convention); 4 *id.* at 145, 171

(remarks of James Iredell in North Carolina ratifying convention); *id.* at 290 (remarks of Rawlins Lowndes at South Carolina ratifying convention); CECELIA M. KENYON, THE ANTIFEDERALISTS 51 (1985) (report of Pennsylvania convention minority).

55. *Compare Patton*, 281 U.S. at 296-97, *with* material quoted *supra* text accompanying notes 27-37. *Patton* suggested that the colonies allowed bench trials in criminal cases, 281 U.S. at 306, but more recent historical studies have called into question the evidence underlying *Patton's* claims. *See* Susan C. Towne, *The Historical Origins of Bench Trial for Serious Crime*, 26 AM. J. LEGAL HIST. 123 (1982). In any event, this history is of only tangential relevance to the meaning of **Notes** Article III and the Sixth Amendment, whose wording **for pp.** differed considerably from various colonial and state **146-148** constitutional antecedents.

56. *See, e.g.*, United States v. Gibert, 25 F. Cas. 1287, 1304 (C. C. D. Mass. 1834) (No. 15,204) (Story, Circuit J.); *Schick*, 195 U.S. at 81-82 (Harlan, J., dissenting); FRANCIS H. HELLER, THE SIXTH AMENDMENT 71 (1951).

57. Albert W. Alschuler, *Plea Bargaining and Its History*, 79 COLUM. L. REV. 1, 1-24 (1979); *see also* WILLIAM E. NELSON, AMERICANIZATION OF THE COMMON LAW (1975), at 100 (noting judicial discouragement of guilty pleas in capital cases).

58. *See* Alschuler, *supra* note 57, at 1, 40 (citing statistics and Supreme Court cases).

59. *See in re* Oliver, 333 U.S. 257, 266 (1948).

60. EDWARD COKE, THE SECOND PART OF THE INSTITUTES OF THE LAWS OF ENGLAND 103 (London: E. and R. Brooke, 5th ed., 1797) (emphasis added).

61. *See in re* Oliver, 333 U.S. at 268-69 and n.22.

62. 3 J. STORY, *supra* note 20, §1785 at 662 (emphasis added).

63. See U.S. CONST. amends. I, II, IV, IX, X.

Notes for pp. 148–151

64. *See generally* Akhil Reed Amar, *The Central Meaning of Republican Government: Popular Sovereignty, Majority Rule, and the Denominator Problem*, 65 U. COLO. L. REV. 749 (1994).

65. *See* Gannett Co. v. DePasquale, 443 U.S. 368, 428-29 (1979) (Blackmun, J., concurring in part and dissenting in part) (quoting Cox Broadcasting Corp. v. Cohn, 420 U.S. 469, 495 (1975)).

66. MATTHEW HALE, THE HISTORY OF THE COMMON LAW OF ENGLAND 344 (London: Henry Butterworth, 6th ed., 1820).

67. 3 W. BLACKSTONE, *supra* note 19, at 372. Though this passage occurs in the context of a discussion of evidence law in civil cases, Blackstone elsewhere makes clear that the same principles apply to criminal cases. *See* 4 *id.* at 350.

68. Sir John Hawles, Remarks upon Mr. Cornish's Trial, *in* 11 Howell's State Trials 455, 460.

69. 3 W. BLACKSTONE, *supra* note 19, at 373. For very similar language, see M. HALE, *supra* note 66, at 345 (quoted *infra* note 73).

70. THE FEDERALIST NO. 83, at 500-501 (Alexander Hamilton).

71. *Cf.* Rock v. Arkansas, 483 U.S. 44, 51-53 (1987) (affirming a criminal defendant's constitutional right to testify).

72. *See generally* Joel N. Bodansky, *The Abolition of the Party-Witness Disqualification: An Historical Survey*, 70 KY. L. J. 91 (1982); Ferguson v. Georgia, 365 U.S. 570, 573-77 (1961).

Notes for pp. 151–157

73. 3 W. BLACKSTONE, *supra* note 19, at 372-73. *See also* 4 *id.* at 350. Blackstone borrowed heavily, it seems, from Hale: "[O]ftentimes witnesses will deliver [in private] that, which they will be shamed to testify publicly. . . .[M]any times the very MANNER of delivering testimony, will give a probable indication, whether the witness speaks truly or falsely. . . . [Cross-examination] beats and boults out the truth much better . . . and [is] the best method of searching and sifting out the truth. . . ." M. HALE, *supra* note 66, at 345.

74. 4 W. BLACKSTONE, *supra* note 19, at 345 (emphasis altered).

75. *See* Wilson v. United States, 149 U.S. 60, 66 (1893); Akhil Reed Amar and Renée B. Lettow, *Fifth Amendment First Principles: The Self-Incrimination*

Clause, 93 MICH. L. REV. 857, 922-24 (1995); Stephen J. Schulhofer, *Some Kind Words for the Privilege Against Self-Incrimination*, 26 VAL. U. L. REV. 311 (1991).

Notes for pp. 157–158

76. The Trial of Sir Walter Raleigh, 2 Howell's State Trials 15-16 (Oyer and Terminer 1603).

77. *See, e.g.*, ZECHARIAH CHAFEE, JR., THREE HUMAN RIGHTS IN THE CONSTITUTION OF 1787, at 127 (1956).

THE NINTH AND TENTH AMENDMENTS
(THE POPULAR-SOVEREIGNTY AMENDMENTS)
(Pages 159-164)

1. THE FEDERALIST NO. 84, at 513 (Alexander Hamilton) (emphasis altered) (Clinton Rossiter ed., 1961) [hereinafter all citations are to this edition].

Notes for pp. 161–163

2. 2 DEBATES ON THE ADOPTION OF THE FEDERAL CONSTITUTION 432, 437 (Jonathan Elliot ed., AYER Co. reprint ed., 1987) (1836) (emphasis added).

3. THE DECLARATION OF INDEPENDENCE para. 2 (U.S. 1776) (emphasis added).

4. THE FEDERALIST NO. 78, at 469 (Alexander Hamilton) (emphasis added; footnote omitted).

5. For further elaboration, see Akhil Reed Amar,

Of Sovereignty and Federalism, 96 YALE L. J. 1425, 1492-1519 (1987).

Notes for pp. 163–164

6. *See* EDWARD DUMBAULD, THE BILL OF RIGHTS AND WHAT IT MEANS TODAY 163 (1957).

THE BILL OF RIGHTS
AS A CONSTITUTION
(*Pages 165-176*)

1. 3 THE RECORDS OF THE FEDERAL CONVENTION OF 1787, at 290 (Max Farrand rev. ed., 1937) [hereinafter M. FARRAND] (Luther Martin's Reply to the Landholder).

2. 2 *id.* at 640 (George Mason's objections to Constitution); 3 DEBATES ON THE ADOPTION OF THE FEDERAL CONSTITUTION 444 (Jonathan Eliot ed., AYER Co. reprint ed., 1987) [hereinafter ELLIOT'S DEBATES] (remarks of Mason in Virginia ratifying convention).

Notes for p. 167

3. *Letters of Agrippa* (XVI), *reprinted in* 4 THE COMPLETE ANTI-FEDERALIST 111 (Herbert J. Storing ed., 1981).

4. 2 ELLIOT'S DEBATES, *supra* note 2, at 401; *see also* 3 *id.* at 445-46 (similar remarks of Patrick Henry at Virginia ratifying convention); Thomas F. McAfee, *The Original Meaning of the Ninth Amendment*, 90 COLUM L. REV., 1241-44 (1990) (discussing and quoting other Antifederalists linking Bill of Rights with states' rights).

5. 2 ELLIOT'S DEBATES, *supra* note 2, at 399.

6. Letter from Thomas Jefferson to James Madison (Dec. 20, 1787), *in* 1 BERNARD SCHWARTZ, THE BILL OF RIGHTS: A DOCUMENTARY HISTORY 607 (1971) (August 18, 1789) (emphasis added).

7. GORDON S. WOOD, THE CREATION OF THE AMERICAN REPUBLIC, 1776-1787, at 520 (1969); *see also id.* at 516 (describing Antifederalists as populists who emphasized widespread participation in government).

8. 1 B. SCHWARTZ, supra note 6, at 615 (letter of Oct. 17, 1788) (emphasis added).

Notes for pp. 167–170 9. THE FEDERALIST NO. 38, at 235 (James Madison) (Clinton Rossiter ed., 1961) [hereinafter all citations are to this edition].

10. *Id.* No. 84, at 515 (Alexander Hamilton) (emphasis added).

11. *Id.; see also* PENNSYLVANIA AND THE FEDERAL CONSTITUTION, 1787-1788, at 252 (John Bach McMaster and Frederick D. Stone eds., Lancaster: Inquirer, 1888) (remarks of Thomas McKean in Pennsylvania ratifying convention) ("[T]he whole plan of government is nothing more than a bill of rights — a declaration of the people in what manner they choose to be governed.").

12. 2 B. SCHWARTZ, *supra* note 6, at 1031 (June 8, 1789).

13. *Id.* at 1031-32.

14. Letter from Thomas Jefferson to James Madison (Mar. 15, 1789), *in* 14 THE PAPERS OF THOMAS JEFFERSON 659 (Julian P. Boyd ed., 1958).

15. Letter from Thomas Jefferson to L'Abbé Arnoux (July 19, 1789), *in* 14 *id.* at 282 (citing book "Jurors judges both of law and fact by Jones").

16. Letter from Thomas Jefferson to Joseph Priestley (June 19, 1802), *in* 8 THE WRITINGS OF THOMAS JEFFERSON 158, 159-60 (Paul Leicester Ford ed., New York: G. P. Putnam's Sons, 1897).

17. *See, e.g.,* 3 JOSEPH STORY, COMMENTARIES ON THE CONSTITUTION OF THE UNITED STATES §1859 (Boston: Hilliard, Gray, 1833) (Bill of Rights "serves to guide, and enlighten public opinion"); *Letters from the Federal Farmer* (XVI), *reprinted in* 2 THE COMPLETE ANTI-FEDERALIST, *supra* note 3, at 324-25 (A declaration of rights "establish[es] in the minds of the people truths and principles which they might never otherwise have thought of, or soon forgot. If a nation means its systems, religious or political, shall have duration, it ought to recognize the leading principles of them in the front page of every family book. What is the usefulness of a truth in theory, unless it exists constantly in the minds of the people, and has their assent. . . . [E]ducation [consists of] a series of notions impressed upon the minds of the people by examples, precepts and declarations."); 1 BLACKSTONE'S COMMENTARIES 308 app. (St. George Tucker ed., Philadelphia: Burch and Small, 1803) ("A bill of rights may be considered, not only as

Notes for pp. 171–173

intended to give law, and assign limits to a government
. . . , but as giving *information to the people* [so that]
every man of the meanest capacity and understanding
may *learn* his own rights. . . . ") (emphasis added).

18. *See* Robert C. Palmer, *Liberties, in* CONSTITU-
TION AND RIGHTS IN THE EARLY AMERICAN REPUBLIC
55 (William E. Nelson and Robert C. Palmer eds.,
1987); IRVING BRANT, THE BILL OF RIGHTS 37-42
(1965).

19. VA. CONST. OF 1776 (Declaration of Rights),
§15.

20. Madison well understood that maxims helped
ordinary citizens to learn and remember. See THE FED-
ERALIST NO. 53, at 330-32 (James Madison); 2 M.
FARRAND, *supra* note 1, at 616-17 (Madison endorsing
anti-standing army maxim for inclusion in Article I, §8);
see also EDWARD DUMBAULD, THE BILL OF RIGHTS
AND WHAT IT MEANS TODAY 207 (1957). (Madison
proposing an amendment that described freedom of the
press as "one of the great bulwarks of liberty"). Hamilton, less of a true populist, was more critical. *See* THE
FEDERALIST NO. 84, at 513 (Alexander Hamilton)
(didactic "aphorisms which make the principal figure in
several of our State bills of rights . . . would sound much
better in a treatise of ethics than in a constitution of
government"). Hamilton was of course also less enthu-
siastic about militias and juries. *See id.* Nos. 26, 29, 83
(Alexander Hamilton).

21. *Letter from a Delegate Who Has Catched Cold,*
reprinted in 5 THE COMPLETE ANTI-FEDERALIST,

**Notes
for
p. 173**

supra note 3, at 268, 273; *see also* 1 WILLIAM BLACK-
STONE, COMMENTARIES ON THE LAWS OF ENGLAND 6
(Oxford: Clarendon, 1765) (in ancient Rome, "boys
were obliged to learn the twelve tables by heart").

22. 3 ELLIOT'S DEBATES, *supra* note 2, at 137, 223.

23. 1 B. SCHWARTZ, *supra* note 6, at 616-17. (Letter of James Madison to Thomas Jefferson Oct. 17,
1788). Madison here prefigured the words of Edmund
Randolph concerning the Virginia Bill of Rights, quoted
in *id*. at 249.

24. 14 THE PAPERS OF JAMES MADISON 218
(Robert A. Rutland et al. eds., 1983) (*National Gazette*
essay on U.S. government, Feb. 4, 1792); *accord* G.
WOOD, *supra* note 7, at 33-35 (Constitution "ultimately
sustained" by "the very spirit of the people"); *id*. at 377
("genius" and "habits" of people prevail over "paper
. . . form[s]" in constitutions and bills of rights) (quoting
Noah Webster).

Notes for pp. 173–175

25. *Quoted in* G. WOOD, *supra* note 7, at 120.

26. *Id*.

27. *Id*. at 426.

28. MASS. CONST. OF 1780, pt. II, ch. V, §II.

ANTEBELLUM IDEAS
(Pages 179-194)

1. 32 U.S. (7 Pet.) 243 (1833).

2. *Id*. at 247.

Notes for pp. 179–180

3. *Id.*

4. *Id.* at 243, 250 (1833).

5. *See generally* Part I.

6. *See* Paul Finkelman, *James Madison and the Bill of Rights: A Reluctant Paternity*, 1990 SUP. CT. REV. 301, 335.

7. *See* Livingston v. Moore, 32 U.S. (7 Pet.) 469, 482, 539, 551-52 (1833) (Fourth and Seventh Amendments); Holmes v. Jennison, 39 U.S. (14 Pet.) 540, 555, 582, 587 (1840) (opinions of Thompson and Barbour, J J.) (Fifth Amendment due process); Permoli v. New Orleans, 44 U.S. (3 How.) 589, 609 (1845) (First Amendment free exercise); Fox v. Ohio, 46 U.S. (5 How.) 410, 434-35 (1847) (Fifth Amendment double jeopardy); Town of East Hartford v. Hartford Bridge Co., 51 U.S. (10 How.) 511, 539 (1850) (Fifth Amendment just compensation); Smith v. Maryland, 59 U.S. (18 How.) 71, 72, 76 (1855) (Fourth Amendment); Withers v. Buckley, 61 U.S. (20 How.) 84, 89-91 (1858) (Fifth Amendment just compensation); Pervear v. Massachusetts, 72 U.S. (5 Wall.) 475, 476, 479-80 (1866) (Eighth Amendment).

The only troubled note in this unanimous chorus was sounded by Justice McLean in a pair of double-jeopardy dissents. *See* Fox, 46 U.S. (5 How.) at 438-40 (McLean, J., dissenting); Moore v. Illinois, 55 U.S. (14 How.) 13, 21-22 (1852) (McLean, J., dissenting). McLean never claimed that the Fifth Amendment barred a state from punishing the same person twice for the same offense; but he did think that the amendment, in tandem with its counterpart double-jeopardy clauses in the state constitutions, prevented the federal and state governments from each punishing the same person once for the same conduct.

8. Bank of Columbia v. Okely, 17 U.S. (4 Wheat.) 235, 240-42 (1819). For a parsing of Johnson's language as inconsistent with the later *Barron* opinion, *see* William Winslow Crosskey, *Charles Fairman, "Legislative History," and the Constitutional Limitations on State Authority*, 22 U. CHI. L. REV. 1, 127-29 (1954).

9. Houston v. Moore, 18 U.S. (5 Wheat.) 1, 33-34 (1820) (separate opinion of Johnson, J.).

Notes for pp. 182–183

10. People v. Goodwin, 18 Johns. 187, 200-201 (N.Y. Sup. Ct. 1820); State v. Moor, 1 MISS. 134, 138 (1823) (citing and following *Goodwin*).

11. WILLIAM RAWLE, A VIEW OF THE CONSTITUTION OF THE UNITED STATES OF AMERICA 120-30 (Philadelphia: H. C. Carey and I. Lea, 1825).

12. People v. Goodwin, 18 Johns. 187, 200 (N.Y. Sup. Ct. 1820).

13. Rhinehart v. Schuyler, 7 Ill. (2 Gilm.) 473, 522 (1845); *see also* Cockrum v. State, 24 Tex. 394, 401-2 (1859) (invoking counsel's claim that state law violated federal Second Amendment, and discussing principles of that amendment without adverting to *Barron*).

14. Fox v. Ohio, 46 U.S. (5 How.) 410, 420 (1847).

15. 39 U.S. (14 Pet.) 540, 555 (1840).

16. *Id*. at 555-56.

17. *Id*. at 556-57.

18. Nunn v. Georgia, I Ga. 243, 250 (1846).

19. *Id*. at 249.

20. *Id*.

21. *Id*. at 250-51 (emphasis omitted).

22. *Id*. at 250.

Notes for pp. 183–188

23. Campbell v. State, II Ga. 353 (1852).

24. *Id*. at 365.

25. Campbell v. State, II Ga. at 365.

26. *Id*. at 367-68.

27. *See, e.g.*, 1 THE RECORDS OF THE FEDERAL CONVENTION OF 1787, at 250, 338, 439 (Max Farrand rev. ed., 1937) (remarks of John Lansing and Luther Martin); CECELIA M. KENYON, THE ANTI-FEDERAL-ISTS 93, 124, 133, 171, 185, 240-41, 251, 254 (1966) (collecting objections to novelty of proposed Constitution from various Antifederalists). For Publius's attempt to blunt this critique, see THE FEDERALIST NO. 14 (James Madison).

28. CONG. GLOBE, 35th Cong., 2d Sess. 982 (1859); *see also* CONG. GLOBE, 37th Cong., 2d Sess. 1640 (1862) (remarks of John Bingham, invoking the congressional "act for the admission of [Bingham's home state of] Ohio on the condition of perpetual freedom to all law-abiding men within her limits"); CONG. GLOBE, 40th Cong., 2d Sess. 2463 (1868) (remarks of John Bingham discussing condition imposed upon admission of Missouri safeguarding privileges and immunities of citizens); Howard Jay Graham, *The "Conspiracy Theory" of the Fourteenth Amendment*, 47 YALE L. J. 371, 395 n.84 (1938) (discussing this aspect of Bingham's thought as possibly influenced by congressional statutes conditioning admission of new states on compliance with due process and other guarantees).

Notes for pp. 190–192

29. *See, e.g.,* MICHAEL KENT CURTIS, NO STATE SHALL ABRIDGE: THE FOURTEENTH AMENDMENT AND THE BILL OF RIGHTS, 36, (1986); WILLIAM GOODELL, THE AMERICAN SLAVE CODE IN THEORY AND PRACTICE 372-84 (Negro Universities Press, 1968) (1853); HAROLD M. HYMAN AND WILLIAM M. WIECEK, EQUAL JUSTICE UNDER LAW, 15, 401-2 (1982); JACOBUS TEN-BROEK, EQUAL UNDER LAW, 38-39, 125-26 (Collier, 1965) (1951); WILLIAM M. WIECEK, THE SOURCES OF ANTISLAVERY CONSTITUTIONALISM IN AMERICA 1760-1848, at 182-83, 280-81 (1977).

30. *See* CONG. GLOBE, 36th Cong., 1st sess. 2595-2601 (1860) (remarks of Sen. Charles Sumner); Michael Kent Curtis, *The 1859 Crisis Over Hinton Helper's Book*, The Impending Crisis: *Free Speech, Slavery, and Some Light on the Meaning of the First*

Section of the Fourteenth Amendment, 68 CHI.-KENT
L. REV., 1129 (1993) [hereinafter *1859 Crisis*].

31. *See* M. CURTIS, *supra* note 29, at 23, 30-38;
KENNETH M. STAMPP, THE PECULIAR INSTITUTION
211-12 (1956); Alfred Avins, *Incorporation of the Bill
of Rights: The Crosskey-Fairman Debates Revisited*, 6
HARV. J. ON LEGIS. 1, 17-26 (1968); *see generally* CLE-
MENT EATON, THE FREEDOM OF THOUGHT STRUGGLE
IN THE OLD SOUTH (1964); RUSSELL B. NYE, FET-
TERED FREEDOM (1963); Micheal Kent Curtis, *The
Curious History of Attempts to Suppress Antislavery
Speech, Press, and Petition in 1835-37*, 89 NW. U.L.
REV. 785, 862 (1995) (quoting A FULL STATEMENT OF
THE REASONS . . . 17 (Boston, 1836) (emphasis in orig-
inal) [hereinafter *Curious History*]; Curtis, *1859 Crisis,
supra* note 30.

**Notes
for
p. 192**

32. *See* Curtis, *1859 Crisis, supra* note 30, at 1134-
35.

33. *See* CONG. GLOBE, 39th Cong., 1st Sess. 1013
(1866) (remarks of Rep. Tobias Plants); K. STAMPP,
supra note 31, at 208, 211; J. TENBROEK, *supra* note
29, at 124-25; Avins, *supra* note 31, at 17; Curtis, *1859
Crisis, supra* note 30, at 1123.

34. *See* Kurt T. Lash, *The Second Adoption of the
Free Exercise Clause: Religious Exemptions Under the
Fourteenth Amendment*, 88 NW. U. L. REV. 1106,
1134 and n.127 (1994).

35. *See* K. STAMPP, *supra* note 31, at 132-40. For
earlier fears, *see* W. WIECEK, *supra* note 29, at 123-24,
128-49.

36. *See* STEPHEN P. HALBROOK, THAT EVERY MAN BE ARMED 96-106 (1984); Robert J. Cottrol and Raymond T. Diamond, *The Second Amendment: Towards an Afro-Americanist Reconsideration*, 80 GEO. L. J. 309, 333-38 (1991).

37. *See* K. STAMPP, *supra* note 31, at 153, 188-91, 193-94, 212, 215-17; M. CURTIS, *supra* note 29, at 40, 50; THOMAS D. MORRIS, FREE MEN ALL (1974).

38. *See* Curtis, *1859 Crisis*, *supra* note 30, at 1162, 1171. On the clear impermissibility of warrants for books, see Entick v. Carrington, 95 Eng. Rep. 807 (C. P. 1765), 19 Howell's State Trials 1029 (Camden, C. J.); Eric Schnapper, *Unreasonable Searches and Seizures of Papers*, 71 VA. L. REV. 869 (1985).

Notes for pp. 192–194

39. For a nice discussion of the influence of this abolitionist theory on the Reconstruction Republicans of the Thirty-ninth Congress, *see* M. CURTIS, *supra* note 29, at 26-56; *see also* Curtis, *Curious History*, *supra* note 31, at 860 (outlining declaratory theory of antislavery leader Gerrit Smith); *see generally* William E. Nelson, *The Impact of the Anti-Slavery Movement upon Styles of Judicial Reasoning in Nineteenth Century America*, 87 HARV. L. REV. 513 (1974); Earl M. Maltz, *Fourteenth Amendment Concepts in the Antebellum Era*, 32 AM. J. LEGAL HIST. 305, 309 (1988).

40. *See, e.g.*, CONG. GLOBE, 39th Cong., 1st Sess. 1065 (1866) (remarks of Rep. John Bingham) (stressing need to protect "thousands of loyal white citizens" in the South from property confiscations and other

Notes
for
p. 194

repressive measures); Charles Fairman, *Does the Fourteenth Amendment Incorporate the Bill of Rights?*, 2 STAN. L. REV. 5, 90 (1949) (quoting October 1866 speech of Vermont Governor Paul Dillingham on need to ratify Fourteenth Amendment to "secure to the original Union men of the South equal rights and impartial liberty"); The Slaughter-House Cases, 83 U.S. (16 WALL.) 36, 123 (1873) (Bradley, J., dissenting) ("The mischief to be remedied was not merely slavery. . . [but also] that intolerance of free speech and free discussion which often rendered life and property insecure, and led to much unequal legislation."); Ex parte Virginia, 100 U.S. 339, 364-65 (1880) (Field, J., dissenting) (discussing importance of protecting various Northerners and Unionists in South); *see generally* S. EXEC. DOC. NO. 2, 39th Cong., 1st Sess. (1865) (report of Carl Schurz) (detailing need to protect white Unionists and Yankees in the South); CHESTER JAMES ANTIEAU, THE ORIGINAL UNDERSTANDING OF THE FOURTEENTH AMENDMENT 24-25 (1981) (collecting similar quotations).

THE FOURTEENTH AMENDMENT
(*Pages 195-218*)

1. 10 U.S. (6 Cranch) 87, 138 (1810).

Notes
for pp.
197–198

2. *See* Piqua Branch of the State Bank v. Knoop, 57 U.S. (16 HOW.) 369, 385, 392 (1853); Cummings v. Missouri, 71 U.S. (4 Wall.) 277, 322, 325 (1866).

3. U.S. CONST. amend. I ("Congress shall make no law . . . abridging . . .").

4. U.S. CONST. amend. I ("freedom" of speech and of the press; "right" to assemble and petition; "free" exercise of religion); *id.* amend. II ("right" to keep and bear arms); *id.* amend. IV ("right" against unreasonable searches and seizures); *id.* amend. VI ("right" to various procedural protections in criminal prosecutions); *id.* amend. VII ("right" to civil jury); *id.* amend. IX ("rights" retained by the people).

5. 12 OXFORD ENGLISH DICTIONARY 522 (2d ed. 1989) (defining "privilege" as, among other things, a "right, advantage, or immunity"); 7 *id.* at 691 (defining "immunity" as, among other things, "freedom from liability to taxation, jurisdiction, etc.").

6. SECOND CONTINENTAL CONGRESS, DECLARATION OF THE CAUSES AND NECESSITY OF TAKING UP ARMS, para. 3 (1775), *reprinted in* 1 GREAT ISSUES IN AMERICAN HISTORY 46, 49 (Richard B. Hofstadter ed., 1958); THE FEDERALIST No. 84, at 513-14 (Alexander Hamilton) (Clinton Rossiter ed., 1961). For more eighteenth-century examples, *see* Robert J. Reinstein, *Completing the Constitution: The Declaration of Independence, Bill of Rights and Fourteenth Amendment*, 66 TEMPLE L. REV. 361, 401 and n. 212 (1993).

Notes for pp. 199–200

7. American Ins. Co. v. Canter, 26 U.S. (1 Pet.) 511, 515, 517 (1828) (reprinting circuit opinion of Justice Johnson).

8. An Act for the Establishment of a Territorial Government in Florida, ch. 10, 3 Stat. 654, 658 (1822).

9. Treaty Between the United States of America and the Ottawa Indians of Blanchard's Fork and Roche De Boef, June 24, 1862, 12 Stat. 1237; Treaty Concerning the Cession of Russian Possession in North America by His Majesty the Emperor of all the Russias to the United States of America, March 30, 1867, 15 Stat. 539, 542; Treaty Between the United States of America and Different Tribes of Sioux Indians, April 29, 1868, 15 Stat. 635, 637; see generally Arnold T. Guminski, *The Rights, Privileges, and Immunities of the American People: A Disjunctive Theory of Selective Incorporation of the Bill of Rights*, 7 WHITTIER L. REV. 765, 789-90 (1985).

Notes for pp. 200–201

10. 1 WILLIAM BLACKSTONE, COMMENTARIES *127-45; see also id. at *164-65 (discussing "privilege of speech" and "freedom of speech" interchangeably and referring to "privilege" against "seizures"). These passages from Blackstone, and their implications for the Fourteenth Amendment, are thoughtfully analyzed in MICHAEL KENT CURTIS, NO STATE SHALL ABRIDGE: THE FOURTEENTH AMENDMENT AND THE BILL OF RIGHTS 64, 74-76 (1986).

11. *See, e.g.*, Act for Declaring the Rights and Liberties of the Subject, and Settling the Succession of the Crown (Bill of Rights), 1689, 1 W. & M., ch. 2, §10 (Eng.) ("excessive bail ought not to be required, nor excessive fines imposed; nor cruel and unusual punishments inflicted"). The language of the Eighth Amendment substitutes "shall not be" for "ought not to be" but is otherwise identical.

12. 60 U.S. (19 How.) 393, 449 (1857) (emphasis added).

13. *Id.* at 403.

14. *Id.* at 404, 410-11.

15. CONG. GLOBE, 39th Cong., 1st Sess. 430 (1866) (quoting *Dred Scott*, 60 U.S. at 404).

16. *See e.g., id.* at 1072 (remarks of Sen. James Nye, describing Bill of Rights as "the natural and personal rights of the citizen"); *id.* at 1153 (remarks of Rep. M. Russell Thayer) (describing due-process clause as one of "those guarantees of the Constitution of the United States which are intended for the protection of all citizens"); *id.* at 1263 (remarks of Rep. John Broomall) (describing "the right of speech," "the writ of habeas corpus, and the right of petition" as "the rights and immunities of citizens"); *id.* at 1118, 1294 (remarks of Rep. James Wilson) (describing "fundamental civil rights" belonging to "citizens of the United States, as such" and rights of "the citizen" "embraced in the bill of rights"); *id.* at 1832-33 (remarks of Rep. William Lawrence) (describing "bill of rights to the national Constitution" as "rights which pertain to every citizen"); *see generally* M. CURTIS, *supra* note 10, at 54, 103.

Notes for pp. 202–204

17. CONG. GLOBE, 39th Cong., 1st Sess. 1090 (1866)(emphasis added).

18. *Id.* at 2765-66.

19. On the significant distinction between citizen and persons, *see, e.g., id*. at 505, 1115, 2560, 2768-69, 2890 (remarks of Sen. Reverdy Johnson, Rep. James Wilson, and Sens. William Morris Stewart, Benjamin Wade, and Edgar Cowan); Ho Ah Kow v. Nunan, 12 F. Cas. 252, 256 (C. C. D. Cal. 1879) (No. 6,546) (Field, Circuit J.); EARL M. MALTZ, CIVIL RIGHTS, THE CON- STITUTION, AND CONGRESS, 1863-1869, at 62-64, 97 (1990); HAROLD M. HYMAN AND WILLIAM M. WIECEK, EQUAL JUSTICE UNDER LAW 411 (1982); ALAN P. GRIMES, DEMOCRACY AND THE AMENDMENTS TO THE CONSTITUTION 49 (1978); 2 WILLIAM WINSLOW CROSSKEY, POLITICS AND THE CONSTITUTION IN THE HISTORY OF THE UNITED STATES 1100-1103, 1109-10 (1953); M. CURTIS, *supra* note 10, at 107; John Harri- son, *Reconstructing the Privileges or Immunities Clause*, 101 YALE L. J. 1385 (1992). On the entitle- ment of aliens to the "protection" of the laws, *see* CONG. GLOBE, 39th Cong., 1st. Sess. 1757, 2890 (1866) (remarks of Sens. Lyman Trumbull and Edgar Cowan).

Notes for pp. 204–205

20. On the importance of war rhetoric stressing the need for national protection as the counterpart to national allegiance, *see* Daniel A. Farber and John E. Muench, *The Ideological Origins of the Fourteenth Amendment*, 1 CONST. COMMENTARY 235, 266-69, 276-77 (1984).

21. THE DECLARATION OF INDEPENDENCE para. 32 (U.S. 1776); 1 JEFFERSON DAVIS, THE RISE AND FALL OF THE CONFEDERATE GOVERNMENT 86 (T. Yoseloff) (1958 1881). For a powerful exposition of the high

place of honor nevertheless held by the Declaration among antebellum antislavery crusaders and Reconstruction Republicans, *see* Reinstein, *supra* note 6, at 361, 389-90. And for a brilliant discussion of Lincoln's use of the Declaration, *see* GARRY WILLS, LINCOLN AT GETTYSBURG (1992).

22. See 1 J. DAVIS, *supra* note 21, at 99-120. *But see* Akhil Reed Amar, *Of Sovereignty and Federalism*, 96 YALE L. J. 1425, 1444-66 (1987) (rejecting secessionist interpretation of Founding).

23. *See generally* M. CURTIS, *supra* note 10, *passim*; William Winslow Crosskey, *Charles Fairman, "Legislative History," and the Constitutional Limitations on State Authority*, 22 U. CHI. L. REV. 1 (1954).

Notes for p. 205

24. In addition to the various sources quoted earlier, *see, e.g.*, CONG. GLOBE, 39th Cong., 1st Sess. 2468 (1866) (remarks of Rep. William Kelley) ("if [provisions of section 1] are not already" in the Constitution, they should be); *id*. at 2539 (remarks of Rep. John Farnsworth) (privileges-or-immunities and due-process clauses of section 1 are "reaffirmation" and "surplusage"); *id*. at 256 app. (remarks of Rep. Jehu Baker) (section 1 is "more valuable for clearing away bad interpretations . . . of the Constitution . . . than for any positive grant of new power"); *id*. at 340 (remarks of Sen. Edgar Cowan) (suggesting Fifth Amendment due process restricts states); *id*. at 1833 (remarks of Rep. William Lawrence) (similar); *id*. at 1151-52 (remarks of Rep. Russell Thayer) (similar); *id*. at 1294 and 157 app. (remarks of Rep. James Wilson) (similar).

25. *See, e.g.*, CHESTER JAMES ANTIEAU, THE ORIGINAL UNDERSTANDING OF THE FOURTEENTH AMENDMENT 62-70 (1981); M. CURTIS, *supra* note 10, at 149-52; E. MALTZ, *supra* note 19, at 116; WILLIAM E. NELSON, THE FOURTEENTH AMENDMENT, 104-9 (1988). On the possibly broad power of Congress to enforce section 1, see C. ANTIEAU, at 40-42, 55-56.

26. CONG. GLOBE, 35th Cong., 2d Sess. 982 (1859).

27. *Id*. at 983-85.

28. *Id*. at 983.

29. CONG. GLOBE, 35th Cong., 2d Sess. 983 (1859).

Notes
for pp.
206–208

30. CONG. GLOBE, 39th Cong., 1st Sess. 430 (1866) (quoting *Dred Scott*, 60 U.S. at 404); *id*. at 1090.

31. CONG. GLOBE, 39th Cong., 1st Sess. 2542 (1866).

32. CONG. GLOBE, 39th Cong., 1st Sess. 1088-94 (1866).

33. *Id*. at 1089-90.

34. *Id*. at 1291-93.

35. CONG. GLOBE, 39th Cong., 2d Sess. 811 (1867).

36. CONG. GLOBE, 42d Cong., 1st Sess. 84 app. (1871) (emphasis altered).

37. *Id.*

38. Cong. Globe, 38th Cong., 1st Sess. 1202-3 (1864). We are especially indebted here to the work of Michael Kent Curtis, who, we believe, first brought this important Wilson passage to light. *See* M. Curtis, *supra* note 10, at 37-38.

Hale echoed Wilson's and Bingham's sentiments on February 27, 1866:

> [T]hese amendments to the Constitution, numbered from one to ten, . . . constitute the bill of rights, a bill of rights for the protection of the citizen, and defining and limiting the power of Federal and State legislation.
> . . . [There is much force in the reasoning that] there has been from first to last, a violation of the provisions in this bill of rights by the very existence of slavery itself . . . .

Notes for pp. 208–211

Cong. Globe, 39th Cong., 1st Sess. 1064-65 (1866).

39. *Id.* at 2459. *See* Reinstein, *supra* note 6, 361, 389-90 (beautifully tracing analytic and historical linkages between the Declaration of Independence and section 1 of the Fourteenth Amendment).

40. Cong. Globe, 39th Cong., 1st Sess. 2765-66 (1866) (emphasis added).

41. Even Senators knew of Bingham's authorship and views. Senator James Doolittle, for example, reminded his colleagues that section 1 had been pre-

pared by "Mr. Bingham," who, Doolittle recalled, had also argued that the Civil Rights Act was unconstitutional under extant case law and required a constitutional amendment (namely Bingham's) to validate it. Doolittle went on to praise Bingham's "very able speech" in the House which argued that only an amendment would suffice to "declare the civil rights of all persons" (Doolittle's paraphrase) — a speech in which Bingham invoked "the bill of rights" a half dozen times. CONG. GLOBE, 39th Cong., 1st Sess. 2896 (1866).

Notes for pp. 211–212

42. *See* Richard L. Aynes, *On Misreading John Bingham and the Fourteenth Amendment*, 103 YALE L. J. 57, 72 and n.84 (1993) (quoting N.Y. TIMES, Mar. 1, 1866, at 5, and JOHN A. BINGHAM, ONE COUNTRY, ONE CONSTITUTION, AND ONE PEOPLE: SPEECH OF HON. JOHN A. BINGHAM, OF OHIO, IN THE HOUSE OF REPRESENTATIVES, FEB. 28, 1866, IN SUPPORT OF THE PROPOSED AMENDMENT TO ENFORCE THE BILL OF RIGHTS (Washington: Cong. Globe Office, 1866).

43. *See* JOSEPH B. JAMES, THE FRAMING OF THE FOURTEENTH AMENDMENT 125 (1956).

44. *See id*. at 135-36; *see* Charles Fairman, *Does the Fourteenth Amendment Incorporate the Bill of Rights?*, 2 STAN L. REV. 5, 68-69 (1949); Crosskey, *supra* note 23, at 102-3.

45. ERIC FONER, RECONSTRUCTION 260-61 (1988).

46. *See* CONG. GLOBE, 39th Cong. 1st Sess. 1034 (1866).

47. *Id.* at 1090.

48. CONG. GLOBE, 39th Cong., 1st Sess. 1072 (1866).

49. *Id.* at 1629.

50. *Id.* at 1617, 1838-39, 1621.

51. *See generally* M. CURTIS, *supra* note 10, at 154-70. Professor Fairman tried to point to various congressional decisions between 1866 and 1870 that he claimed were implicitly inconsistent with incorporation. Fairman, *supra* note 44, at 122-32. In admitting or readmitting states, Congress (claimed Fairman) appeared to approve without comment various state constitutions that did not perfectly comport with the federal Bill of Rights. Fairman's chief evidence focused on silence about grand juries. The alleged inconsistencies Fairman points to are truly de minimis in light of the basic facial consistency of these state constitutions with the privileges and immunities of the federal Bill of Rights. Given this basic consistency and the centrality of many other factors in the (re)admission process, it is unsurprising that little attention was paid to microscopic details about the precise incidents and triggers of grand juries. For similar responses to Fairman on this point see E. MALTZ, *supra* note 19, at 116-17; Crosskey, *supra* note 23, at 85-88.

Notes for pp. 213–216

52. CONG. GLOBE, 42d Cong., 2d. Sess. 844 (1872).

53. United States v. Hall, 26 F. Cas. 79, 82 (C. C. S. D. Ala. 1871) (No. 15,282).

54. Letter of January 3, 1871 (photocopy on file with authors).

55. PROCEEDINGS IN THE KU KLUX TRIALS AT COLUMBIA, S.C., IN THE UNITED STATES CIRCUIT COURT, NOVEMBER TERM, 1871, at 147 (Columbia: Republican Printing, 1872) (discussing United States v. Mitchell, 26 F. Cas. 1283 (C. C. D. S. C. 1871) (No. 15,790)).

Notes for pp. 216–218

56. 83 U.S. (16 Wall.) 36 (1873); *see also* Blyew v. United States, 80 U.S. (13 Wall.) 581, 596 (1872) (Bradley, J., dissenting) (Civil Rights Bill of 1866 designed to protect blacks in "having firearms, . . . exercising the functions of a minister of the gospel, . . . [in] being taught to read and write," and against "laws which subjected them to cruel and ignominious punishments not imposed upon white persons").

57. 83 U.S. (16 Wall.) at 114-18 (Bradley, J., dissenting) (emphasis added).

58. *Id*. at 121-22.

THE INCORPORATION PROCESS
(*Pages 219-224*)

1. Henry J. Friendly, *The Bill of Rights as a Code of Criminal Procedure*, 53 CAL. L. REV. 929, 934 (1965).

Notes for p. 220

2. William W. Van Alstyne, *Foreword* to MICHAEL KENT CURTIS, NO STATE SHALL ABRIDGE: THE FOUR-

TEENTH MENDMENT AND THE BILL OF RIGHTS, at ix
(1986).

3. This phrase is meant to suggest the importance
of the cases and not necessarily their correctness.

4. 376 U.S. 254 (1964) (freedom of speech and
press).

5. 374 U.S. 203 (1963) (nonestablishment of religion).

6. 367 U.S. 643 (1961) (exclusion of evidence
obtained by unreasonable search and seizure); *see also*
id. at 661-66 (Black, J., concurring) (relying in part on
right against compelled self-incrimination).

7. 384 U.S. 436 (1966) (privilege against compelled self-incrimination and right to counsel).

**Notes
for pp.
220–222**

8. 372 U.S. 335 (1963) (right to counsel).

9. 391 U.S. 145 (1968) (right to criminal jury).

10. Indeed, before undergoing stylistic surgery in the
Senate, the amendment as passed by the House in
1789 read as follows: "A well regulated militia, composed of the body of the People, being the best security
of a free state, the right of the People to keep and bear
arms, shall not be infringed. . . ." EDWARD DUMBAULD,
THE BILL OF RIGHTS AND WHAT IT MEANS TODAY 214
(1957).

11. *See supra* Chapter 3.

12. *See, e.g.*, Burton v. Sills, 248 A.2d 521 (N.J. 1968), *appeal dismissed*, 394 U.S. 812 (1969); Quilici v. Village of Morton Grove, 695 F.2d 261 (7th Cir. 1982), *cert. denied*, 464 U.S. 863 (1983).

13. *See supra* Chapter 3.

RECONSTRUCTING RIGHTS
(*Pages 225-257*)

1. On Zenger, see *supra* Chapter 2; on Callender, see *supra* Chapter 5.

2. For an account, *see* 1 HENRY WILSON, HISTORY OF THE RISE AND FALL OF THE SLAVE POWER IN AMERICA 578-82 (Boston: Houghton and Mifflin, 1872).

3. *See* CONG. GLOBE, 38th Cong., 1st Sess. 2984, 2990 (1864) (remarks of Reps. William Kelley and Ebon Ingersoll); CONG. GLOBE, 38th Cong., 2d Sess. 193, 237 (1865) (remarks of Reps. John Kasson and Green Smith); CONG. GLOBE, 39th Cong., 1st Sess. 41, 157-58, 474-75, 1263 (1865-66) (remarks of Sen. John Sherman, Rep. John Bingham, Sen. Lyman Trumbull, and Rep. John Broomall); *id.* at 142 app. (remarks of Sen. Henry Wilson); *see also* CHESTER JAMES ANTIEAU, THE ORIGINAL UNDERSTANDING OF THE FOURTEENTH AMENDMENT 24 (1981) (quoting 1866 remarks of Rep. Columbus Delano); Charles Fairman, *Does the Fourteenth Amendment Incorporate the Bill of Rights?*, 2 STAN. L. REV. 5, 22 (1949) (Samuel Hoar episode was "stock example" in Reconstruction Congress).

4. CHARLES EDWARD STOWE AND LYMAN BEECHER STOWE, HARRIET BEECHER STOWE: THE STORY OF HER LIFE 202-3 (1911).

5. On the ways in which the Slave Power specially targeted "outside agitators," *see* Michael Kent Curtis, *The 1859 Crisis over Hinton Helper's Book*, 68 CHI.-KENT L. REV. 1134, 1161 (1993) [hereinafter *1859 Crisis*].

6. C. ANTIEAU, *supra* note 3, at 24; CONG. GLOBE, 42d Cong., 1st Sess. 84 app. (1871).

7. CONG. GLOBE, 39th Cong., 1st Sess. 474-75 (1866); *see also* JACOBUS TENBROEK, EQUAL UNDER LAW 124-25 (Collier, 1965) (1951) (discussing centrality in abolitionist theory of right to "teach or be taught the Gospel" to nourish the "immortal mind").

Notes for pp. 227–229

8. CONG. GLOBE, 39th Cong., 1st Sess. 142 app. (1866).

9. CONG. GLOBE, 38th Cong., 2d Sess. 138 (1865); CONG. GLOBE, 38th Cong., 1st Sess. 2990 (1864); *see also id.* at 2615 (1864) (remarks of Rep. Daniel Morris) (discussing incarceration of "*Christian* men and women for teaching the alphabet" (emphasis added)); *id.* at 2979 (remarks of Rep. John Farnsworth) (denouncing Slave Power assault on "churches" and censorship of those who spoke against "the evil and sin of slaveholding").

10. 2 PROCEEDINGS OF THE BLACK STATE CONVEN-

TIONS, 1840-1865, at 302 (Philip S. Foner and George E. Walker eds., 1980) [hereinafter PROCEEDINGS].

11. *See* Kurt T. Lash, *The Second Adoption of the Free Exercise Clause: Religious Exemptions Under the Fourteenth Amendment*, 88 NW. U. L. REV. 1106, 1133 n.125 (1994) [hereinafter *Free Exercise*].

12. *See* KENNETH M. STAMPP, THE PECULIAR INSTITUTION 211 (1956) (emphasis added).

13. *See* Curtis, *1859 Crisis*, *supra* note 5, at 1135.

14. *See id.* at 1136.

Notes for pp. 229-230

15. *See id.* at 1159-67.

16. For an early illustration, *see* Michael Kent Curtis, *The Curious History of Attempts to Suppress Antislavery Speech, Press, and Petition in 1835-37*, 89 NW. U. L. REV. 785, 862-63 (1995) [hereinafter *Curious History*] (discussing efforts in 1830s of Massachusetts antislavery society to invoke Virginia statute of religious freedom on behalf of a general right of freedom of opinion and expression encompassing free speech and free press).

17. *See* Curtis, *1859 Crisis*, *supra* note 5, at 1157; ABRAHAM LINCOLN: SPEECHES AND WRITINGS 1859-1865, at 128, 149 (Don E. Fehrenbacher ed., 1989).

18. *See* Curtis, *1859 Crisis*, *supra* note 5, at 1156 (quoting 36th CONG. GLOBE, 1st Sess. 1857 (1860)).

19. *Id.* at 1159 (quoting 36th CONG. GLOBE, 1st Sess. 205 app. (1860); *see also id.* at 1155 (quoting similar language of Rep. Sidney Edgerton).

20. *See generally* 1 ALEXIS DE TOCQUEVILLE, DEMOCRACY IN AMERICA 315 (Vintage ed., 1945); SARA M. EVANS, BORN FOR LIBERTY 67-92 (1989).

21. See WILLIAM M. WIECEK, THE SOURCES OF ANTISLAVERY CONSTITUTIONALISM IN AMERICA 1760-1848 at 152, 154, 167, 184, 195 (1977) (discussing Elizabeth Heyrick, Sarah Grimké, Lucretia Mott, and women's voices more generally in petitioning and in organizations like the Boston Female Anti-Slavery Society); Curtis, *Curious History*, *supra* note 16, at 863 (discussing women like the Grimké sisters who joined abolitionist crusades and were prominent speakers); S. EVANS, *supra* note 20, at 67-118 (describing women's increasingly visible political role); Lea S. VanderVelde, Their Presence in the Gallery (1997) (unpublished manuscript) (discussing visible and vocal presence of women in the gallery of the Reconstruction Congress).

Notes for pp. 230–231

22. *See* Nina Morais, Note, *Sex Discrimination and the Fourteenth Amendment: Lost History*, 97 YALE L. J. 1153, 1155-56 (1988).

23. *See id.* at 1156

24. 2 HISTORY OF WOMAN SUFFRAGE 78-79 (Elizabeth Cady Stanton, Susan B. Anthony, and Matilda Joslyn Gage eds., AYER Co. reprint, 1985) (1882); *see*

also LINDA K. KERBER, WOMEN OF THE REPUBLIC 112-13 (1980) (discussing "the women's abolitionist petitions that flooded Congress in the 1830s and forced confrontation of the slavery issue").

25. Crandall v. State, 10 Conn. 339, 340-41 (1834).

26. For excellent accounts of the Crandall affair, *see* Howard Jay Graham, *The Early Antislavery Backgrounds of the Fourteenth Amendment*, 1950 WIS.L. REV. at 498-506; HAROLD M. HYMAN AND WILLIAM M. WIECEK, EQUAL JUSTICE UNDER LAW, at 94-95 (1982); W. WIECEK, *supra* note 21, at 162-67.

27. On the centrality of the black church, see generally ERIC FONER, RECONSTRUCTION 88-95, 282 (1988).

Notes
for pp.
231–232

28. *See* CONG. GLOBE, 39th Cong., 1st Sess. 474 (1866).

29. *See e.g., Report of the Joint Committee on Reconstruction,* 39th Cong., 1st Sess. 7, 12, 15 (1866) (distinguishing between "civil" and "political" rights, and linking section I with "*civil* rights and privileges") (emphasis added); CONG. GLOBE, 39th Cong., Sess. 476, 599, 606, 1117, 1151, 1159, 1162, 1263, 1293, 1757, 1832, 1836, 3035 (1866) (remarks of Sen. Lyman Trumbull, Reps. James Wilson, M. Russell Thayer, William Windom, John Broomall, Samuel Shellagarger, and William Lawrence, and Sen. John Henderson) (Civil Rights Bill does not encompass political rights like voting); *id.* at 2542, 2766 (remarks of John Bingham and Jacob Howard) (clearly stating that section 1 did not encompass right of suffrage); *id.* at

2462, 2469, 2508, 2530, 2539, 3038 (similar observa-
tions froms Reps. James Garfield, William Kelley,
George   Boutwell,   Samuel   Randall,   and   John
Farnsworth, and Sen. Richard Yates); JOSEPH B.
JAMES, THE FRAMING OF THE FOURTEENTH AMEND-
MENT 163 (1956) (quoting 1866 campaign speech of
Thaddeus Stevens conceding that section 1 "does not
touch . . . political rights"); PHILADELPHIA N. AM. AND
U.S. GAZETTE, SEPT. 28, 1866, at 2, *quoted in* C.
ANTIEAU, *supra* note 3, at 50-51 ("In making native
born and naturalized persons citizens, this section does
not make them voters, for if it did, then would all
women and minors have the right of suffrage, since they
are just as much persons. . . . The fact that this section
does not give the colored man the right of suffrage con-
stitutes the main reason why the extreme advocates of
Negro suffrage oppose the Amendment."); *see also*
Minor v. Happersett, 88 U.S. (21 Wall.) 162 (1875)
(right of suffrage not a section 1 privilege or immunity);
H.R. Rep. No. 22, 41st Cong., 3d Sess. 1-4 (1871),
reprinted in THE RECONSTRUCTION AMENDMENT'S
DEBATES 466-67 (Alfred Avins ed., 1967) (Victoria
Woodhull petition report authored by John Bingham)
(similar); MICHAEL KENT CURTIS, NO STATE SHALL
ABRIDGE: THE FOURTEENTH AMENDMENT AND THE
BILL OF RIGHTS 149 (1986); EARL M. MALTZ, CIVIL
RIGHTS, THE CONSTITUTION, AND CONGRESS, 1863-
1869, AT 118-20 (1990).

Notes for p. 232

To see the same point textually rather than historically, recall that women and children were paradig-
matic (or typical models of) citizens — enjoying many
rights that Dred Scott, as a free black, could not,
according to the Supreme Court — but not voters. Citizenship did not entail suffrage. Nor did the common

nineteenth-century phrase *civil rights*, which was often
invoked in contradistinction to four clustered "political
rights" (the rights to vote, hold office, serve on juries,
and serve in militias). Gender helped to crystallize this
civil/political distinction — men enjoyed "political
rights," but not women — and so did the language of
the Constitution's Article IV comity clause. Under this
clause, a Massachusetts man would enjoy many equal
"civil" rights in South Carolina — the right to own real
property for example, a right often denied to aliens. But
a Massachusetts man could not vote in a South Carolina election, serve in a South Carolina legislature, sit
in a South Carolina jury box, or participate in a South
Carolina militia. The Article IV comity clause did not
extend to these political rights, *see* Bank of Augusta vs.

**Notes
for pp.
232–233**

Earle, 38 U.S. (13 Pet.) 519, 552 (1839) (oral argument of Daniel Webster), and neither did the similar
language of section 1, which also spoke of "privileges"
and "immunities" of "citizens." *See* CONG. GLOBE,
39th Cong., 1st Sess. 1836, 3035 (1866) (remarks of
Rep. William Lawrence and Sen. John Henderson); id.
40th Cong., 3d Sess. 1003 (1869) (remarks of Sen.
Jacob Howard); *Minor*, 88 U.S. at 174; THE RECON-
STRUCTION DEBATES, *supra*, at 466 (Woodhull petition
report). In viewing the Fourteenth Amendment as a
source of equal voting rights, modern courts have
stressed the language not of privileges or immunities
but of equal protection. *See, e.g.*, Reynolds v. Sims,
377 U.S. 533 (1964). Textually, the equal protection
clause embraces all persons — most typically nonvoting
aliens — making the clause a most unsturdy foundation
for political rights.

30. CONG. GLOBE, 39th Cong., 1st Sess. 337 (1866).

31. W. E. BURGHARDT DU BOIS, BLACK RECONSTRUCTION IN AMERICA 230 (Russell and Russell, 1962) (1935).

32. On the abundance of black petitions generally, *see* W. DU BOIS, *supra* note 31, at 230-35; E. FONER, *supra* note 27, at 115; *see also* KENNETH M. STAMPP, THE ERA OF RECONSTRUCTION, 1865-1877, at 165 (1965) (discussing how Tennessee blacks first petitioned their state legislature for suffrage and then asked Congress not to seat the state delegation till the petition was granted).

33. J. TENBROEK, *supra* note 7, at 124-25.

34. *See* Lash, *Free Exercise*, *supra* note 11, at 1134 n. 133 (quoting Virginia Code of 1833, §31) (emphasis added). For similar antebellum laws in South Carolina and the District of Columbia, *see id.*

Notes for pp. 233–237

35. *See* GERARD V. BRADLEY, CHURCH-STATE RELATIONSHIPS IN AMERICA 98 (1987) (describing the events of July 21, 1789); 1 ANNALS OF CONG. 685; 1 Stat. 50, ch. 8.

36. For an overview, see G. BRADLEY, *supra* note 35, at 99-104.

37. *See* STEVEN D. SMITH, FOREORDAINED FAILURE 28 (1995).

38. IOWA CONST. OF 1846, art. I, §3; IOWA CONST. OF 1857, art. I, §3.

39. *See* 9 SOURCES AND DOCUMENTS OF UNITED STATES CONSTITUTIONS 380 (William F. Swindler ed., 1979) (reprinting Constitution of the State of Deseret, art. VII, §3); *id.* at 388 (reprinting Utah Draft Constitution of 1860, art. II, §3).

40. 2 *id.* at 18 (reprinting Constitution of Jefferson Territory, art. I, §3).

41. THOMAS M. COOLEY, A TREATISE ON THE CONSTITUTIONAL LIMITATIONS WHICH REST UPON THE LEGISLATIVE POWER OF THE STATES OF THE AMERICAN UNION 469 (Boston: Little, Brown, 1868).

Notes for pp. 237–240

42. T. COOLEY, *supra* note 41, at 469 (emphasis added). Cooley went on to defend nonpreferential, nonsectarian governmental endorsements of religion, such as government-sponsored fast days and thanksgivings, while warning that care must "be taken to avoid discrimination in favor of any one denomination or sect." *Id.* at 471.

43. *See, e.g.*, CONG. GLOBE, 38th Cong., 1st Sess. 1202 (1864) (remarks of Rep. James Wilson); CONG. GLOBE, 39th Cong., 1st Sess. 156-57, 1072, 1629 (1866) (remarks of Rep. John Bingham, Sen. James Nye, and Rep. Roswell Hart). *See generally* CONG. GLOBE, 36th Cong., 1st Sess. 198 app. (1860) (remarks of Rep. W. E. Simms); CONG. GLOBE, 42d Cong., 1st Sess. 84-85 app., 475 (1871) (remarks of Reps. John Bingham and Henry Dawes); *see also* M. CURTIS, *supra* note 29 (quoting similar speeches outside of Con-

gress by Judge Lorenzo Sherwood and Judge Preston Davis); United States v. Hall, 26 F. Cas. 79, 81 (C. C. S. D. Ala. 1871) (No. 15,282) (Woods, J.) (stressing speech, press, assembly, and free-exercise rights as Fourteenth Amendment privileges and immunities while omitting mention of establishment clause); WILLIAM D. GUTHRIE, LECTURES ON THE FOURTEENTH ARTICLE OF AMENDMENT TO THE CONSTITUTION OF THE UNITED STATES 58-59 (Boston: Little, Brown, 1898) (defining as Fourteenth Amendment privileges and immunities each of the five rights and freedoms of the First Amendment, but omitting nonestablishment).

44. For a somewhat similar suggestion, see Michael W. McConnell, *Free Exercise Revisionism and the* Smith *Decision*, 57 U. CHI. L. REV. 1109, 1145-46 (1990).

Notes for pp. 240–241

45. What if a religious group indulged voluntary sacrifice of its own adult members? If we strictly applied the autonomy principle, these acts of religious "suicides" and "suicide assistance" could be criminalized only in the event that the volunteers were mentally incompetent. Otherwise, how could government bar an adult of sound mind from literally dedicating his life to God in an act of supreme sacrifice? This hypothetical may tempt us to bend the autonomy principle here, but before we do, we should remember that many churches were built by martyrs who gave up their earthly lives to win something they deemed even more precious.

46. *See* Lash, *Free Exercise, supra* note 11.

47. *See supra* text accompanying note 6; CONG.

GLOBE, 39th Cong., 1st Sess. 783 (remarks of Rep. Hamilton Wood).

48. CONG. GLOBE, 39th Cong., 1st Sess. 337, 474, 585, 651, 654, 1073, 1182, 1266, 1621, 1629, 1838, 2765, 3210 (1866) (remarks of Sens. Charles Sumner and Lyman Trumbull, Reps. Nathaniel Banks, Josiah Grinnell, and Thomas Eliot, Sens. James Nye and Samuel Pomeroy, Reps. Henry Raymond, Leonard Myers, Roswell Hart, and Sidney Clarke, Sen. Jacob Howard, and Rep. George Julian); *see also id.* at 2774 (remarks of Rep. Thomas Eliot quoting General Fisk).

Notes for pp. 241–243

For a more general discussion of firearms and the Fourteenth Amendment, see STEPHEN P. HALBROOK, THAT EVERY MAN BE ARMED 106-53 (1984); Robert J. Cottrol and Raymond T. Diamond, *The Second Amendment: Toward an Afro-Americanist Reconsideration*, 80 GEO. L. J. 309, 342-49 (1991); Stephen P. Halbrook, *Personal Security, Personal Liberty, and "The Constitutional Right to Bear Arms": Visions of the Framers of the Fourteenth Amendment*, 5 SETON HALL CONST. L. J. 341 (1995) [hereinafter *Fourteenth Amendment*]; Sayoko Blodgett-Ford, *The Changing Meaning of the Right to Bear Arms*, 6 SETON HALL CONST. L. J. 101 (1995); *see also* M. CURTIS, *supra* note 29, at 138-41.

49. For a theoretical discussion of how this can occur, *see* J. M. Balkin, *Deconstructive Practice and Legal Theory*, 96 YALE L. J. 743 (1987).

50. To cast the point within the felicitous framework of Professor Rubenfeld, our claim here, and throughout this chapter, is that the Founding and Reconstruction

visions of various rights featured slightly different "paradigm (or model) cases." *See generally* Jed Rubenfeld, *Reading the Constitution as Spoken*, 104 YALE L. J. 1119, 1169-71 (1995).

51. E. FONER, *supra* note 27, at 203; *see also* CONG. GLOBE, 39th Cong., 1st Sess. 40 (1866) (remarks of Sen. Henry Wilson) ("In Mississippi rebel State forces, men who were in the rebel armies, are traversing the State, visiting the freedmen, disarming them, perpetrating murders and outrages upon them"); *id.* at 914, 941 (remarks of Sens. Henry Wilson and Lyman Trumbull, each quoting Dec. 13, 1865, letter from Colonel Samuel Thomas to Major General O. O. Howard) ("Nearly all the dissatisfaction that now exists among the freedmen is caused by the abusive conduct of [the ex-confederate Mississippi] militia."); HARPER'S WEEKLY, Jan. 13, 1866, at 3, col. 2 ("The militia of [Mississippi] have seized every gun and pistol found in the hands of the (so called) freedmen"); *see generally* Halbrook, *Fourteenth Amendment*, *supra* note 48.

Notes for pp. 243–246

52. For general discussions of congressional use of the military in Reconstruction, see E. FONER, *supra* note 27, at 271-77, 307-8, 438; MICHAEL LES BENEDICT, A COMPROMISE OF PRINCIPLE 223-43 (1974); K. STAMPP, *supra* note 32, at 144-47.

53. *See supra* note 29.

54. *See supra* note 48.

55. 14 Stat. 173, 176 (1866) (emphasis added).

56. 14 Stat. 173, 176 (1866) [emphasis added]. The "bear arms" clause was understood as declaratory, simply clarifying what was already implicit. HORACE EDGAR FLACK, THE ADOPTION OF THE FOURTEENTH AMENDMENT 17 (1908); CONG. GLOBE, 39th Cong., 1st Sess. 743 (1866) (remarks of Sen. Lyman Trumbull). All of this suggests that the right to bear arms — and presumably all other rights and freedoms in the Bill of Rights — were encompassed by both the Freedman's Bureau Act and its companion Civil Rights Act.

57. 1 WILLIAM BLACKSTONE, COMMENTARIES *141-44. The link between Blackstone and the language of this Act is nicely illuminated by Professor Curtis. See M. CURTIS, supra note 29, at 74-76.

58. See Cottrol and Diamond, supra note 48, at 333-38; S. HALBROOK, supra note 48, at 96-106.

59. JOEL TIFFANY, A TREATISE ON THE UNCONSTI-TUTIONALITY OF AMERICAN SLAVERY 117-118 (Cleveland: J. Calyer, 1849) (emphasis deleted).

60. On Tiffany's importance and influence, see J. tenBROEK, supra note 7, at 72-74, 108-13.

61. 2 BLACKSTONE'S COMMENTARIES 65 app. (St. George Tucker ed., Philadelphia: Burch and Small, 1803).

62. See Cottrol and Diamond, supra note 48, at 333-49; E. FONER, supra note 27, at 119-23, 148; W. DU BOIS, supra note 31, at 166-67, 223. See generally Halbrook, Fourteenth Amendment, supra note 48.

63. 2 PROCEEDINGS, *supra* note 10, at 284, 302.

64. CONG. GLOBE, 39th Cong., 1st Sess. 474 (1866).

65. *Id.*

66. *Id.* at 651.

67. *Id.* at 1073 (emphasis added).

68. *Id.* at 1182. Pomeroy's next sentence made clear that he also supported political rights for blacks; but his rhetoric tended to privatize the arms right. *But cf. id.* at 1183 (discussing right to vote and right to bear arms in the same sentence; but not describing arms-bearing as a political rather than a civil right). *See also id.* at 371 (remarks of Sen. Garrett Davis) (both parties "were for every man bearing his arms about him and keeping them in his house, his castle, for his own defense").

69. *Id.* at 1266. Similarly, Congressman Henry Dawes in 1871 declared that the privileges and immunities of the American citizen included "the right to keep and bear arms in his defense." CONG. GLOBE, 42nd Cong., 1st Sess. 475 (1871).

70. *See* HORACE E. FLACK, THE ADOPTION OF THE FOURTEENTH AMENDMENT 42 (1908).

71. LOYAL GEORGIAN, Feb. 3, 1866, at 3, col. 4, *quoted in* Halbrook, *Fourteenth Amendment*, *supra* note 48, at 380, n.198. This editorial borrowed language from a December 22, 1865, Freedman's Bureau

circular. *See* Ex. Doc. No. 70, House of Representatives, 39th Cong., 1st Sess., at 65 (1866). For discussion, *see* Halbrook, *supra*, at 380-81, 396.

72. *See supra* Chapter 11, text at note 6.

73. 4 W. BLACKSTONE, *supra* note 61, at *349. Modern scholars have questioned Blackstone's historical claims about Magna Carta's original meaning — but his views on the point were utterly orthodox in the eighteenth and nineteenth centuries. *See* A. E. DICK HOWARD, THE ROAD FROM RUNNYMEDE 340-41 (1968); ALVAN STEWART, A CONSTITUTIONAL ARGUMENT ON THE SUBJECT OF SLAVERY (1837) *reprinted* in J. TENBROEK, *supra* note 7, at 281-84; Murray's Lessee v. Hoboken Land & Improvement Co., 59 U.S. (18 HOW.) 272, 276 (1856); Strauder v. West Virginia, 100 U.S. 303, 308-09 (1880).

74. *See, e.g.*, CONG. GLOBE, 35th Cong., 2d Sess. 985 (1859) (remarks of Rep. John Bingham) (acknowledging that states could deny blacks the vote but not the right to be tried by jury); CONG. GLOBE, 39th Cong., 1st Sess. 2765-66 (1866) (remarks of Sen. Jacob Howard) (similar).

75. *See* J. TENBROEK, *supra* note 7, at 50, 64-69; M. CURTIS, *supra* note 29, at 106.

76. SALMON P. CHASE, SPEECH OF SALMON P. CHASE IN THE CASE OF THE COLORED WOMAN, MATILDA 31, 36 (Cincinnati: Pugh and Dodd, 1837).

For a nice overview of the case, *see* H. HYMAN AND W. WIECEK, *supra* note 26, at 106-7.

77. *See id.* at 97, 107, 158-59; W. WIECEK, *supra* note 21, at 197-99. *See generally* THOMAS D. MORRIS, FREE MEN ALL (1974).

78. *See* T. MORRIS, *supra* note 77, at 138.

79. EMANCIPATOR AND REPUBLICAN, Nov. 14, 1850 (emphasis deleted). Bingham agreed that the 1850 act violated rights of due process and jury trial. *See* CONG. GLOBE, 36th Cong., 2d Sess. 83 (1861).

80. See CONG. GLOBE, 39th Cong., 1st Sess. at 1117, 1294, 1832 , 156 app. (1866) (remarks of Reps. James Wilson and William Lawrence). *See also id.* at 632 (remarks of Rep. Samuel Moulton). For representative statements in Reconstruction Congresses about the importance of jury trial, *see* CONG. GLOBE, 38th Cong. 1st Sess. 114, 1971-72 (1864) (remarks of Reps. Isaac Newton Arnold and Glenni Scofield); CONG. GLOBE, 38th Cong., 2d Sess. 215 (1865) (remarks of Rep. Chilton White); CONG. GLOBE, 41st Cong., 2d Sess. 515 (1870) (remarks of Sen. Joseph Fowler); CONG. GLOBE, 41st Cong. 3rd Sess. 1245 (1871) (remarks of Rep. William E. Lawrence); CONG. GLOBE, 42d Cong., 1st Sess. 475, 84-85 app. (1871) (remarks of Reps. Henry Dawes and John Bingham); CONG. GLOBE, 42d Cong., 2d Sess. 844 (1872) (remarks of Sen. John Sherman).

Notes for pp. 254–256

81. *See* E. FONER, *supra* note 27, at 204, 245; H.

HYMAN AND W. WIECEK, *supra* note 26, at 322-24,
425; M. CURTIS, *supra* note 29, at 136-37; Ronald F.
Wright, *Why Not Administrative Grand Juries?*, 44
ADMIN. L. REV. 465, 469 n.18 (1992); CONG. GLOBE,
42d Cong., 1st Sess. 158, 820, 220 app. (1871)
(remarks of Sens. John Sherman and Allen Thurman).

82. *Cf.* CONG. GLOBE, 42d Cong., 1st Sess. 220 app.
(1871) (remarks of Democratic Sen. Allen Thurman)
(arguing that problem of white southern jury nullification in Klan trials was insoluble "unless you intend to
transport these offenders [north], as our forefathers
were transported to Great Britain for trial"; such a
strategy would be "a plain violation of the Constitution"). For a prescient anticipation of the problem of
white nullification and a plea for black representation
on juries, *see* CONG. GLOBE, 38th Cong., 2d Sess. 289
(1865) (remarks of Rep. William Kelley).

**Notes
for pp.
256–257**

83. Act of March 1, 1875, ch. 114, 18 Stat. 335
(codified as amended at 18 U.S.C. §243 (1988)).

84. *Compare id.* ("no *citizen* . . . shall be disquali-
fied for service as grand or petit jurors in any court of
the *United States, or of any State, on account of race,
color, or previous condition of servitude*") (emphasis
added), *with* U.S. CONST. amend. XV ("The right of
citizens of the United States to vote shall not be denied
or abridged by the *United States, or by any State on
account of race, color, or previous condition of servitude*.") (emphasis added).

For a discussion of the legislative history of this
statute, and its connections to the Fifteenth Amend-

ment, *see* Vikram David Amar, *Jury Service as Political Participation Akin to Voting*, 80 CORNELL L. REV. 203, 238-41 (1995).

85. This is not to say that voting is the only thing jurors do. They also deliberate (as should voters in ordinary elections). *See* Douglas Gary Lichtman, *The Deliberative Lottery: A Thought Experiment in Jury Reform,* 34 Am. Crim. L. Rev. 133, 145, 153 n.76 (1996).

Above and beyond the simple textual argument that the Fifteenth Amendment right to vote encompasses a right to vote on juries (and in legislatures), three additional arguments are at work here. First, if the Fourteenth Amendment is best understood as protecting all civil rights (though it does not use this phrase), the Fifteenth is best understood as protecting all political rights, of which the right to vote was emblematic. Second, even if the Fifteenth Amendment did not ipso facto make blacks jurors, it did redefine the electorate in each state, and many state laws and state constitutions themselves made voters ipso facto jurors. Finally, the Fifteenth Amendment worked a kind of estoppel argument. States were estopped from claiming that blacks as such lacked what it took to be voters — and if blacks had the right stuff for the ballot box, why not the jury box, too? Any jury exclusion of black voters would seem very hard to defend rationally. For much more elaboration and historical documentation, see Vikram David Amar, *Jury Service as Political Participation Akin to Voting*, 80 Cornell L. Rev. 203 (1995).

Notes for p. 257

86. *See supra* Chapter 5, text at note 30.

A NEW BIRTH OF FREEDOM
(*Pages 259-268*)

1. See *generally* Kenneth R. Bowling, *"A Tub to the Whale": The Founding Fathers and Adoption of the Federal Bill of Rights*, 8 J. EARLY REPUBLIC 223 (1988); Paul Finkelman, *James Madison and the Bill of Rights: A Reluctant Paternity*, 1990 SUP. CT. REV. 301.

2. Letter from James Madison to Richard Peters (August 19, 1789), in 12 THE PAPERS OF JAMES MADISON 346 (R. Rutland et al. eds., 1979).

Notes for pp. 262–263

3. Dred Scott v. Sandford, 60 U.S. (19 How.) 393, 450 (1857) ("An act of Congress which deprives a citizen of the United States of his liberty or property, merely because he came himself or brought his property into a particular Territory of the United States . . . could hardly be dignified with the name of due process of law.").

4. Robert J. Reinstein, *Completing the Constitution: The Declaration of Independence, Bill of Rights and Fourteenth Amendment*, 66 TEMPLE L. REV. 361, 365 n.25 (1993).

5. For general affirmations of this point, *see* William J. Brennan, Jr., *Why Have a Bill of Rights?*, 26 VAL. U. L. REV. 1, 7 (1991); John Paul Stevens, *The Bill of Rights: A Century of Progress*, 59 U. CHI. L. REV. 13, 19-21 (1992); Geoffrey R. Stone, Foreword, *The Bill of Rights in the Welfare State: A Bicen-*

tennial Symposium, 59 U. CHI. L. REV. 5, 6 (1992). In specific doctrinal areas, *see, e.g.*, Mary Ann Glendon and Raul F. Yanes, *Structural Free Exercise*, 90 MICH. L. REV. 477, 479 (1991) (religion); Daniel Shaviro, *The Confrontation Clause Today in Light of its Common Law Background*, 26 VAL. U. L. REV. 337, 338 (1991) (confrontation clause).

6. Although the Court pretended to assume, for the sake of argument, that speech and press clause principles applied against states in *Patterson v. Colorado*, 205 U.S. 454, 462 (1907), in retrospect it is clear that its sustained drive for First Amendment incorporation began in *Gitlow v. New York*, 268 U.S. 652, 666 (1925).

7. *See* Fiske v. Kansas, 274 U.S. 380 (1927); Stromberg v. California, 283 U.S. 359 (1931); Near v. Minnesota, 283 U.S. 697 (1931); Cantwell v. Connecticut, 310 U.S. 296 (1940).

Notes for pp. 263–264

8. *See generally* HARRY KALVEN, JR., A WORTHY TRADITION: FREEDOM OF SPEECH IN AMERICA (1988).

9. *See* Lamont v. Postmaster General, 381 U.S. 301, 306 (1965).

10. *See* Texas v. Johnson, 491 U.S. 397 (1989); United States v. Eichman, 496 U.S. 310, 315 (1990).

11. *See, e.g.*, Henry J. Friendly, *The Bill of Rights as a Code of Criminal Procedure*, 53 CAL. L. REV. 929, 937 n.42 (1965); Ker v. California, 374 U.S. 23, 45-46 (1963) (Harlan, J., concurring in the result); Duncan v.

Louisiana, 391 U.S. 145, 182 n.21 (1968) (Harlan, J., dissenting).

12. *See* Edmond Cahn, *The Firstness of the First Amendment*, 65 YALE L. J. 464, 468-70 (1956).

13. *See generally* Thurgood Marshall, *Reflections on the Bicentennial of the United States Constitution*, 101 HARV. L. REV. 1 (1987).

14. *See* 4 DEBATES ON THE ADOPTION OF THE FEDERAL CONVENTION 316 (Jonathan Elliot ed., AYER Co. reprint ed., 1987) (1836). Major portions of this quotation appear in TIMOTHY FARRAR, MANUAL OF THE CONSTITUTION OF THE UNITED STATES OF AMERICA, §439, at 394 (Boston: Little, Brown, 1867).

GLOSSARY

Appellate: Of or relating to an appeal from the decision of a lower court, or appeals generally.

Attainer: A law that extinguishes a person's civil rights.

Bicameral: Having two legislative houses (in our federal government, the House of Representatives and the Senate).

Bill of Attainder: A special legislative act prescribing capital punishment, without a trial, for a person guilty of a high offense such as treason or a felony. Bills of attainder are prohibited by the Constitution.

Black Codes: Laws enacted shortly after the Civil War in the former Confederate states to restrict the liberties of the freed slaves and maintain white supremacy, thus preserving as much as possible the prewar way of life in the South.

Capitation (poll tax): A tax levied on each person within a jurisdiction. The Twenty-fourth Amendment prohibits the federal and state governments from imposing poll taxes as a condition of voting

Cause of action: A group of operative facts giving rise to one or more bases for suing; a factual situation that entitles one person to obtain a remedy in court from another person.

Challenge for cause: During the selection of a jury, a party's challenge supported by a specified reason, such as bias or prejudice, that would disqualify a potential juror.

Coercion: (coercive, *adj.*) To compel by pressure or threat.

Comity Clause: The clause of the U.S. Constitution (art. IV, § 2, cl.1) giving citizens of one state the right to all privileges and immunities enjoyed by citizens of the other states.

Common law: The body of law originated and developed in England, based upon court decisions in individual cases, rather than from statutes or constitutions.

Compensatory damages: Damages sufficient in amount to indemnify the injured person.

Declaratory judgment: A binding adjudication that establishes the rights and other legal relations of the parties without providing for or ordering enforcement.

De minimis: Trifling, minimal. So insignificant that a court may overlook it in deciding an issue.

Demurrer: A pleading stating that although the facts alleged in a complaint may be true, they are insufficient for the plaintiff to state a claim for relief and for the defendant to frame an answer.

Directed verdict: A judgment entered on the order of a trial judge who takes over the fact-finding role of the jury because in his opinion the evidence is so compelling that only one decision can reasonably follow, or because the evidence has failed to establish a prima facie case.

Estoppal: A doctrine that prevents a party from asserting a claim or right that contradicts what he said or did before.

Ex parte: [Latin "from the part"] Something done or made at the instance and for the benefit of one party only, and without notice to, or argument by, any person adversely interested.

Ex post facto: [Latin "from a thing done afterward"] After the fact: retroactively.

Federalism: The relationship and distribution of power between the national and regional governments within a federal system of government.

Federal question: A legal issue involving the interpretation and application of the U.S. Constitution, an act of Congress, or a treaty. Jurisdiction over federal questions rests with the federal courts.

Forum-shopping: The practice of choosing the most favorable jurisdiction or court in which to file a claim.

General verdict: A verdict by which the jury finds in favor of one party or the other, as opposed to resolving specific fact questions.

Grand jury: A body of people (often 23) who are chosen to sit permanently for at least a month — and sometimes a year — and who, in ex parte proceedings decide whether to issue indictments. If the grand jury decides that evidence is strong enough to hold a suspect for trial, it returns a bill of indictment charging the suspect with a specific crime.

Habeas corpus: A writ employed to bring a person before a court, most frequently to ensure that the party's imprisonment or detention is not illegal.

Impressment: One method by which armed forces were formerly expanded, when so-called press-gangs seized men off the streets and forced them to join the army or navy.

Imprimatur: [Latin "let it be printed"] A license required to publish a book. Once required in England, the imprimatur is now encountered only rarely, and only in countries that censor the press.

In pari materia: [Latin "in the same matter"] An interpretation doctrine, providing that statutes regarded as being *in pari materia* may be construed together, so that inconsistencies in one statute may be resolved by looking at another statute on the same subject.

Ipso facto: [Latin "by the fact itself"] By the very nature of the situation.

Jury nullification: A jury's knowing and deliberate rejection of the evidence or refusal to apply the law either because the jury wants to send a message about some social issue that is larger than the case itself or because the result dictated by law is contrary to the jury's sense of justice, morality, or fairness.

Libertarianism: A doctrine of absolute and unrestricted liberty, especially of thought and action.

Malfeasance: A wrongful or unlawful act; especially wrongdoing or misconduct by a public official.

Per se: [Latin "of, in, or by itself"] Something which stands alone, without reference to additional facts.

Petit jury: A jury (usually consisting of 12 persons) summoned and empanelled in the trial of a specific case.

Prima facie: [Latin "at first sight"] An adjective used to describe evidence that will establish a fact or sustain a judgment unless contradictory evidence is produced.

Prior restraint: A governmental restriction on speech or publication before its actual expression. Prior restraints violate the Constitution's First Amendment, unless the speech is obscene, is defamatory, or creates a clear and present danger to society..

Punitive damages: Damages awarded in addition to actual damages when it is determined by the jury that the defendant acted with recklessness, malice, or deceit.

Special verdict: A verdict that gives a written finding for each issue presented to a jury, leaving the application of the law to the judge.

Star Chamber: A now defunct English court, operating at the king's discretion, that had broad civil and criminal jurisdiction. This much detested and feared court operated with secretive, arbitrary, and oppressive procedures, including compulsory self-incrimination, inquisitorial investigation, and the absence of juries.

Suffrage: The right to vote.

Tort: A civil wrong for which a remedy may be obtained, usually in the form of damages; a breach of duty that the law imposes on everyone in the same relation to one another as those involved in a given transaction.

Villein: One of a class of feudal serfs who held the legal status of freemen in their dealings with all persons except their lord.

TERMS AND ABBREVIATIONS USED IN NOTES

art., article
c., chapter
cf., compare
ed., editor, edition
eg., for example
id., the same

infra, below
n., note
para, paragraph
passim, throughout
rev., revised
supra, above

INDEX

ABOUT THE AUTHORS

Akhil Reed Amar is Southmayd Professor Law at the Yale Law School, where he teaches courses in constitutional law, criminal procedure, federal jurisdiction, and American legal history. He received his B.A., *summa cum laude*, from Yale College, and his J.D. from Yale Law School, where he served as editor of the *Yale Law Journal*. He is the recipient of numerous awards and honors, including the Paul Bator award from the Federalist Society for Law and Public Policy, the ABA Certificate of Merit, the Yale University Press Governors' Award, and an honorary doctorate of law (LL.D.) from Suffolk University. *The National Law Journal* named him as one of the 40 "Rising Stars in the Law" in 1995. He has delivered endowed lectures at over two dozen colleges and universities, and has written widely on constitutional issues for such publications as *The New York Times, The Washington Post, The Los Angeles Times, The American Legion* and *Slate*. He is a contributing editor to *The New Republic* and *The American Lawyer*. His many law review articles have been widely cited by scholars, judges, and justices. He is the author of four recent books: *The Constitution and Criminal Procedure: First Principles*, *For the People* (with Alan Hirsch*), The Bill of Rights: Creation and Reconstruction*, and *Processes of Constitutional Decisionmaking* (editor, with Paul Brest, Sanford Levinson, and Jack Balkin).

Les Adams is a lawyer, publisher, writer, and chairman of Palladium Press. His academic degrees include a B.A. in English from the University of North Carolina, an M.A. in English from Columbia University, a J.D., *cum laude*, from the Cumberland School of Law of Samford University, where he was editor in chief of the law review, and an honorary doctorate of law (LL.D) from William Penn College. He is the author of *The Second Amendment Primer*. He is a member of the Alabama Bar Association, The National Rifle Association, and the American Civil Liberties Union.